Walking North

Walking North

Mic Lowther

Excerpts from *Pilgrim at Tinker Creek* by Annie Dillard used with permission of Harper & Row Publishers.

Cover photograph courtesy of Jerrianne Lowther

Cover design by Beth Farrell

ISBN: 1-58619-020-2

Library of Congress Card Catalogue Number: 00-109659

First edition (hardcover) published privately in Anchorage, Alaska, March 1990.

Second edition (softcover) published by Elton-Wolf Publishing in Seattle, Washington, January 2001.

ELTON-WOLF PUBLISHING
2505 Second Avenue Suite 515 Seattle, Washington 98121
Tel 206.748.0345 Fax 206.748.0343
www.elton-wolf.com info@elton-wolf.com
Seattle • Los Angeles • Portland

The Appalachian Trail

**A 2,000-mile
mountain footpath
from Georgia to Maine**

Learn of the green world what can be thy place.

- EZRA POUND

Contents

Walking North

CHAPTER 1

_____

Reality Is All Uphill

*The first day of spring is one thing, and the first
spring day is another. The difference between
them is sometimes as great as a month.*
                                    - HENRY VAN DYKE

W E STOOD AT ONE END of an endless trail. Three backpacks
leaned against still-leafless trees. Three sets of tentative boot-
prints tracked Georgia dirt where a path wound two thousand
miles north. Endless, the Appalachian Trail, or intended to
seem so. It led to Maine. We were going to walk.

Our friend Rosemary Passano had driven us eighty miles
from Atlanta to Amicalola State Park, dropped us near a wooded
lake at pavement's end and wished us a pleasant trip. Then
she'd gone. I'd watched her drive our car down the steep hill
from the lake, down and out of sight onto Georgia Highway 52,
and expected to take it calmly. We'd planned this journey for
more than a year, after all. The sudden, hollow feeling of that
moment came as a surprise.

The car, my last link with the city and surroundings I found
most familiar, headed south taking Rosemary home. A foreign,

silent wood crowded round me and I heard little but the wind. To say I felt apprehensive hardly told the story at all.

It was March 21. We'd begun our hike on spring's first full day as an optimistic gesture but the weather took no notice. A biting wind nipped our ears and fingers and swirled dead leaves about our feet and along the trail. The lake rippled and danced with shifting patterns, with broken reflections of trees and clouds. Weak sunshine offered the faintest of shadows. Spring was late, it seemed. We'd hoped for a much warmer welcome.

We dug out hats and gloves to fend off the cold, stood for pictures under a sign reading *Springer Mt 7m*, then put on our packs and started north. It was 2:30 in the afternoon.

The trail proved easy to follow. Blue blazes painted on trees led around Amicalola Lake on a dirt road for two miles, then turned up a well-worn path into the woods. The forest pushed closer, closed behind us, and the grade steepened. Our hearts and lungs and muscles switched to lower gears. Uphill: a mile-long climb of Frosty Mountain.

Jerri walked in front. The walk had been her idea, though she wouldn't always remember it that way. She'd wanted to see spring come to the southern Appalachians and follow it north. Pleasant spring days would last longer that way. From the looks of our barren surroundings, we'd arrived in plenty of time.

Five-foot-five, brown hair, smile radiating confidence from the depths of warm clothes she'd bundled in, Jerri already seemed at ease. She'd grown up in the country and knew the outdoors. Time in the woods was like a visit with friends to her, and she would likely fall quickly to watching birds and identifying flowers and lose all apparent interest in our destination.

Photographer, writer, and self-taught naturalist, Jerri had gladly left the Arizona desert to be among things growing and green. She wouldn't rush to get anywhere, she said. She'd come to see things and to watch the seasons change. In front, she had first chance to look.

2

Ten-year-old Kyra (rhymes with Vera) followed along in the middle. She wore the blue knitted cap she'd made, with its bobbing, softball-sized tassel, and her blonde hair flowed from beneath it to wave in the wind. Already nearly as tall as her mother, Kyra shouldered her pack with nonchalance. She flashed a ready grin but it didn't quite mask her wary look. Seven months' vacation from school had come as riches beyond measure to her; she wasn't sure this was the best way to spend them.

"Oh, it's okay," she allowed, not wanting to commit herself one way or the other. Better than sixth grade, at least. "But why did we have to keep it such a big secret?"

"Since no one knew," Jerri explained, "we weren't bombarded with reasons it couldn't be done. And we avoid making excuses if we don't get very far."

Walking close behind Jerri, Kyra kept up the pace. We hadn't even considered the possibilities, she was probably thinking ... surely we could have done something else with our time....

No stranger to the outdoors, Kyra had accompanied us on trips since she could toddle and had traveled through twenty-eight states. But none, she pointed out, on foot.

At the end of the line, I looked around at the quiet woods. I'd grown up in town. I thought of the forest as a place. One went there to do things, to hike, to camp, to find adventure. I'd walked and slept in the woods and in desert as well, and I'd come to the Appalachians for my most ambitious adventure so far.

I'd designed and programmed computer systems for eleven years. The work was interesting enough, but the prospect of walking through two thousand miles of new experiences came with a force I couldn't resist. The Appalachian Trail seemed awesome in concept and scale. I'd seized it at once as a fascinating problem to work.

We'd settled matters of equipment, supplies, routing, and timing as months passed and arrived at Amicalola ready to go. Georgia to Maine, over scenic mountain trails — it sounded great. But like other times I'd come to the woods, the surroundings seemed just out of reach. I felt remotely uncomfortable, like a guest whom the host did not know.

I looked the part, at least. Dressed in jeans like the others, plus similar rugged boots and down jacket, I stood six-three and had long hair showing beneath a wide-brimmed black hat. Years before I'd grown a full beard. I hadn't trimmed it in quite a while.

The Chattahoochee National Forest around us gave no sign of bursting to life. Past summers' leaves covered the ground and crinkled softly as we shuffled along. Pine trees lent touches of dusty green but deciduous trees stood stark and bare. Views from ridge-tops showed the drab Georgia countryside. Atop Frosty Mountain, we stopped for a look. A thousand mountains, likely more, marched in random heaps to the horizon and beyond, their colors fading with distance.

Chattahoochee: the Cherokee word meant "flower-painted rock." Sorry, no flowers today, and too little sun to paint the sky and far-off peaks. Lots of rocks, though, and the wind still blowing. We didn't stop for long.

The trail led on from Frosty's summit a mile and a half to Nimblewill Gap. We walked downhill quickly then started back up, another mile to the top of Black Mountain. The trail guidebook used discouraging words, like "steeply," and we shifted gears once more.

Uphill: hardly ever fun, especially with a pack. I wondered if I'd get used to it, or forget to notice the soreness already beginning in my shoulders and legs. Other hikers' accounts described the trail as *all* uphill, in either direction. "I climbed the Appalachian Trail," went the suggested T-shirt message.

We reached the base of Springer Mountain weary, out of

breath, and only too glad to set down our packs. We'd walked three hours, covered six miles, and the next climb looked like it went on forever. The uphill business had gotten serious.

"Zigzag steeply up slope," directed the guide in terse dismissal of another mile. Jerri sat down, back to the wind, and pulled off her boots.

"Blisters," she said. "Where's the moleskin?"

Jerri cut protective patches for both heels with supplies I retrieved from the first-aid kit.

"Don't the boots fit?" I asked, knowing we'd broken them in, jogging and clumping fifty miles around the block back home.

"They slip a little at the heels," she admitted. "For short walks on level ground, it wasn't enough to matter."

Great ... and we'd barely started. She must have felt them coming on ... we could have stopped sooner....

She'd felt them for miles. Annoyed that expensive, carefully fitted, properly broken-in boots had failed to protect her narrow heels, and wary of my reaction to trouble so soon, she'd walked on. Her blisters were too big to ignore now.

Springer Mountain gave way slowly. The trail rose steeply on switchbacks and the wind blew stronger and colder with each upward step. A rhythmic creaking came from my pack as I moved from foot to foot. The ache from packstraps spread through my shoulders, to my neck, down my back. I felt mounting strain all through my legs as I climbed on, pushing upward, following the two figures just ahead. Looking up, hoping to catch a glimpse of the top, I noted frost on the grass and trees. Patches of white thickened as we advanced.

"How much farther?" Kyra asked, pulling her cap tighter around her ears. "I'm tired, and cold."

"There's a shelter on top," I said. "Pretty soon we'll be out of the wind." A dull orange glow through the trees foretold sunset. Daylight wouldn't last much longer. We climbed higher, following turn after turn of zigzagging trail.

Gaining the 3,782-foot summit at last, we came to a dead stop. New snow outlined the scene ahead in sharp relief. The trail led through woods nearly devoid of color, through stark, twisted black brush, through undergrowth white and bent with frost. Trees hung heavy with ice. Wind-blown branches clattered together like drumsticks in a grade-school rhythm band.

"But there were cardinals and daffodils and new green leaves in Atlanta." Jerri protested.

It had rained there, too, and rain had come as ice and snow to Springer Mountain.

A signboard marked the southern end of the Appalachian Trail. The walk officially began at that point for northbound hikers, where two-by-six-inch white paint blazes replaced the side-trail blue. We could start counting there. Everything so far had just been practice, warm-up for the big event. We leaned wearily against the sign for pictures, against words that told of a mountain footpath leading to Mount Katahdin in Maine. It suddenly seemed like a long, long way.

"Where's the shelter?" Kyra asked.

"A little farther on," I replied. "We'll get there soon."

"Brrrr, I want to get in my bag."

I looked around for the register to record our names. The guidebook had mentioned it and on my way up the mountain I'd imagined the scene. I'd find a rusting iron box chained to a tree, and inside, safe from the weather, an aging bound volume. Paging carefully, reverently, through years of signatures, I would pause at names well known ... Avery ... Gatewood ... Shaffer. I would nod at those whose books I'd read ... Sutton ... Garvey ... Baker. Then, in a history-making moment, I'd add ours. Thousands had started; we would be among them. A few had finished. So, perhaps, might we.

Right. I found a two-foot-square board mounted at waist level on a pipe driven into the ground. A dented metal sheet covered the board, shielding what valued contents there might be. I pried the cover loose. A sudden gust sent torn, wet, random scraps of paper fluttering like confetti over the frozen mountaintop. I watched, shrugged, and dropped the cover to the ground with a loud clang.

On one reasonably dry sheet, I signed us in: *Mic, Jerrianne, & Kyra Lowther - Phoenix, Arizona.* I added *Georgia →Maine* with very little ceremony. I stuffed remaining papers inside and hammered the cover back in place with my hand. So much for history.

We filled canteens from a stream beyond the summit and walked to the newly built shelter. Its three sturdy wood walls, platform floor, and pitched shingle roof looked inviting in the wintry scene. It was the first of more than two hundred such structures we would find along the trail. As we approached, a man stepped from behind the canvas tarp that covered the shelter's open side.

"This one's full," he said. "Sixteen of us. There's another lean-to just down the mountain."

This wasn't part of the plan ... Big Stamp Shelter lay a mile and a half farther on ... darkness would soon close in.

"It will be warmer down there," Jerri said. "We'll just have to hurry." She set off in a rush down gently descending trail. Kyra followed without a word.

Regular white blazes led us off the mountain and out of winter's ice and snow. Wind still stirred branches above and brush around us and light faded fast, but smooth footway kept our steps from straying in the dark. Trees loomed black and ghostly as we passed. Restless forest sounds came from every side. We hurried on.

Details vanished in the dark. We saw no blazes, no trail, only shapes that gave a sense of passage through the night. The path leveled. Jerri pointed to something dim, black, rectangular off to one side. Big Stamp: refuge at last.

This shelter seemed older and smaller and wind blew directly into the front. A tarp was stretched part way across the opening to block it. We looked inside, around the tarp's flapping edge, and in the gloom saw a picnic table heaped with gear. A large, pointed rock protruded from the dirt floor beneath it. Wrapped tight in sleeping bags, four hikers filled the remaining space. Big Stamp was full, too.

"Hello," Jerri said.

"Hullo," said two of the four.

"Where ya headed?" I asked.

Maine, they allowed.

So were we, Jerri replied.

Silence ... now what?

"And how old are you?" asked a voice.

"Ten," Kyra answered.

Silence.

"... A *ten-year-old* going to *Maine?*"

Four male visions of hiking the long, rugged trail suffered measurably. Grandmothers and girls in their teens had done the AT; that was bad enough. Now a ten-year-old. Was nothing sacred? Was there no escape from amateurs, even on a howling, freezing night on Springer Mountain?

They said nothing for a few moments more, then one by one offered to scoot forward and make room for Jerri and Kyra to sleep along the back wall. That left no space for me. I lit our sputtering candle lantern and petted the small collie pup that came over to me from one corner. We couldn't cook dinner in such cramped quarters so I handed out jelly-bread as Jerri and Kyra settled in.

One of the four, Peter Home Douglas, resumed the conversation our arrival had interrupted. He'd hiked long distances before, he said, and planned to cover at least fifteen miles a day. We hoped for ten, I said. He talked about his backpacking gear, why he'd chosen what he carried, and told of techniques he'd developed walking the 260-mile Long Trail through Vermont. I mentioned lessons we'd learned hiking in the West. Basic things, like staying on the trail, bringing warm clothes, and not running out of water.

Peter thought it best to have clean equipment. He planned to keep his so at all times, he said, especially his expensive goose-down sleeping bag. I nodded agreement, just as a full slice of jelly-bread slipped from my freezing fingers and landed on his bag, jelly-side down.

The crowded shelter grew suddenly quiet.

"Th-that's okay ..." Peter managed, as I apologized and quickly cleaned up. What timing ... no need to worry now about where I would sleep. I packed up, ducked around the tarp, and got out of there fast. Silence returned to Big Stamp.

I leaned my pack against the back of the shelter and rolled out my bag in a pile of wind-drifted leaves. Getting in brought a satisfying crunch. Wind still howled and beat at the front of the shelter. I felt safe and out of its reach. And soon, for the first time in hours, I was warm.

What if it rained, a passing thought asked. Clear sky, stars ... not likely. Long day. Nine miles, we'd walked, or just under. Not bad for a mid-afternoon start. We'd done that much in a day only once before ... Yosemite ... in the rain. We'd have to do that every day. I turned over on my side. Leaves crackled beneath me.

Quite an ordeal to get this far ... a year of planning a "different" family adventure ... months of research and preparation ... three weeks to move everything we owned to a storage warehouse ... the drive to Atlanta. On the trail at last. Only a few people knew where we were.

Noises. Wind in the trees ... no, something crunched through the leaves. Squirrel. They had squirrels in Georgia didn't they? Chipmunk, maybe. What if something big did come by? We'd had bears in Yosemite. Lumpy ground. Colder, too. Nine miles ... not bad ... could we keep it up? Would all days be this odd? Why did things seem less possible in the dark?

This was it ... the Appalachian Trail. A narrow path grooved into the earth leading up mountain and down. Or maybe just up. A centerline for the very different lives we would live for a time ... till nearly winter, I figured. And we were on our way.

I scrunched around in the leaves and finally went to sleep. Whatever adventures lay beyond Springer Mountain could wait....

Machine-gun fire startled me awake at four in the morning. Bombs exploded in the distance and the whirring and chopping of a battle-ready helicopter filled the air directly overhead. Searchlights stabbed the trees and ground nearby. Rifle shots barked from the woods. I watched without moving. I knew that U.S. Army Rangers used the area for training, and we'd expected to meet them. But on the first night?

The attackers weren't concerned with us so I settled back to sleep, first pulling a canteen from my pack for a drink. Frozen solid. I couldn't help but laugh. This adventure would be different, all right.

CHAPTER 2

Of Rain, and Things
That Go Chomp in the Night

*"I think," said Christopher Robin, "that we ought
to eat all our Provisions now, so that we shan't
have so much to carry."*

— A. A. MILNE

LOSING THE TRAIL NEXT MORNING took no more than half an hour.
We all noticed the symptoms; we'd gone astray on hikes a time
or two before. There were no trail markers ahead or behind.
The road we were on didn't match the trail guide description.
And the four hikers who'd gone before us somehow had left no
footprints. We walked nearly all the way back to Big Stamp
before Kyra spotted a double white blaze on a tree. "Turn here,"
that meant. Many sets of footprints had turned. Three sets
had not. So went lesson one in trail-finding.

We had started very late. Long climbs and short rations the
day before left us tired and dispirited, even after a night's rest.
The last of the hikers camped with us had gone long before we'd
organized a hot breakfast, loaded the packs, and departed at

eleven o'clock. Cold wind had diminished by then, however, leaving a clear sky. By noon we felt the encouragement of warm sunshine. We needed it.

Simply stated, hiking the trail was a lot of work. I hadn't expected it to be easy, but I had thought we were in better condition. I'd thought the same thing backpacking into Grand Canyon, through Yosemite, and in the Superstition Wilderness outside Phoenix. We'd struggled along steep trails saying we would just have to get into better shape.

We'd walked, jogged, and exercised in preparation, yet following the AT tired us as quickly as ever. Our packs weighed heavy on not-yet-hardened hips and shoulders to make the going uncomfortable and slow. The guidebook laughed at our efforts as the path drew us ever up and down, describing the day's route as a restful walk on old logging roads with gentle grades. It didn't seem that easy to me.

We reached Hickory Flats Cemetery in late afternoon. Tilting headstones trailed shadows on the leaf-covered ground and occasional inscriptions told of people from another age. Odd-sized pieces of blank marble marked a few graves. Ordinary rocks stood by others. We shuffled through leaves as we looked about, briefly disturbing the quiet, then we went on.

We made camp early on the south slope of Hawk Mountain. I rolled out sleeping bags in soft grass and Jerri cooked dinner. She listed the day's positive things: we'd camped before dark, the packs were now one day's food lighter, and she'd seen new leaves and tiny flowers, violets and bloodroot, poking cautiously from the ground. And Kyra, looking up just in time, had pointed — "Oh, look!" — to three deer fleeing as we'd approached. Some compensation for seven miles of aches and pains.

"You'd better hang up the packs," Jerri said.

"We shouldn't have any problem here."

"We said that in Death Valley," she said, "and fought off kangaroo rats all night."

"Squirrels got our breakfast in Grand Canyon," Kyra added. "Remember?"

"Then we had the bear and salami incident," Jerri went on.

"Okay, okay, I'll hang them up."

I loaded my pack with all the food and dug out a fifty-foot length of nylon cord. Tying one end to the crossbar of my red Kelty pack, I tossed the cord's other end over a tree limb and pulled the pack aloft. The other packs contained no food so could stay on the ground.

"That'll discourage disrespectful beasts," I said. "Although, those fraying mouse holes and bear-bite marks do give the packs a certain flair."

After distributing everything to its proper place again next morning, I held packs for the others to put on. Kyra's weighed twenty pounds, Jerri's thirty, and mine came in around fifty. Extra food and water would add to each at times, sending mine as high as sixty-five pounds. This broke all the rules. Popular books of the day recommended lighter loads, urged us to do without, economize, take only essentials. Heavy packs were stuffed with frivolous things that "only weighed a few ounces."

Wonderful.

We preferred being prepared.

"On the third day, we started the morning tough at eight o'clock by climbing up Hawk Mountain." So reported Kyra's journal for March 23 and we surely felt renewed. We reached the 3,619-foot summit with ease. Down the other side, in Hightower Gap, we completed the guidebook's first section.

Progress.

One hundred eighty-one sections to go.

The forest lay quiet as we made our way along. I paused atop a ridge to look through a break in the trees. Peaceful plains and mountains ... was it scenery or just countryside?

Scenery meant thundering waterfalls, spectacular sunsets, New England autumn to me. These drab, uneventful views didn't pack much punch. Jerri seemed to see them a different way, I noticed, as if finding something remotely of interest in quiet, dead-brown hills. She was a photographer. She saw things ... subtleties of light and shadow ... composition of forms. I wasn't all that impressed. I walked on, stopping to look from other points from time to time.

"Halt!" whispered the camouflaged U.S. Ranger on the trail ahead of us. We'd come upon him suddenly rounding a bend. "What are you doing here?"

"Hiking this trail," I said. "Can we get by?"

He looked at us a moment, then raised a radio to his lips and cautiously spoke:

"Requesting clearance for three civilians on foot."

Words crackled out of the speaker advising of an hour's delay. We sat in the trail and waited. Other troops crept about the brush laying ambush for an unseen enemy.

Wait? ... I didn't want to wait. We had plans for the day. Now we'd have to push on later to make up. I looked at the ranger sourly but it had no effect. An hour: no more, no less.

We continued in the allotted time. No fireworks greeted us in the besieged area, but a face bearing a wide grin did pop from a foxhole to urge us along.

"There's troops comin' over the mountain soon gonna be in for a big surprise. You might want to hightail it up that hill!"

We moved out, but heard no more from the rangers.

Mountain after mountain crowded in front of us and the way grew hard again. We plodded up to their summits, over, then down to gaps hundreds of feet below. Climbing peaks in the three- to four-thousand-foot range may have sounded trivial but it was no piece of cake. One took an hour or two; four or five could eat up a day.

We labored through the miles, helped a lagging Kyra, and our pace slowed. Thirty-four hundred feet of elevation gained, all but two hundred given back.

"Go and look behind the Ranges — Something lost behind the Ranges," Kipling urged. Intense words that made me feel I could tramp on forever, ignoring the torturous route. The Georgia guidebook said, "Follow trail thru woods...." Hardly so inspiring. I couldn't quite ignore the trail's upward reach.

Occasional woodland roads helped us along and we stopped often at streams to rest, dropping our packs at the least excuse.

"Wild water!" Jerri would say, and we'd pause for a refreshing drink. But always the trail went on.

I wondered what Kyra was thinking. Dumb idea, perhaps. Who wanted to climb all these stupid mountains? Maybe she thought she'd been conned. I'd tried to gain her support during the trip's planning stage by presenting it in a convincing way....

"We've been thinking about a long vacation," I'd said, "longer than we've ever had before."

"What kind of vacation?" she'd asked, interested at once.

"Walking the Appalachian Trail. It would take about six months, I suspect. You'd have to get time off school."

"How far *is* it?"

"Well, you walk about a mile back and forth to school every day, right?"

"Uh-huh."

"This would be like doing that two thousand times."

Her look of interest changed then, to a wide-eyed, mixed-emotion stare.

"Walk two thousand miles?"

The conversation went disappointingly on to questions like "Why?" and "Do I have to go?", whereupon my repertoire of persuasive gambits had run dry. I didn't know what would make her want to go. I didn't know much about Kyra at all, for that matter. She'd lived with us ten years. We were friends and did things together. But I'd never really felt close.

She accepted the idea in time and we'd come to the AT, to walk to school and back ten times a day. So far she hadn't pointed out that she'd never climbed a mountain to get to school.

We reached Gooch Gap Shelter toward evening and mustered a spirited "Hoo-ray!" The ten-mile day was our longest ever. Mice appeared once we'd settled into our bags, but couldn't get into the food. They took to running up and down walking sticks we'd leaned against the shelter wall. Playful scampering sounds kept us company as we drifted off to sleep.

Sunrise filled the sky with warnings. I woke to watch the sun climb slowly behind a long band of clouds and turn the horizon brilliant red. Lines of trees on distant mountaintops stood in sharp silhouette against the glow. Rain for sure ... I dressed quickly and walked alone toward Gooch Gap.

The small town of Suches lay three miles off the trail. We'd mailed a box of supplies to ourselves there, care of general delivery. I didn't know when the Post Office might close on a Saturday, or if it were open at all, but I guessed I had until noon. The easy way to town still lay miles ahead at Woody Gap on Georgia Highway 60. I preferred to take the back roads early to be safe. Reaching Gooch Gap, I turned left on a gravel road and the trail dropped quickly behind.

Nineteen miles ... we'd walked that much of the white-blazed trail. What lay ahead? Sixty more miles of Georgia, then trail through North Carolina, Tennessee, Virginia, and ten other states following the very crest of the Appalachian Mountain range. We would climb to remote peaks and high places. We would drop into valleys, cross rivers and highways, pass through small towns. The route would seek out national parks, forests, and state preserves wherever possible, lead along back roads at times, cross sections of private land. We would sometimes follow highways where access to better surroundings was denied.

Our walk would end in Maine, one faraway day on Mount Katahdin. We would see it for days as we approached, a solitary, mile-high mountain growing to dominate the skyline. What a sight it must be after walking all those miles! Katahdin ... still too far away to seem real.

My boots crunched steadily on gravel. Occasional birds and barking dogs added the only other early morning sounds.

Too far away ... that was the whole idea. Proposing the trail in 1921, Benton MacKaye wrote: "The Appalachian Trail should be a seemingly endless trail that would link the wilderness areas along the eastern seaboard." He'd wanted a place for people to walk and look and always feel they'd find more up ahead. Sixteen years of building by volunteers followed his proposal.

By 1971, the trail's fiftieth year, traffic had grown from a few hardy souls to numbers measured in millions per year. Most came for short walks. Fewer than a hundred people had walked it all. Barely half those finished the same year they'd started.

The typical end-to-end hiker walked fifteen to twenty miles a day, reaching his or her goal in about five months. At our intended pace, we would reach Mount Katahdin around October 6. The park surrounding the mountain would close nine days later. Permits and special gear for climbing would be required as winter drew nearer. The margin for error seemed small....

Too early for such concerns, I thought, as Suches came into view. We wouldn't even be keeping score until Fontana, according to Jerri. Fontana Village, the first sizable town on the trail, was still 140 miles away. We would do our best till then, Jerri had said, but take time to notice what we passed through. That's what MacKaye said the trail was for: "To walk. To see. And to see what you see."

In town, I met postmaster Lloyd Gooch.

"This is Suches, such as it is," he confirmed as he dug around behind the counter. "But no box for Lowther — just a minute." He walked into the small building's back room.

He appeared with our box moments later. I loaded ten days'

prepackaged meals into my pack as he talked about the trail in a quiet, reserved way.

"Never saw so many hikers this early in the year before," he said. "Some of them have had real bad weather." But the season was changing, he went on. Storms wouldn't last five or six days anymore; they'd come and go more quickly.

I mentioned my wife and daughter back at camp and our hopes of reaching Maine.

"A long way for such a little girl," the old-timer answered thoughtfully. "But she'll probably make it."

His weather forecast came as no surprise: rain.

I bought more supplies at local stores, then walked back to camp. I noticed Jerri off in the woods, washing something in the cookpot, and found Kyra sitting up in her bag, crocheting. She'd become interested in knitting, needlework, and other hand crafts through her sixth-grade teacher.

"Did you get my candy bars?" she asked.

"Two kinds. Did you get lots of sleep?"

"Sure, and I crocheted five granny squares for my poncho and Mom bandaged her feet forever. When do we eat?"

Jerri appeared just then to check my load of groceries.

"You've been foraging, I see — peanut butter, Hershey bars, doughnuts. Not bad."

"Have some, then let's pack up and go. And what's with the cookpot?"

"I washed the socks. They were getting a trifle dirty."

"In the cookpot?"

"Soap pollutes the streams. Clothes and dishes and people should be washed away from water sources."

"Do socks pollute the dinner?"

"Only if you worry about it. I'll boil the pot out first."

Overcast sky turned to dark clouds and cold winds by late afternoon. Rattling branches and creaking tree limbs orchestrated our climb of Big Cedar Mountain. On top, we looked out

18

at the view — rain, as promised, and soon. We found a spring and secluded flat spot beyond the summit and put up the tent.

Muffled splattering woke me around midnight.

Rain ... no problem, we had rain gear ... we could keep going. Rain wouldn't last long anymore, Mr. Gooch had said. Good ... never cared much for hiking in the rain....

I dropped back to sleep, snug, dry, unconcerned, never guessing the storm would continue seven days.

"Where's the rain gear?" Jerri asked. It was morning. We sat in the tent's dim glow staring out at drops pattering onto shiny-wet leaves.

"In your pack," I answered.

"Which is in a tree," she politely observed.

"Which is in the rain!" snickered Kyra from deep in her bag.

"Clever of you to notice. I'll get it."

"Maybe we should bring rain gear in at night, hmmm?" advised Jerri.

"Maybe so, maybe so."

"Or we can stay in bed till the rain stops," said Kyra.

We broke camp later and I packed up the tent. Jerri had made the two-man tent from a kit. It really had room inside for three people, if one was ten and no one thrashed around much. Jerri and Kyra had already departed by the time I was ready to go. I heaved the fully loaded pack onto my shoulder and felt a strap tear loose from the frame.

We carried spare pack parts but I knew we had nothing to fix a grommet ripped right out the end of a shoulder strap. I buckled the torn strap around the frame crossbar and hurried to catch up. I felt uneasy. We were alone here; solutions to problems would have to be our own.

We walked all day in rain and blowing fog. Mountain summits wrapped in clouds offered no distant views but Jerri pointed out things close by: stark trees and tiny flowers, rain-rippled puddles, two deer just visible in the fog, bounding off as we came near. The trail led around a mountain sometimes, instead of straight up and over (we cheered), but remaining climbs proved tough and steep as ever. Rain kept on. Leaves no longer crunched underfoot. We only heard soft sounds of rain falling on the forest. We met two other hikers. They rushed past in soaking wet clothes, hurrying to get home.

Home. Did we have one? We'd left no warm refuge behind; everything was in storage. Was this home? I wasn't sure.

We reached the top of Blood Mountain by evening, the highest point (4,461 feet) on the trail in Georgia. Rain still followed us as we crossed the bleak summit and wind-swayed trees faded and reappeared in swirling fog. A grim stone building swam slowly into view. I approached and walked around the moss-grown structure, then opened creaking wooden doors and went in.

My eyes adjusted gradually to dim light. I was in a dirt-floored room with two narrow windows blocked by wooden shutters. A doorway led through a stone dividing wall to a larger back room. Campfire smoke had blackened the interior in places. Dark stains in the littered dirt showed where water dripped from the roof and seeped down inside walls. Every stone and timber felt damp and cold. A musty odor lingered in the air. The building blocked the wind and gave shelter from rain, but offered no welcome, only formless feelings of unease. A faint warmth in the front-room fireplace indicated recent guests, but they'd gone. We had the place to ourselves.

Jerri closed and latched the doors and we set up camp in the back room. Opening shutters let in light, puffs of fog, and gusts of wind. I draped the tent and rain suits from rafters to dry and hung up my pack as well. After leveling dirt in the one dry corner of the room, we spread out the bags.

"I get to sleep in the middle," Kyra said. We all wanted to sleep in the middle that night.

The guidebook told how Blood Mountain had gotten its

name, along with nearby Slaughter Creek and Slaughter Gap. Creek and Cherokee Indians had fought a fierce battle there, according to legend, till the mountain and streams "ran red with blood." Lichens and plants on the mountain's rocky slopes still showed the crimson hue. Other explanations crossed my mind as light faded and our dungeon rooms grew dark. We got into our bags and pulled them close around us, huddling in a corner to sleep on a night already grown long.

I woke suddenly to scurrying sounds that came from every corner of the room. Shadowy figures darted along ledges, walls, and floor amid a flurry of scampering and scratching. Something small and fast raced along my bag toward my head. I felt each leap come nearer. I rolled and turned my face aside. I fumbled for the flashlight and turned it on. Mice. Four hundred of them ... or were there just four? Nothing stirred as I shined the light around.

I turned it out and settled back into my bag. Soon they were back, chewing, gnawing, dashing back and forth. The food hung out of reach ... what could they harm? I pulled my bag over my head and went back to sleep.

I woke again at midnight to the same persistent sounds and heard a faint rustling in one of the packs. I got up and searched. A mouse bolted for freedom as I shined the light into Kyra's pack. It had chewed holes all through a plastic bag of trash. I hung up the other two packs and went back to bed. Traffic diminished, but whistling wind, banging shutters, and scraping of tree branches along the roof and walls outside kept night sounds alive.

I dozed off again but woke at three o'clock to noises in the next room. Clawing ... rattling at the door ... something was trying to get in. What next? Visions of doom and bears and savage, ghostly Indians flashed by. I found the light and shined it through the doorway. The sounds stopped. The creature returned an hour later but again retreated when I turned on the light. Jerri and Kyra slept soundly as the standoff continued. I sat up the whole early morning, hoping for dawn, chasing mice and phantoms trying to break down the door.

I found no tracks or other calling cards outside in the morning, only clouds and another red sunrise. Days later we learned that skunks and raccoons paid regular visits to Blood Mountain Shelter and we had no reason for concern. Just the same, the stick Jerri had wedged in the door latch was all that had kept the night creature out. We were glad it held.

CHAPTER 3

If Daisies Won't Tell,
Ask a Daffodil

A good deal of nonsense has been written about
April showers, most of it by indoor poets and
those who write rhymes for sentimental songs.
April rain is warmer than sleety March rain, but it
isn't really green rain and it isn't full of violets.

— HAL BORLAND

FOG, COLD WINDS, AND THREATENING CLOUDS stayed with us. We
saw the sun only once the next three days; the rest of the time
we walked in rain or mist or chilling dampness that always
seemed but moments from a driving downpour. We kept the
rain gear handy and trudged north through wet Georgia woods.

Sometimes forests of budding hardwoods took us in and
promised a roof of summer's sunlit leaves. We passed through
laurel and rhododendron stands and Jerri talked of huge, fragrant blossoms that would later grace our path. Mountains led
us ever higher, hinting at distant views their summits could
reveal. Promises for someday — meanwhile, views were fogged,

trees were bare, and rhododendron leaves were rolled up like cigars, retreating from the cold.

At times the fog would part and we'd glimpse a world perhaps better left obscured: skies of endless gloomy gray, rows and rows of mountains in dreary purple-brown. And fog that slid through gaps and spilled down mountain slopes toward winding muddy roads.

By day we followed the trail to every peak and knob, then walked obediently down to cross a creek or road and climb back up. Thirty miles passed. It all looked about the same.

"The woods were bleak indeed," Jerri wrote in one day's log. "I even wished, on uphill stretches, that I'd mailed my heavy flower book ahead to Fontana. If I actually saw a flower, I was pretty sure I'd remember it the whole way."

We spent nights wherever we'd had enough, once carrying six quarts of water — twelve extra pounds — three miles to a supposedly dry camp, only to find an unmarked spring. Twice in the rain we slept in our tent. The other night we found a shelter and rain held off. We saw lights in the valleys at night. I thought of people in warm, dry houses.

The sky seemed about to clear one morning, then clouds converged in featureless gray and rain began again. We walked spongy, muddy trail through dripping forest, thinking it better to move on than to wait it out in the cold. Kyra dropped far behind on uphill, then sped ahead going down. We didn't like having her out of sight but said nothing to discourage what games she could invent.

We reached the side trail to Addis Gap Shelter at noon our ninth day. Jerri suggested a lunch stop there to get out of the rain for a while. Kyra had other ideas.

"Let's take the afternoon off," she urged. "We can rest and dry out and try again tomorrow."

"Maybe," I said, "if there's room. We can't get to any other shelter soon anyway, and we're all pretty wet."

Kyra eagerly led the way down the quarter-mile trail. We found one hiker in the shelter, asleep on one of its four wooden bunks. We moved in to claim the other three.

A wet and shivering collie pup peered around the corner of the shelter partway through lunch, then bounded in. Larry Parker and Craig Clark followed right behind. We'd met them our first night out at Big Stamp. We moved aside on the two bottom bunks to make room. The sleeping hiker briefly stirred.

Art Baggett arrived soon after, then came companions, Sue and Jeff. Jeff carried a guitar in a canvas case. We moved down again. Lenny Adler woke up, looked out from his bunk, and wondered aloud how his lonely retreat had come to resemble a downtown bus station.

The hikers, all college age, had traveled from New Jersey, Virginia, Ohio, and Florida, they said, to walk the Appalachian Trail. Some were "through-hikers" like us, headed for Maine. Others were just walking north. Rain had left them looking much wetter and worse off than we were.

We ate lunch and told trail stories, watched the rain and groused about the weather, and all the while I wondered who would get to be the big hero. Nine people and a dog couldn't sleep in bunks designed for four. Even after a few took the meager floor space there would be too little room. Jerri faced the issue first.

"I think we should go," she quietly told me. "We're better prepared than they are."

"You can stay," Art said as we put rain gear back on. "We'll sleep on the floor. It'll work out."

"Thanks," I said, "but there's daylight left. We should put on a few more miles."

Kyra held her disappointment until we were out of ear-shot, then burst into tears.

"We were there first," she sobbed. "Now we don't get our day off and we'll have to sleep in the rain again."

She understood, of course, but still preferred shelter and friends to uphill and rain. Talking about it only brought more sobs. She maintained a steady pace in the middle as the trail turned to puddles and muck, and in places a flowing stream, but her unhappiness remained. She walked in gloomy silence, her buoyant smile gone.

Quite the opposite mood gripped Jerri. As miles passed, she experienced a soaring feeling that took her far beyond conditions that beset us. She described it later in the log:

"We came out here to experience spring, to feel it as Muir did, and Thoreau, and Eiseley, and the others who are able to express it because they have actually experienced the weather and the seasons firsthand. But when it rains and the wind blows, your boots and socks are wet, and the prospect of spending another night in a still wetter tent looms, the resolve gets a little soft.

"Yet today in the wind and the rain, trudging up a hill that seemed ten miles long and forty thousand feet high, the 'mountain madness' hit as it had in Yosemite and at Christmas time in the Superstitions. Absolutely everything about the situation was miserable. But I was alone in it and I wasn't miserable — I was exhilarated, flying.

"Suddenly, in the midst of my attack, I thought of Kyra: cold, tired, and unhappy about leaving Addis Gap Shelter. The mood evaporated like bubbles in stale champagne.

"But children are resilient and soon after we came upon one large, perfect daffodil...."

I saw Jerri stop and wait and point to something off to one side of the trail.

"Look, Kyra," she said, "a bright yellow telephone. Why don't you call ahead for a weather forecast to see how long the rain will last?"

Kyra hesitated a moment, then crouched low and poked her finger in the air, pretending to dial. She spoke into the daffodil.

"Rrrriinnng ... rrrriinnng ... rrrriinnng ... Hello, Weather Bureau? Could you tell me what the weather will be like for the next few days? ... Thank you, goodbye."

Looking up at us she reported, "It will be cloudy for three days, then sunny."

Kyra's smile quivered faintly, broadened to a grin, then spread to all three of us. And for the rest of that day as we walked in the rain, set up a wet tent in the rain, ate dinner in the rain, and crawled into wet sleeping bags in the rain, we held onto our moment of make-believe. We'd need all the smiles we could muster till the sun came out again.

Morning. Rain continued. A deer crashed through the still-ness and came to an abrupt halt a few feet away. I stood star-ing just outside the tent; Jerri and Kyra watched astonished from within. The deer's blazing eyes met mine and its every muscle tensed. I could nearly reach out to feel its pulsing breath. I stood still, watching.

It sprang away with a sudden leap, stopped once to look back, then flipped its tail and vanished. The sounds of its bounding flight over brush and fallen trees faded quickly. I remained motionless long after it was gone. Our tenth day on the trail had begun.

We were camped at Dicks Creek Gap. Nine miles had taken us over four mountains the day before but promised "fine" and "splendid" views remained a foggy mystery. Seventy miles of distant sights had passed in much the same fashion — scenes gray-clouded and obscured. But close by, Jerri had seen yellow violets, bloodroot, and budding leaves that offered hints of green. And a startled deer had paused in the early morning damp. We broke camp and walked on.

Rain subsided but every saturated branch and bush stood ready to douse the careless passer-by. Water puddled in the trail. Parts of the route turned to squooshing, sliding mud which could have easily sent us slipping down the mountain, especially in the steepest places. Mud splashed our jeans; icy water soaked our boots and socks once more.

"Bird," I said, pointing to a spot just ahead. "What is it?"

"Never mind," Jerri said, "you won't believe it."

"Believe what?"

"It's a yellow-bellied sapsucker."

"They really exist?"

"That one does."

The trail led on through the northernmost section of the Chattahoochee Forest in Georgia's Blue Ridge Mountains. The path still led up far more than down, or so it seemed, but climbing of peak after peak began to go easier. We seldom felt stiff in the mornings anymore or ready to die at day's end. Practice made a difference, and wet weather gave us something else to complain about.

We'll soon be cruising right along, I figured in my usual optimistic way, walking lots of miles and taking in great views ... when there got to be any. Once we're in shape, ten miles a day will be routine....

Climbing still slowed us for the moment, however, and clouds persisted on mountain summits. When occasionally they parted, the scene ahead looked no greener than where we stood. We still had quite a walk to find spring.

We began a winding traverse along overlapping ridges late that afternoon. Following the trail along each slope, we would see what appeared to be the top up ahead where the path crossed the crest and turned out of sight. Around that bend we'd find another ridge, another climb, another turn. The repetitive, zigzag pattern gave no sense of forward progress, only a feeling of wandering back and forth.

"Where are we?" asked Kyra.

"In Georgia," I replied.

"No, I mean, are we getting anywhere?"

"Getting dizzy, maybe, and tired."

"What does the guidebook say?" asked Jerri.

"Nothing that matches this," I said. "We're either half a mile from where we want to be or a mile and a half. I can't tell."

"Doesn't it say, 'Wander back and forth over ninety-two ridges until you go crazy?'" said Kyra.

"No, it doesn't mention ridges at all, only '... ascend over side spur thru mature forest.' That's the half-mile option and most likely where we are."

We rounded the final bend near six o'clock and found a sudden change of scene. The mountain we'd been crossing dropped sharply away to a valley and another mountain rose steeply on the other side. A narrow ridge joined the two, punctuated on our side by one twisted, wind-shaped tree. A wooden sign marked the trail at the middle of the crossing: *Bly Gap GA-NC Line.* We had finished our first state.

I put up the tent on the Georgia side and hung wet gear in the tree, hoping the whipping wind would dry things before rain began again. Clouds rolled dark and heavy in all directions. We watched them settle down around us as fog moved in. Jerri cooked dinner in the lee of the ridge and at dusk I gathered in gear for the night.

I heard motors sputtering in the distance as I laid out dry sleeping bags in the tent. The sound grew to a popping and crackling rumble, then a deafening roar that shattered the quiet of our camp. Headlights gleamed around a bend and noise hit us full force. Three thundering motorcycles skidded to a stop just across the ridge. Six North Carolina boys had come to join us for a Friday-night campout.

They gunned and raced their engines, riding back and forth over the same forty feet of ground for what felt to my aching ears like hours. Parking at last to set up camp, they began a whooping, arm-waving debate regarding the best place to bed down. A campfire smoked to life. Poptops snapped, releasing pressure in a hiss from soda cans well-agitated on the bumpy ride. The boys drained them quickly, tossing empties in random directions. Darkness and cold finally drove them to their bags, spread around the fire on damp grass. We settled in as well. I hoped our visitors would not be interested in the packs I'd hung in the gnarled old tree.

I fell into uneasy, dream-filled sleep. Vivid color images came and went in flickering sequences; I tossed and rolled in my bag. A pattern emerged. Real sounds from outside the tent added dimension. It seemed very real....

I was standing outside by the tree. Rain stung my face in the dark and wind beat the packs hung above me, setting dim flashes of red spinning and twisting back and forth. Yelling and shouting came again from across the ridge. Six rain-soaked campers were packing and calling it quits.

A roar of motors filled the air. Car headlights gleamed around the bend. Their mothers had come to take them home. The boys loaded the cars and departed; the sound of engines diminished and faded away, just as it had come. Then we were alone in the dark, in the quiet of wind and rain. I turned from the tree and looked toward the flapping blue tent ... and woke up.

Four-thirty in the morning and raining ... I unzipped the tent flap to look out. The campers had gone. Their campfire lay dead and black. Our packs still swayed in the tree and I heard only wind blowing rain against the tent. Had their mothers really driven up a roadless mountainside? I wondered.

Jerri cooked breakfast in the tent at dawn. I read from the guidebook about the trail into North Carolina as rain poured down.

"'Ascend steeply,' it says here, and 'steadily,' too — four times in the first two miles."

"What happens after that?" Jerri asked.

"Well, after the 'unusually fine views' and 'abundant' wild-flowers — those come in May — it appears to get easier."

30

"There won't be many views in this rain, but I'll bet we see some new flowers near the trail," Jerri said, handing out cups of steaming oatmeal.

"No French toast again today, I see ..." I said, digging out my spoon.

Mileages, elevations, place names, and editorial description came from the *Guide to the Appalachian Trail*, published by the Appalachian Trail Conference in Harpers Ferry, West Virginia. Instructions were given in both north-to-south and south-to-north formats to assist hikers traveling in either direction.

"Where's the next shelter?" Kyra wanted to know.

"The book says six miles, but my note on the map says it's been torn down. Must have read that somewhere. Eight more miles to the one after that."

"Super," Kyra grumped, "another soggy tent night."

Breakfast-time research complete, packs on our backs, and bravely singing "Nothing could be finer than to be in Carolina in the morning," we marched out of Georgia in the rain. We scrambled up steep, muddy climbs, saw nothing special from foggy summits, then picked our way carefully down. We slipped in mud and on thick mats of wet leaves that littered the trail. Perspiration from the grinding uphill effort soaked through our clothes inside our rain gear, then chilled us quickly when we stood to rest. We walked hour after hour through wind-driven rain that showed no inclination to end.

Grouse blasted into the air nearby from time to time and Jerri noted the season's first pussy willows, but relief didn't last long. Kyra dropped far behind and Jerri forged ahead until we were strung out widely along the trail. I waited for Kyra so we wouldn't lose her on rain-drenched twists and turns.

We found an A-frame shelter at noon and climbed in to console ourselves with lunch. Kyra dragged in last, showing little enthusiasm for anything but lying down right there to wait for the sun.

"You just have to keep up, Kyra," Jerri insisted. "You could get lost if you don't."

"I thought this was supposed to be *fun*," the tired ten-year-old grumbled.

"It will be," I said, "if the rain ever quits and we get more used to uphill."

"Sure."

"Tell you what," Jerri said; "if you quit falling behind and making us wait we'll give you a chocolate bar."

"Today?"

"Every day."

Kyra put forth her best and charged along between us without complaint. Rain kept on, however, and we decided to end our eleventh day early. But the shelter had been moved, I'd read, taken from the south side of Standing Indian Mountain and rebuilt farther on. I hadn't noted where. Perhaps on the other side. I lacked enthusiasm for crossing the 5,498-foot peak to find out.

A hiker out for the weekend joined us from a side trail in mid-afternoon, so I asked him.

"It's on this side," he assured me as he walked on ahead. "Follow me. It's about half a mile."

"Are you sure?" I asked.

"Well," the lanky fellow said, plodding on without a backward glance, "it was there last week."

Three-thirty in the afternoon seemed early to stop when we'd covered only six miles for the day, but the roomy shelter looked as good right then as home on the trail ever could. We moved in, hung wet gear to dry, and settled into our bags to watch the rain out our big front door. This time, no matter what, we would stay.

More and more hikers arrived. By evening the shelter had filled and tents and tarps dotted the surrounding area. We chatted through dinner with weekend campers from nearby towns. Kyra smiled and ate chocolate as locals assured us of good weather the following day.

Darkness approached. Steady drizzle outside turned to blowing, pounding sheets of rain, booming thunder, jagged streaks of lightning. The sky crackled and roared and rain lashed the shelter roof and walls.

Surely the townsfolk were right ... the storm would break; the sky would clear. The daffodil's promise would come true on schedule: "Cloudy for three days, then sunny."

CHAPTER 4

Descent into Spring

stay together
learn the flowers
go light
  - GARY SNYDER

RAIN ON THE SHELTER ROOF induced long, restful sleep. Thunder woke me now and then, I saw trees flash briefly white, and each time I enjoyed anew the safety of my dry, sheltered bag. Mice conducted their usual night patrols. Twice I saw a skunk meander through the sleeping camp. By daylight all was quiet. Dawn revealed puffy clouds tinged pink in a bright blue sky — a sunny day for sure.

Through-hikers Art and Sue looked out of their dripping tent and cheered with gratitude. Weekenders David Bankston and Bill McClure stretched and yawned from the safety of their tarp, then settled back to sleep. Up early to walk back to town, the grandfather and grandson camped with us noted blue sky and the accuracy of their forecast. The end of seven stormy days meant something to each, and we all were glad at the sun's return.

"When you get to Maine, could you send me a card?" Bill stopped by to ask. "I'll give you my address."

"We'll let you know if we make it," I said, jotting the details in my journal, "but it won't likely be soon."

We packed up early to see the sights. We reached the top of Standing Indian Mountain in an easy two miles and followed a side trail on to the summit, 5,498 feet, the highest point so far. The world enlarged around us for our first clear view in days.

Rows of mountains lay strewn across the scene, extending in all directions, fading and vanishing on the distant horizon. Farms and towns dotted level areas. Houses clung to hillsides. Tiny roads wound up and over passes and snaked through slowly greening valleys. Clouds crawled lazily by, mottling the land with moving, irregular shadows.

Jerri took pictures; other hikers talked excitedly of what they saw. I stood looking at the outstretched world. The view was nice, quiet, far ... better than fog and clouds, for sure. What more might one see? Writers went into terminal rapture on mountaintops, overflowing with feeling about one thing or another. Why was that? I felt more subdued ... perched on one heap of rock, I looked out at others. Later I'd stand on one of those and look back. So?

"Something hidden. Go and find it." Kipling again ... I wondered what *it* was.

Seven hikers toting bags of trash broke my reverie. A clean-up hike, they said, and as we met, one man was fighting his way out of tangled brush with a rusting soda can.

"Y'know," he said, brushing leaves and broken twigs from his shirt and dirt from his knees, "it's bad enough that people leave their junk all over the trail, but why must they pitch it so deep in the bushes?"

We set a brisk pace on the six-mile descent through alternating open sections and thick stands of laurel and rhododendron. The path grew faint at times in expanses of dried and flattened grass where no trees made handy markers. We found our way without misstep as though we'd been there many times. We reached the shelter chosen for the night just after lunch, so set off at once for the next one. Kyra sped along without urging. At times I thought I might have trouble keeping up.

We arrived at Big Spring Gap well before dark. Kyra found the shelter deep in a rhododendron thicket, and three hikers already camped there moved aside to let us in. Darkness at five thousand feet brought cold that even down mummy bags and insulating pads could not dismiss. One by one we each hauled in down jackets to wear zipped tight in our protective cocoons.

Fourteen and a half miles ... a good day. We'd make up short days easily at that rate.

We pitched our tent near a road through Wayah Gap after another fourteen miles the next day. Jerri made dinner from the last of the food picked up in Suches. I prepared mail orders for dehydrated food to be sent to Hot Springs, North Carolina, 150 miles up the trail.

I'd find a store three miles down the road, my information said. I'd make an early morning grocery run, mail the orders, and get food to last till the next town.

But I found no store three miles away. I kept walking, caught a ride, and finally located a gas-station grocery six or seven miles from camp. The proprietor lounged behind the counter as I searched the few stocked shelves, and included me in his conversation with another customer. The two asked questions about our walk, but eventually agreed to leave the hiking to us.

"I got quite enough of that in the Service," the customer said. "Don't think I'd want to be that long away from a shower again."

"Mind mailing these letters?" I asked the proprietor as he rang up my purchases.

"Not at all," he replied. "Not at all."

Two hours of waiting, walking, and thumbing put me back at

the trail around noon. I walked the short distance to camp, expecting to find everyone set to leave. Not so. Everything from socks to sleeping bags lay draped over branches and bushes and the tent still stood where I'd pitched it.

"I thought you'd be ready to go," I said sharply.

"We're airing things out," Jerri replied.

"Jeez, I just blew the whole morning getting supplies. I didn't think I'd have to pack up, too."

"How were we supposed to know when you'd get back?"

"You could have taken down the tent, at least."

"Saving ten minutes," Jerri said. "Is that important?"

I unloaded my supply of "town food" — doughnuts, fresh fruit, ice cream — onto a picnic table and sat down.

"Have some lunch," I said grumpily.

We got underway a short while later and started up 5,336-foot Wayah Bald. The route had originally followed an auto road. A recent trail relocation, still sporting its builders' colored marker ribbons, led instead along a more difficult path on a different side of the mountain. We labored slowly upward back and forth on switchbacks, expecting to find viewpoints along the way. There were none. The route's only virtue seemed to be avoidance of an occasional passing car. Kyra dropped behind. I stopped and yelled for her to hurry. She caught up, only to fall behind again.

On top, we climbed the stone observation tower for a look around. We saw mountains — mountains in every direction. To the north stood the Great Smokies. Behind rose Standing Indian and peaks in Georgia. Sunlit browns and blues reminded me of the view from thirty miles back. It looked about the same. "Magnificent," extolled the guide, "... one of the finest mountain areas in the East."

We noticed something else as well: rain, headed our way. Five miles separated us from shelter and the day ticked on toward quitting time. We hit the trail.

Long downhill runs and graded ridges took us swiftly to Licklog Gap. We raced over Whiteoak Ridge, then steamed into Burningtown Gap just as the sinking sun prepared to leave the spacious meadow in shade. Rays slanting through jumbled clouds glowed red on hardwood trees and streaked growing shadows across the ground.

We skirted five bald summits as clouds moved in, then hurried up the last incline to Cold Springs Shelter as rain began. Nine miles in an afternoon; not bad for amateurs.

"Breakfast time, sleepy bug," Jerri said next morning to the pumpkin-colored bag next to hers. Kyra lay inside not answering, the bag drawn tight over her head.

"Oatmeal with apples and raisins — c'mon, wake up."

"I *hate* raisins," came the muffled reply.

"Time to get going," I said, poking the inert form.

"Nobody home."

Jerri hauled out M&Ms then and sprinkled a handful over Kyra's porridge. Kyra brought one eye and a cautious nose to the peephole left by her bag's drawstring.

"Still raining," she grumped.

"Eat your breakfast."

Rain ended by the time we reached the top of Wesser Bald. The trail led down from there to the Nantahala River winding through a deep, green valley twenty-nine hundred feet below. We began in a rush.

But the farther we went, the slower Jerri walked. Each hundred-foot drop took us to greener and greener regions of the budding mountainside. Each was like a day forward into time, Jerri said, a day forward into spring. Bright flowers of pink, yellow, white, and blue soon surrounded us. She waded through them like in a dream. As if greeting old friends, she introduced them all by name.

"These were still the earliest of spring flowers," she later wrote, "but even so, what a variety! The bloodroot was mixed with similar flowers like rue anemone, sharp-lobed hepatica, and chickweed. I saw spring beauties, trout lilies, and carpets of violets. Trilliums were in bud. Trailing arbutus gave way to buttercups and birdfoot violets.

"Most of these I'd never seen before, but hours of flower-book reading made new discoveries seem like old acquaintances. The whole afternoon was spring. I forgot my pack and nearly walked off ends of switchbacks, fell into creeks, and bumped into trees. Paradise! How I dreaded to go up into winter again."

The descent took hours. We stopped every few yards to admire and photograph some new variety of blossom, then went on and stopped again, and again. Wesser Creek grew in size and volume as we followed it down and the sound of cascading water drew us to stop along its banks. We stopped again at the bottom, resting amid creekside grasses and flowers, staying a long time until Jerri finally tore herself away. Then we turned down a dirt road toward U.S. Highway 19 and the Nantahala River.

A light mist began as we walked along the highway shoulder. Trucks howled by in a blast of spray and fumes, jarring us back to the everyday reality we thought we'd left behind. The small town of Wesser lay ahead a quarter-mile off the trail. We hoped to find a motel there for the night and a store to buy food for the three-day walk to Fontana.

But the motel was closed. Had been since October, Jerri noted from a calendar inside the dirty front window. The gas station — closed; the grocery store — closed. At quarter-past three in the afternoon, the whole town was closed. The next twenty-five miles of mountains, the Stekoahs, were the most difficult on the whole trail, many said. Even the guidebook switched to italics to warn us. We had to find a store open somewhere, and soon.

We walked back to the footbridge across the Nantahala and tried to figure out what to do.

"Look at the map," Jerri said. "Are there any towns within reach?"

"Nothing close by," I said, pulling the map case from her pack and checking our position. "Nothing we could walk to, anyway."

"We could hitch a ride."

"Which way? These other places might be closed, too."

"We're just too early in the season, I guess," she said.

"The store looked like it had been open today. I wonder for how long...."

I leaned against the bridge railing and watched the river splash noisily underneath. Traces of white showed where rocks broke the surface and water surged in rippling hollows and swells. Droplets fell from my hat brim as the rain increased. I watched them fall to be swept away below. I looked upstream and down, watching rain on fast-moving water.

Would we have missed the store if we'd gotten here sooner ... if we hadn't stayed so long on the mountain?

A battered blue Chevy pulled off the road and stopped near the bridge. Fishermen downstream gathered their gear and headed toward the car. So did I. I said hello, explained our situation, and asked about stores or towns nearby.

"There's a station 'bout four miles from here that sells groceries," one said. "Jump in, we're goin' right by."

Loaded with eight people, four fishing rigs, and three backpacks, the blue Chevy headed west on U.S. 19. Four miles stretched to seven before a gas-station grocery came into view. Our rescuers offered to wait and take us back to the trail when we'd finished shopping. Eying tourist cabins across the road, we thanked them and said we'd rather stay.

"Well, give them the fish," said one.

"Oh, yeah, the fish," agreed another, and he dug into a bag at his feet. "Here," he said, handing me four fresh rainbow trout, "we just go for sport anyway."

Then five strangers drove off, waving. I hardly knew what to say.

Jerri and Kyra went to the store while I walked down the road to check out the cabins. None were occupied, but a car parked in the office driveway implied the proprietor was in.

"Why, yes," came the answer to my knock. "We just opened today — come right in."

We moved into a cabin and carried sacks of groceries to the kitchen. Rooms felt shivering cold. Heaters gradually warmed us and set the wooden structure creaking. We shed jackets and shirts a layer at a time to keep pace. Hot showers washed away dirt from fifteen days on the trail. Fresh fish and biscuits, followed by ice-cream sundaes, brought unaccustomed variety to "dinner out." Like few times before, we reveled in a night indoors.

And Kyra was overjoyed. Motel rooms usually offered only one bed and she'd expected to sleep on the floor. I'd gotten an extra bed for a dollar. She fell asleep soon after dinner with soft, clean sheets and blankets pulled up to her nose.

CHAPTER 5

To Mountain Vistas, Steeply

*It's risky business being a spring ephemeral, pok-
ing your tender nose up into what seems like the
dead of winter. But it's a living. And that's all
any organism asks of evolution.*

— MICHAEL GODFREY

I THUMBED DOWN A VOLKSWAGEN BUS in under ten minutes. A
young couple on vacation returned us to Wesser, where we
found the store open.

"Where were you yesterday?" I asked the proprietor as he
rang up my handful of candy bars.

"I closed at three o'clock," he said.

We'd missed him by fifteen minutes.

Crossing the Nantahala River footbridge again, we followed
railroad tracks for half a mile before turning up into the woods.
We would regain 3,000 feet of elevation on the mountain before
us, 4,730-foot Swim Bald. The sky hung gray and overcast and
we felt a cold, warning wind. The guidebook promised "panoramic views." We started up. Then I noticed Kyra had lost her
walking stick.

Intent on unwrapping a candy bar, she'd forgotten the stick in the store.

"You'll have to do without for a while," I told her. "Pay attention to what you're doing next time." I'd cut each of us a shoulder-high staff from dead agave stalks on our Christmas hike in the Superstitions. The lightweight sticks lent stability on tricky crossings and steep descents.

We began climbing again. I reached for the guidebook to check our location.

"Um ... anyone seen the guidebook?" I asked.

"You took it out of your pocket when you retied your boots a while ago," said Jerri.

I walked back a quarter-mile and found the book on a stump. Kyra was giggling as I returned.

"Better keep track of your stuff, Dad," she said.

"Uh-huh," I said. "Here's a new walking stick." I handed her a sapling I'd stopped to cut.

"Are we ready now?" Jerri asked.

"Onward," I said. "'Ascend steeply,' it says here."

We struggled up Swim Bald for nearly five hours. The climb began steeply, as promised, and led straight up for as far as we could see. We got tired and frustrated and rested often — at Tyre Top after two miles, at Grassy Top after three, at several points in between. We were in better shape after two weeks on the trail but were still no match for such a mountain. The temperature dropped as we climbed higher and wind increased.

The trail seemed more like a wall than a path at times. We climbed holding onto trees, pulling ourselves upward from trunk to trunk. Loose dirt and rocks gave way and sent us sliding back more steps than we'd gained. Looking down, we noted points we'd struggled toward moments, or maybe hours, before. We couldn't measure progress looking up.

Just when we thought we were nearing the top, the going got worse. Mud slicked the trail. We held onto trees and rocks to move forward, even to stand up. A sign identified *The Jump-Up*, a much steeper knife-edge of rock rising in front of us. We struggled up it, following a jagged, narrow ridge and climbing higher.

When we gained the summit at last, no one looked for "splendid views of the Great Smokies." We watched snow fall from a solid gray sky instead and again stood under trees drooping heavy with ice. The chilling wind made us shiver. Discouragement set in quickly. My phone call to Rosemary the night before suddenly didn't seem so well-timed.

"Everything's going fine," I'd said. "You can send our car on." I'd asked her to have the car driven to friends in New York, adding, "We won't need it till fall."

We walked glumly on another mile to Sassafras Gap Shelter and found hikers already camped. Several hours of daylight remained. Choosing between shelter and a warm fire in mid-afternoon, or a snowy tent site farther on was easy for Jerri and Kyra: we stayed.

The group at the fire invited us to crowd around.

"I'm Richard," said one, "and this is Charlie." A third hiker lay asleep in the shelter.

"Sassafras tea, I see," Jerri said, spying the bubbling pot on the fire.

"We dug sassafras tree roots and boiled them," Charlie said. "Have some."

"Know anything about the town up ahead?" I asked.

"Fontana? Sure don't," said Richard. "Why?"

"We'll get there Saturday. I thought you might know when the Post Office closed. We mailed supplies there."

"Anybody's guess," said Charlie. "We've never been there."

"I sure don't want to wait till Monday for them."

The fire and companionship renewed our sagging attitudes for a time, but couldn't dispel the persistent wind that grew steadily colder. Jerri huddled close to the flames to keep warm.

44

As the conversation slowed, she sank deeper into gloom. We'd climbed far above spring. It seemed forever to her until we would find it again.

We cooked dinner early and crawled into our bags wearing down jackets and pants. Wind slammed against the shelter, whistled underneath its raised floor, and shook trees nearby. We scrunched into our bags and drew them tight around our heads. I wondered whether it was too late to reach Rosemary.

Questions ... people we met asked questions. Why did we leave the city to live in the woods? Why so early in the season? Why these woods, the Appalachians?

We wanted a family adventure, Jerri would tell them — one that would keep us outdoors for several seasons to see and feel and smell things that grew. We needed a simpler life for a time, in simple surroundings, where we could live in harmony with the natural world. We wanted time to be and work together so we could leave behind the separate goals that always occupied our lives.

Jerri's reasons ... they sounded good, anyway. My answers were different.

I'd wanted adventure, a change of scene and occupation. Bored with office routine, I'd wanted a new problem to work, one with an ambitious objective that would capture my interest. I'd wanted to do something I would always remember.

Walking the Appalachian Trail was a natural choice, whatever the motive. This was a journey with a single theme, with ample opportunity for adventure, and it would take several seasons. Much was known about the trail, so we could focus on seeing and doing, rather than surviving.

Thus we'd turned our backs on the Rocky Mountains to walk from Georgia to Maine ... from spring, through summer, into fall. From the looks of things, we'd see winter, too.

Darkness engulfed us and the other hikers sought refuge in their bags. Wind drove snow in shadowy streaks across the shelter opening and in shifting swirls along the ground. I huddled in two layers of down, my thoughts turning to keeping warm ... to prospects of deep snow and tough going in the morning ... to the little girl in the bag next to mine....

Why was she doing this? No choice, really ... she was "just along." Yet she hadn't asked to go home. She was trying hard to keep up. And her initial complaints had begun to fade.... Might she have reasons of her own to walk these mountains? I wondered....

"Goodnight, Kyra," I said, rolling over and touching my cold nose to hers.

"G'night," she replied. "... um, Dad?"

"What?"

"You know what I'd like?"

"I give up."

"A strawberry parfait."

"We're short on ingredients right now."

"I mean when we get to town."

"Sure, in town."

"How far is town?"

"Nineteen miles."

"Goodnight, Dad."

Jerri's spirits soared next morning as we woke to sunshine and clear blue sky. Snow mantled the mountains in brilliant white and trees stood stark against the sky, snow and ice tracing each delicate branch. I checked the thermometer I'd found on the trail a few days before: twenty-four degrees.

Charlie and Richard built up the fire and gathered close for warmth. Charlie sat with his sleeping bag draped upside-down over his head and shoulders and pulled close about him.

"I sure didn't think it would be this cold," he said, peering out through the zipper-toothed opening.

Richard, dodging smoke on the other side of the campfire, talked of hiking in the West where it might be warmer.

46

The tea had frozen solid and cracked in the metal pot but the fire soon warmed it for passing around. Eventually, the third hiker stirred from his bag to join us. Charlie introduced Mr. Weatherford, the first over-thirty backpacker we'd seen so far, besides ourselves.

Mr. Weatherford was a different kind of hiker. He'd retired to build a house, he said, and with nothing left to do after that but attend cocktail parties, he decided to walk the Appalachian Trail. He'd departed Springer Mountain three days before us. Everyone else started days and days after and caught up. He hiked in an extremely relaxed manner. When the weather looked bad, he didn't get up. If he felt like hitchhiking to town, he did. He took frequent days off. If he didn't complete the trail this year, next would be fine. A "gentleman stroller," he said he was.

"I counted nineteen different varieties of flowers on the descent into Wesser," he told us. "I think I spent the whole afternoon there."

"You surely could have," Jerri said.

"Have you ever stood quietly and listened to the forest on a sunny day after a rain?" he asked.

"No," I said. "There haven't been many sunny days."

"Try it sometime. You'll hear a soft, crinkling sound as leaves on the ground dry out and curl up again."

We could learn much from this Mr. Weatherford, Jerri said, pointedly.

Charlie and Richard packed off early to the top of Cheoah Bald. We followed their footprints, the only break in several inches of new snow. Atop the sparsely wooded 5,062-foot peak, we looked at mountains turned white all around us, their trees outlined sharply on steep slopes like a four-day growth of beard. The Great Smoky Mountains stood far in the distance, hazy, blue, blending with the sky. In a few days we'd be there.

The scene *did* look dramatic, I had to admit, in shades of

gray, white, and blue ... what more might we find ahead? Cold seeped through our clothes and boots as we rested. We headed down.

The trail down Cheoah dropped to the bottom as if following the track of a plummeting boulder. We slipped and fell on the plunging path, leaving odd-shaped patches where we floundered in the snow. Kyra's feet shot out from under her at one point and she landed sitting down with a thump. Her long fish-net shirt worn outside her jeans left a waffled sitzmark.

The trail turned to mud below the snow line. We picked our way cautiously down, using walking sticks for balance on nearly all of the sheer descent. We crossed a dirt road that had become a stream of yellow, oozing mud. Slime sucked at our boots and splattered and smeared our jeans.

We stopped in Stekoah Gap in mid-afternoon. The trail crossed a road there, continued into the woods, and led on fourteen miles to Fontana Village. The road wound down the mountain and eventually led to Fontana as well. We set down our packs to hitchhike.

It was Friday, April 6. We'd decided to thumb to town early, retrieve supplies from the Post Office and prepare for the Smokies, then return to finish the Stekoahs.

Ingenious plan. We were missing only traffic. Two cars passed in the half-hour we stood there. Neither stopped.

"Let's walk down to the main highway," I suggested. We walked. After half a mile of downhill, Jerri stopped.

"This is silly," she said. "Instead of wasting Sunday, we're wasting today."

Reviewing potential problems — rain, no rides, the uphill back to the trail — I'd reached the same conclusion.

"It's warm and still down off the peaks," Jerri went on. "Why spend nice days in town?" We turned around.

"I wish you guys would make up your minds," Kyra said, none too happy about the abrupt switch in plans.

Back in Stekoah Gap, Mr. Weatherford was hitchhiking.

"I've had enough for today," he said. "I'm going to town to get a steak." A car pulled over just then to give him a ride. "Want to come along?" he asked, opening the car door.

"I do!" Kyra said.

Jerri looked at me and shook her head.

"No, thanks," I said. A look of despair passed across Kyra's face.

We camped near a spring in Brown Fork Gap and spent a quiet evening watching stars through breaks in the trees. The afternoon had been sunny and warm. We'd sat in sunshine on rest stops, listening to leaves rustle quietly as they dried out on the forest floor. Wind stirred branches around our camp and the chirping and buzzing of tiny creatures set a peaceful mood.

"It won't rain," I said. "Let's not put up the tent." A classic line. We laid out our bags in the open on the flattest place around. It had a noticeable downhill slant.

I woke to rain falling on my face around two-thirty. I pulled the rain fly from the tent bag and tossed Jerri one end. We spread it over us and went back to sleep. Kyra, in the middle, slowly slid downhill out from under the rain cover. I rolled over and pulled the cover off Jerri. Rain pattered down and everyone woke up. We resumed places and went back to sleep. Kyra slid downhill and Jerri rolled over and pulled the cover off me. Rain fell harder; everyone woke up. I turned on the flashlight and looked at my watch: half-past three. Wonderful, I thought, plenty of time for several more rounds.

Driving rain soaked us by dawn and Kyra woke up doubly grumpy. Not only had we snatched away her motel bed in Fontana, but she'd spent the night on a "stupid, lumpy sidehill" and was drenched besides.

"For this we turned down a ride with Mr. Weatherford?" she said, scowling. "And passed up a warm motel and a strawberry parfait?"

"This had to happen sometime," I said. "It's part of the experience." She glared at me, unconvinced.

"Let's go to town," Jerri ordered. We packed away dripping bags, donned rain gear, and hit the trail.

We soon turned onto a newer section of trail. More gradual ups and downs replaced the "steeplies" and our speed and dispositions improved. The views did not. Clouds and fog obscured whatever mountain vistas the new route might have offered, and leaking boots and mud-wallow trail kept our minds on more practical concerns.

We overtook Charlie and Richard shortly before noon. Caught without rain gear, they lounged in their bags in Cable Gap Shelter watching the pouring rain. Midway through our lunch, the conversation took a hesitant turn.

"Um ..." Charlie began, "do you have extra food we could buy? We don't have a stove and it's too wet for a fire. Everything we have left needs cooking."

"We're down to Crisco and pepper without a fire," added Richard. "We just looked through both packs."

We gave them what remained of our lunch supplies — crackers, peanut butter, chocolate, powdered milk, and a bacon bar. Jerri even shook up an instant pudding.

"I wasn't going to say anything," Charlie said, a trifle embarrassed. "But then you started into the peanut butter...."

He offered payment, but I declined. The chance to pass on the kindness of the fishermen seemed compensation enough. But that would not do.

"Do you have a pocket knife?" Richard asked Kyra, determined to reciprocate. When she answered no, he dug into a pocket for his.

"Here," he told her, "I have an extra one."

Her smile and thank you put everyone at ease.

A mob of nineteen drenched Boy Scouts arrived so we took our cue to leave. We resumed our slog through rain and mud, following new trail till it returned to the original route. We finished late Saturday afternoon. Cheering the passing of twenty-five miles of rugged mountains, half their distance covered in a day, we walked down the highway toward town.

Fontana Village was built in 1944 as home for construction crews working on nearby Fontana Dam. The village was made a recreation area in 1946 and its three hundred cabins were opened to visitors. We settled into one offering kitchen, living room, and two bedrooms — a bargain at twelve dollars a night.

We gathered ten days' trail supplies in the hour before the grocery store closed for the weekend, plus a mountain of delights for our stay in town. We cooked a festive dinner, then began preparations for coming days on the trail.

The cabin quickly became a jungle of strewn gear. We waded through ankle-deep groceries and equipment from unpacked packs, stumbled over boots drying under heaters, dodged wet bags and clothes hanging from every corner, hook, and knob. We sorted and resorted supplies at hand, but our efforts to package trail meals were blocked at every turn. We could do nothing more without the boxes in the Fontana Post Office.

I grew more frustrated by the minute, thinking surely we could do something ... surely we wouldn't have wait till Monday morning. I put on my jacket and left the cabin.

At the drugstore, I learned the name and number of the postmistress: Mrs. Faye Stewart. I dropped a dime into the pay phone and dialed. Post Office personnel along the trail often went out of their way to help hikers, I knew. They held mail beyond time limits, maintained trail message boards sometimes, and occasionally gave weather and trail condition reports. What I wanted seemed heavy trade on such good will, but we needed the supplies.

Mrs. Stewart answered and I explained our situation. I asked if she would open the Post Office that rainy evening to retrieve our mail. Something in her voice told me she'd heard this story before.

"I'd be happy to," she told me in a friendly tone. "I'll meet you there in ten minutes."

Jerri and I arrived just as the general delivery window slid open. Mrs. Stewart located our packages, pushed them across the counter, and smiled as we expressed our thanks.

"Glad to help out," she said.

We were back in business.

The boxes we'd mailed from Atlanta contained things we needed in town but preferred not to buy at each stop or carry on the trail. Stocks of plastic bags, shampoo, stove fuel, repair parts, and other necessities were available when needed that way, along with reserves of dehydrated food. With these items in hand, we could replenish things used from the packs and package meals for the next section of trail.

When chores were complete, I would tape the box shut and mail it to our next stopping point: Hot Springs, North Carolina. We would repeat the procedure there. Our mobile pantry would thus precede us to Maine in one- or two-hundred-mile jumps. The "Leapfrog Box," Jerri called it.

We finished packing by Sunday noon. Jerri hung the last hand-washed clothes on lines throughout the cabin to drip onto newspapers, and we set departure for early Monday morning.

"How about my strawberry parfait?" Kyra reminded. We left at once for the drugstore.

"I can't make parfaits," said the soda-fountain man, "and I don't have strawberry today. How about a sundae?"

"Pineapple," Kyra ordered. And there we left her, thoughtfully savoring each spoonful.

Outside, rain and gloom had vanished and Fontana Village was alive with sunshine and flowers.

Jerri and I went for a walk.

Larry and Craig hailed us and stopped to talk. We'd last

seen them in Addis Gap ten days before. They were leaving the trail, they said. Rain had left them very discouraged; they didn't see much chance of making it to Maine.

We were going on, I told them. We were doing okay.

Following nature trails and wandering through spring-awakened meadows with camera and wildflower guidebook, Jerri had a photographic field day. The first purple trilliums were blooming and she found toadshade, both maroon and yellow. She showed me Dutchman's breeches and squirrel corn, pointing out differences in their blossoms and leaves. We picked dandelion greens and dug wild onions from road ditches to add something new to dinner.

"We aren't exactly burning up the trail," she wrote to a friend. "We only aim to average about ten miles a day, so we have time to smell all the flowers and hear all the birds sing." That was how Benton MacKaye had imagined it, she said.

Sunshine warmed the grass where we sat. We looked toward mountains where we'd seen a day of snow and ten days of rain and hoped the weather there would change. We didn't have long to wait.

CHAPTER 6

Al^2

*The national parks belong to everyone. To the
people. To all of us. The government keeps
saying so and maybe, in this one case at least,
the government is telling the truth. Hard to
believe, but possible.*

- EDWARD ABBEY

"IT'S RAINING," Jerri said as we entered Great Smoky Mountain
National Park and began climbing Shuckstack Ridge. A light
mist had just started.

"Super," I replied.

"Do you think we need rain gear?"

"Maybe it'll stop."

No one liked wearing rain jackets on uphill, so we avoided
the issue and walked on. Mist became drizzle.

"It's getting worse. Maybe we ought to," Jerri urged.

"Pretty soon, I suppose."

The drizzle slackened a quarter-mile later, ever so slightly.

"Seems to be letting up," I said.

"Maybe, but I'm getting wet."

"You know it'll stop as soon as we put the damn rain gear on," I grumped.

"And if we don't," Kyra observed, "it'll pour."

Then, the deluge.

"Arrrgh!" I yelled, and we quickly dug out rain suits and pulled them on. Too late. We had wet clothes under waterproof nylon and three miles of climbing ahead. The ascent would be a steam bath.

"Waited too long again, huh?" Jerri said.

I didn't reply.

We reached the top of Shuckstack Ridge near dinner time and walked the remaining mile to Birch Spring Lean-to. Seven hikers greeted us as we entered. We threaded our way through a disarray of packs, boots, clothes, and cooking gear strewn about the dirt floor and found an empty corner for ourselves. Wire screen stretched over two log platforms along the back of the shelter offered sleeping space for twelve. I chose three empty bunks on the top level and spread out our bags.

The shelter had thick stone walls on three sides and a built-in fireplace near the front. A chain-link fence enclosed the open fourth side. The fence, standard on Smoky lean-tos, kept out bears. We felt little cause for concern in early April.

We gathered at the fire after dinner but soon left as wind increased and night air turned cold. Bundled in nearly all our clothes, we crawled into our bags and zipped them tight. Awakening later, I understood why top bunks were chosen last. Wind howled under the eaves at my feet to chill me through every layer. Tiny flakes blew across my bag and melted in icy pinpoints on my face. Snow.

We departed first next morning. The seven hikers in the shelter stayed behind to wait out the weather and enjoy a more leisurely breakfast. We heard them singing and laughing around the fire as we plodded on. Snow blew horizontally across the trail, swirling into drifts to make the going slow.

The trail joined the Tennessee-North Carolina border after two miles at the crest of the Great Smokies. We turned east to follow it through the park. We would walk with one foot in each state for the next two hundred miles.

I noticed improvement in the route. Graded trails and switchbacks moderated frequent ups and downs and the path was well-maintained. No blazes marked the AT in the park, but its meandering course was usually obvious. We looked for wide spaces between the trees where the trailway might go and for a slight indentation where the path lay under accumulating snow.

And the way led up, back to the five-thousand-foot level. We would reach six thousand feet at several points in the Smokies, including 6,643-foot Clingmans Dome, the highest point on the Appalachian Trail. With canteens already freezing in the pack as we walked, we could expect little warmth at those elevations. Kyra noticed tracks of mice and rabbits crossing the trail. Business as usual for them, it appeared.

Snow ... pretty, somehow. Under heavy gray skies, it gave the world the look of a black and white photograph. Snow fell lightly but steadily as we walked, clinging to packs, jackets, Kyra's tossle cap. Snow hung on trees, heaping each branch with a delicate mound. Pine boughs held more ... to dump down my neck when I bumped them with my pack. Walking wasn't bad — slippery at times, deep in the drifts, cold on the feet. We'd be warm if we kept moving.... How cold would it get up higher? How many freezing nights to go? Good thing we had warm clothes....

We entered Spence Field at dusk. We'd reserved space in New Spence Shelter on the edge of the forty-acre clearing, but the story told in small footprints outside indicated a change in plans. I opened the tarp-covered gate and found what I expected: Boy Scouts, wall to wall.

Weary eyes in small weary faces peered from sleeping bags everywhere. Wet socks, shoes, sneakers, and combat boots hung from bunks and were scattered on the floor. Rucksacks, day packs, and outsized backpacks added to the pile. A still- ness hung in the air and looks of apprehension greeted us on every side. The boys looked cold and wet and not at all eager to move. The shelter reservations we'd made wouldn't do us much good here. We turned to go.

"Plenty of room," the scoutmaster called out from where he stood warming by the fire. "The boys can double up."

Dressed in striped pants wet part way to his knees, flowered shirt under a stained down vest, and a polka-dotted painter's hat, he walked toward the crowded bunks to clear a space.

"No, thanks," I said. "We'll try the next one." Old Spence Shelter had room for six and was half a mile away.

We arrived near dark and were welcomed by three hikers who'd passed us during the day. We'd camped with them at Birch Spring the night before — Lenny Adler, whom we'd seen in Addis Gap, and two bearded college students bound for Maine with very heavy packs.

"Which one of you is Al?" I asked, remembering I'd heard the name an unusual number of times.

"We both are," said one who wore steel-rimmed glasses and a weathered brown fedora. "I'm Al Sax from Pennsylvania. My partner is Al Kesselheim from Massachusetts."

"People have started calling us Al^2," said the slightly taller of the two, who wore down jacket, jeans, and standard blue work shirt.

"Crowded back there," Jerri said.

"Yeah," said Al S. "We figured you'd be coming here."

"That place'll be a zoo if they ever thaw out," I added.

We got into our bags at once. I set packs within reach, and with our small stove balanced on the elevated bunk, Jerri soon had a pot of stew underway. Similar smells drifted toward us from the other end of the shelter.

"What'ya cooking?" asked Al S.

Al^2 57

"Meat bar stew," said Jerri.

"We've got spaghetti."

"Why don't we stir it all together?" suggested Lenny.

"Okay," said Al S.

"Well ..." Jerri said.

"Sure, Mom," urged Kyra. "Sounds good."

Al dumped our dinner into theirs.

"Anybody got anything else to add?" he asked.

"Bacon bar," offered Al K.

"Dehydrated green peppers," said Lenny.

"Carrots...."

"Peas...."

"Onions...."

An undefinable goulash soon bubbled noisily in the pot. Al served it up and we finished it off within minutes. Only Jerri noticed the decided disimprovement on what she'd planned.

"We need something hot to drink after that," she said.

"Hot Tang," said Al S. "I'll make some."

"I was thinking of cocoa."

"Okay," he said. "We'll have both."

We drank hot orange Tang and cocoa.

"I'm still hungry," Kyra said.

"Let's pop the rest of your popcorn," said Jerri. "What could it hurt?"

Two pots of popcorn made the rounds.

"Caramels for dessert," said Al K., digging out a handful.

"Great," said Al S., "but mint cake would be just the thing. Kendal Mint Cake. I've never tried it but it's supposed to be good."

"We have some," I said. I passed a few chunks around.

"Thank you, my good man," he said. Paraphrasing a testimonial from Hillary's Everest expedition quoted on the package, he continued, "... and we topped it all off with Kendal Mint Cake. Easily the high point of the trip!"

Frigid night air invaded the shelter as the hours passed, yet good cheer seemed to keep the cold at bay. We finally blew the candles out, drew sleeping bags tight around our noses, and fell asleep.

My boots felt oddly cold and stiff next morning. I jammed my feet into them, kicked against the shelter wall, and finally got them on. I clumped around getting things out for breakfast as my feet slowly turned numb. The Als looked on in wonder. What kind of crazy is this? they thought, as they confided days later; he puts on frozen boots and doesn't even notice.

"Eighteen degrees," I reported, tossing the thermometer into my pack. Useless gadget ... why did we need precision readings on things we didn't care to know?

"What's the good news?" someone asked.

Jerri looked outside and saw good news all around: clear blue sky and unbroken snow, bushes and tree branches bristling with frosty filigree, rhododendron leaves curled tight and traced with delicate lacy white.

Leaving snow angels, spent snowballs, and fox-and-goose circles behind, we struck off for nearby peaks. Only a few inches of snow had fallen, but breaking trail through drifts two and three feet deep slowed us down. Sightseeing slowed us even more, as did stops to identify tracks that crossed and followed the trail. Rounding one bend, Jerri stopped us with a sudden hush. A wild pig snuffled in the bushes just ahead, then trotted up the trail.

We'd walked two miles by noon. Scant progress, I thought, but the view from Thunderhead Mountain brought us to a stop again. Eight hundred square miles of national park spread out below. We looked around at thick forest: spruce on the highest snowy summits; fir, oak, and slowly greening birch on slopes; a host of others turning valleys springtime green. Flowering dogwood, mountain laurel, and rhododendron filled in lower growth.

Looking back, we saw Fontana Lake and Stekoah peaks we'd climbed the week before. Ahead stood more snowy mountains, waiting for the trail of footprints that traced a narrow path. Jerri photographed the near and far and Kyra built a snowman. Al^2 passed by.

"Some view!" said Al Sax.

"We'll break trail for a while," Al Kesselheim said. "See you folks later."

Here it was again ... a view with substance. I'd wondered if we'd be stuck with monotonous brown ridges until leaves finally grew. Snow made a difference. Jerri seemed to find it spectacular, in some special way that moved a lot of film through the camera. Kyra liked it, too.

Funny ... I felt more at ease than at first. We'd been walking three weeks. Nothing terrible had happened ... we'd just kept going. And we were still going when others had dropped out....

We approached Clingmans Dome the next afternoon, climbing through beech forest that swayed overhead and filled the view on all sides. Wind-driven clouds raced above. Branches rustled around us. We felt only a trace of breeze in the protection of the trees.

Beeches thinned in half a mile, disappeared in another. Spruce and balsam took their place. Still we saw trees blowing on every side. Another mile brought a ridgecrest into view and we climbed toward it. There the forest ended. Looking along barren ridge to where trees resumed, we saw the mountain's summit — a mile to go. We crossed the ridge, entered the woods, and climbed again.

I saw cloudy skyline through treetops ahead where light defined the nearing summit. Soon the rounded top itself lay within reach. I climbed the last few yards in a rush to reach the highest point on the Appalachian Trail. But that wasn't it. Beyond lay another ridge and another climb. Clingmans Dome was the next peak over. We crossed and climbed once more.

Fir and spruce so thickly covered the summit that an observation tower had been built a short distance off the trail. We
dropped our packs and climbed the ramp. Ice slicked the
walkway. A chilling wind buffeted us forty feet up on the
tower's circular deck. We stood at the railing and looked at
mountains just visible over tops of frosted trees. I walked
around the perimeter, picking out peaks identified in photographs displayed along the rail. Places we'd been, places we'd
yet to go — all moody blue mounds under a sky of sullen gray.

"Mount Collins is the second one over, Kyra," I said, pointing
to a distant peak. "That's where we're headed for tonight."

"It looks pretty far. Haven't we walked ten miles already?"

"Yeah, but that's where we're scheduled to be. Al^2 said
they'd meet us there if we could make it, remember?"

"Uh-huh." A faint sparkle came to her eyes and she said no
more.

We stayed a few moments, then walked back down.

"Where does that go?" Kyra asked about a path leading right.

"To the parking lot," I said.

"Parking lot?"

"Yeah, you can drive up here."

"What a drag. We worked hard to get up this mountain. It
isn't fair."

"They don't build towers just for hikers," Jerri said, "and
without it, we wouldn't have seen the view."

"Poo!"

Three more miles took us steeply over Mount Love and
Mount Collins, then down a half-mile trail at dusk to Mount
Collins Shelter. Al and Al rushed out in welcome as we arrived,
cheering and banging spoons on cookpots the last fifty yards.

"Yaaaayyyy, Kyraaaaa! Thirteen miiiiiles!"

Kyra marched in beaming.

"We were starting to worry," said Al S. "It was getting so
late...."

"I knew Kyra would make it," said Al K. "She's a real through-hiker." Kyra's eyes twinkled brightly.

After dinner, she dug a bag out of her pack.

"We're out of popcorn," she said. "Anyone want a roasted marshmallow?"

"Sure!" said both Als at once. She'd had no friends like this in sixth grade.

Night grew even colder camped above six thousand feet. We huddled in our bags on elevated bunks, shivering, sleeping fitfully, looking at watches every three minutes and hoping for dawn.

Morning brought a red sunrise, clear sky, and an unobstructed view of blue, hazy mountains. We saw it right from our bunks as red fox squirrels, chipmunks, and juncoes came into the shelter to chatter and chirp us awake. The sun streaked patches of light through the spruce forest around us, highlighting clumps of snow on the branches.

"We're headed for Gatlinburg to resupply," said Al Sax. "You guys can have the food we have left."

"Thanks," Jerri said. "We're running short in this cold. Are you sure you won't need it? Can we pay you for it?"

"Nope," Al Kesselheim replied. "You can send us a copy of that book you're gonna write, though."

"Damn," I said to no one in particular.

"What's the matter?" Jerri asked.

"Stove's clogged. Can't get it lit."

"You can use ours," offered Al S.

Our Gerry stove fired up just then.

"Thanks," I said. "It's okay now."

We forced on frozen boots at the last moment, donned packs, and made our way stiff-footed down the trail. The Als moved quickly ahead.

"See you in a couple of days," they called out as they disappeared around a bend.

We met Edward Stewart, a dapper gentleman from Virginia, a short while later. He was out alone for a week's hike.

"Tell me," he asked earnestly of Jerri, "what does a man have to do to get his wife to hike?"

"This was my idea," she replied.

"It's so lovely out here and I've tried so often to get her to join me, but I always end up hiking alone."

"A lot of men expect women to walk too far, I think," Jerri said, "and carry too much, and go too fast. One bad experience is usually enough."

"I'm sure you're right. Too bad she's not here now to talk to you."

We reached Newfound Gap and U.S. Highway 441 at noon. Newfound Gap was a popular starting point for short hikes; already that Friday, April 13, parking areas were filled with cars of sightseers and weekend hikers.

Kyra met one such visitor when she and Jerri stopped to visit heated restrooms. Lady Tourist approached as Kyra washed her hands, noticed the pack leaning against the wall nearby, and sought to make conversation.

"How long have you been hiking, little girl?"

"Since the twenty-first of March," said Kyra, dead-pan, her two-hundredth mile of Appalachian Trail just logged.

"Since March thirty-first!"

"No, *twenty*-first."

"Oh. Well, um ... how long will you be out?"

Kyra hoisted on her pack and replied without expression, "Till October."

Exit Lady Tourist. Jerri, doubled up from barely restrained laughter, looked at Kyra in the mirror. The blase ten-year-old giggled, then strolled outside.

Our jovial mood vanished an hour later. Kyra wandered on while we talked with other hikers and afterwards we couldn't find her. She wanted time alone to think, she'd said. Being sandwiched between our conversations made it difficult. We quickened our pace, expecting to find her around the next bend.

Hikers coming our way said they'd seen her just ahead. We kept on, growing concerned at frequent icy spots and steep drop-offs. Still she eluded us. We stopped at Ice Water Springs Shelter, thinking surely she would wait there. She hadn't. Scenery on either side became more dramatic. We rushed past with hardly a glance.

Another group of hikers told us they'd helped her up from a fall on a slippery patch of trail. They'd thought it odd, they said, for such a little girl to be hiking alone. We raced on, anxiety mounting, thinking we would have to catch her soon.

When at last we spied her rounding a bend, nothing seemed out of the ordinary. A small figure with a bright red pack bobbed along, apparently confident she knew the way to Maine.

Jerri was furious. She admonished Kyra to be more careful, to avoid chances of getting lost or hurt, and to be less casual about causing us concern.

"You stay in sight from now on," Jerri said, "so we know where you are."

Kyra stood stoically through it all, puzzled at the fuss.

"I was okay," she said. "I just wanted to be by myself."

Minutes later we reached Charlies Bunion, a jagged knob of rock jutting out into the valley on the Tennessee side. The trail swung around its outside edge and led between sun-struck rock walls on the right and a plunging drop on the left. Views north, east, and west showed the region's characteristic mountain colors — mixed green and reddish-brown nearby, purple and ever-lighter shades of blue in the distance. Smoky haze increased until the farthest ranges became faint, wavy lines and finally merged with the sky.

Grade-school geography came back to me as I looked over the scene. Appalachians were "old, worn-down" mountains, I'd learned, not "young, rugged" mountains like in the West.

I noted jagged peaks, steep slopes, and deep valleys repeated on every side. I followed our route over the knife-like peaks of the Sawteeth Range, over the thousands of feet of elevation steeply gained and lost. I remembered our climb of Clingmans Dome, of peaks in the Stekoahs and in Georgia, and knew I'd been misled.

Appalachian Mountains were healthy and fit, I wanted to report. Those who thought them worn-down and flat should come out and walk — and see for themselves.

CHAPTER 7

Town

Getting up too early is a vice habitual in horned owls, stars, geese, and freight trains. Some hunters acquire it from geese, and some coffee pots from hunters. It is strange that of all the multitudes of creatures who must rise in the morning at some time, only these few should have discovered the most pleasant and least useful time for doing it.

— ALDO LEOPOLD

WHY AM I GETTING UP at five-thirty in the morning?

For an early start — nearly fifteen miles to do today.

Could I wait till dawn perhaps?

Nope, there's a long way to go to finish the Smokies by evening ... you never know what might slow us down.

So I got up. The cold, clear day would bring five mountains to climb, then a long descent to lower and warmer elevations.

I woke Jerri and Kyra, who responded with somewhat less than wild enthusiasm.

"Go away," Kyra growled.

"What time is it?" Jerri mumbled sleepily.

"Morning. Here's the breakfast stuff."

Jerri rubbed her eyes and rolled her bag over to where I'd set out stove, cookpot, utensils, and other breakfast supplies. Delays began at once — the stove wouldn't light.

"Let me know when it's working," Jerri said, nodding off again.

I took the stove apart, cleaned and poked at areas that might be clogged, but without success. The familiar morning sputter would not come forth. I packed it for repair in Hot Springs, four days away, and borrowed a stove from the fellow in the next bunk.

We soon departed in pursuit of Mount Guyot, Cosby Knob, and the last of the peaks in the park. We followed high, narrow ridges much of the way and covered miles easily, pausing only at viewpoints or for snacks or lunch. One stop featured Dutch-oven biscuits we'd baked the night before. Our oven was a cookpot with a small fire underneath. Another fire in the pie-pan lid provided slow heat all around for even baking. Biscuits in the sunshine, with butter, honey, and brown sugar, added much to the day.

I noticed a marked change in the terrain. The trail crossed broad, rounded peaks and ridges in the southern part of the park; ridge crests north of Newfound Gap were often only three feet wide. Except for high sections around Clingmans Dome, trail south of the gap often led through fields and over balds, giving an open, distant feeling. In the north the forest surrounded. The trail bored through it like a tunnel with only occasional breaks to see out. We walked through miles of trees whose branches merged overhead — virgin fir and spruce along the ridges; oak, beech, and maple at lower elevations. The sun made bright patches on the trail ahead, urging us on to better weather just around the bend.

Beyond Mount Cammerer, the last peak of the day, we

rambled four miles downhill to Davenport Gap Shelter. A group of Tennessee high-schoolers made us welcome with an evening of stories around the campfire. The night stayed warm at 1,975 feet. We hardly needed to zip our bags.

We finished the Smokies early next morning and stopped at a small creek called State Line Branch. Jerri spotted new flowers growing along its banks and got out her camera.

"Look, showy orchis!" she said to Kyra as the two roamed about.

"Is that related to the showy lady slipper?" Kyra asked.

"Same family. Similar colors, too, white and rose, but it's much smaller."

"I sure hope we see a showy lady slipper somewhere. Those white ones are trilliums, right?"

"Right. Lily family. *Trillium grandiflorum.* Oh, and those magenta flowers are wild geraniums!"

"I know that. What are those over there?"

"Yellow toadshade. It's a lily, too...."

It looked like a long session. I leaned my pack against a tree and sat down to wait; flowers were pretty and all that, but this level of detail was a bit much for me. I checked landmarks in the guidebook. I got a drink from a canteen and idly glanced around. Pleasant day ... nice place ... wonder how long they'll be at it. Time to get going soon ... many miles to go before evening....

Toadshade ... the name conjured up images. A swarthy toad in sunglasses and spotted swim trunks, sipping lemonade under a large, striped mushroom ... or wearing a ragged, hooded robe, dragging chains and moaning, "I am the Tooooad of Christmas Paaaaast" ... or on a dark and foggy San Francisco waterfront, trenchcoat wrapped close, hat brim pulled low, with the power to cloud mens' minds....

Income tax returns were due; it was Monday, April 16. I'd mailed mine long before, but some fitting observance seemed in order. Something appropriate, especially in that restful setting, that quiet glade with cheerful gurgling creek, that real garden with imaginary toads.... I leaned back against my pack and fell asleep.

We walked over Big Pigeon River bridge, under the Interstate 40 bridge, and entered Pisgah National Forest on a wooded trail. Rain began as we started up Snowbird Mountain and fell steadily as we climbed. We walked slowly and with effort, sweating quickly through clothes inside our rain gear, shivering in icy wind each time we stopped. We would regain twenty-eight hundred feet of elevation in four miles, bringing total uphill since Springer Mountain to nearly sixty thousand feet. Uphill: I'd expected it to be getting easier.

We labored up the steep slope for six hours and still the rain came down. Water glistened on every leaf and branch and flowed in the trail. It dripped from our rain hoods and ran down our faces.

We camped after ten miles and walked another ten by the following afternoon. Still the rain poured down. Jerri's head throbbed with a cold, her resistance overcome by hours of alternating chilling and overheating. A southbound hiker mentioned a cabin four miles up the trail. I could have made it easily, and wanted to, but Jerri wouldn't go on. We stopped instead at tumbled-down Walnut Mountain Lean-to and shared the meager space with five others.

Our food reserves were low. We'd eaten more than planned in the freezing weather and still had been hungry for days. I built a fire when rain subsided and we cooked all that remained. Darkness came and we lay down on sagging, sloping bunks to sleep.

Town soon ... food ... dry clothes ... hot showers. We'd have been in better position in the cabin. It wasn't that far. She could have made it. We'd need an early start now to cover thirteen miles to town ... and few delays.

Long before daylight a voice came from far away. Something shook my shoulder. I pulled away, slept on. The voice came again, closer. I tried in total blackness to sort it from my dreams. Something shook me again.

"... raining," I faintly heard, "... packs aren't covered ... cameras and books getting wet."

I groped for the drawstring to loosen the sleeping bag pulled tight around my face. Behind me ... I'd rolled over inside my bag. I found it, widened the opening, and looked out — total darkness, air extremely stuffy. I strained to see some shadow, some edge of light and dark. Oh ... I'd worn a down jacket hood to bed ... it had turned to cover my face. I took it off and looked again. Still dark. Then the shelter's black wall came into focus inches away. I turned around, found Jerri, and muttered, "... huh?"

"Why do we keep doing this?" she asked.

I went out in the rain in shorts and socks, retrieved cameras and books, and covered each pack with its rain fly. Why do we keep doing what? Leaving packs uncovered at night when rain before morning was obvious? I shook mud from my socks and crawled back into my bag. Overly optimistic, probably. Or was that what she meant?

We were back on the trail at seven o'clock. Dull, water-soaked scenery persisted, offering little of interest to slow our brisk march to town. I glanced at the cabin as we passed. Open and large — much better than where we'd stayed.

Jerri stopped us briefly for birdfoot violets sprinkled with raindrops, and a newcomer she knew at once as fringed polygala, but her heart wasn't in it somehow. Her thoughts lay in town where she could rest her pounding head. We'd walked nine miles by the time rain ended at noon. The final four went easily. We emerged from the woods at the edge of town in early afternoon. We'd walked 29 days and 262 miles, to Hot Springs, North Carolina.

I saw a man clearing brush nearby so stopped to ask about facilities in town. He mentioned stores, restaurants, motels, but no tourist cabins with kitchens. Disappointed, I turned to go.

"Wait," he said, "I think I have just the thing for you." He led us to a two-story cabin just off the trail.

He opened the front door and we entered a large, dusty room with fireplace and upstairs loft. Faded couches and chairs sat randomly about and a worn, ornate rug covered all but the perimeter of the wooden floor. A lamp with a yellowed shade stood on a table against one wall. Wooden chairs, tables, and mattresses furnished adjoining rooms. Bare light bulbs hung on cords from the ceilings. The kitchen offered stove, refrigerator, and a cupboard full of dishes.

"I'm Father Carmody," our host informed us, "from the Catholic Chapel of the Redeemer just across the way. We open this cabin to hikers on occasion. Do you think it will meet your needs?"

The offer would have answered any hiker's prayers. We said a grateful yes and moved in.

I wrote a note describing our good fortune and thumb-tacked it to the trail signboard outside. Hikers always read signs, and we'd been expecting Al^2 for days since their detour to Gatlinburg. If they passed by before we moved on, this "trail mail" would flag them down.

We noticed again that many stores were closed in town. The Post Office was open though, and as I retrieved the Leapfrog Box, supplies ordered in Wayah Gap, and a box of forwarded mail, I asked if it were some special occasion.

"It's Wednesday," the postmaster said. "Most stores close up around noon on Wednesdays."

"Why is that?" I asked, recalling we'd arrived in Wesser on a Wednesday afternoon.

"Folks here in the South figure they need an extra half-day

of rest to get them through the week. In some towns, even the Post Office closes."

Part way through dinner we heard banging at the front door. Kyra ran to open it. Whoops of recognition followed — "Hey, look, it's Kyra! This *must* be the place!" — bringing us all in a rush. Al[2] stood on the porch, clutching our note. Broad smiles eased for a moment the weariness etched in their faces, the obvious discomfort of wet clothes and heavy packs. We welcomed them in, along with their companions Adele Joyes and Jonathan Coe.

"You can all stay here," I said. "Nice shelter, don't you think?"

"I can't believe this place," said Al S., setting down his pack, "and right on the trail! When we found your note we expected miles of complicated directions."

"How far have you walked today?" Jerri asked.

"Twenty-two miles and we're dead. We just kept walking and walking, saying, 'Maybe we'll find something in town ... maybe we'll find something in town....'"

"Hey, Kyra, we brought you a present," said Al K., digging deep into his sixty-pound pack. He produced a two-pound bag of popcorn. "This replaces what we used up in Old Spence."

"Oh, thank you," she said with a smile. "We'll make some tonight."

Al had carried it sixty miles to give to her, never expecting us to stay ahead five days.

Popcorn by the panful followed dinner, along with brownies, lemonade, and ice cream. We traded stories and news as heavy rain lashed windows and drummed the porch roof outside, and we debated merits of hiking in snow versus hiking in rain.

"You don't get as wet walking in snow," said Adele, an expert in these matters. She'd earned the name Hard-Core Adele trudging through a snowstorm wearing shorts.

"You don't have to break trail in the rain," said an Al.

72

"Are rain and snow the only options?" Jerri asked, drinking steaming lemonade to help break her cold.

So it appeared, everyone agreed.

"How are you doing, Kyra" asked John. "Tired of walking yet?"

"I'm sick of rain and cold and uphill. The rest is okay."

"That doesn't leave much," he said, as everyone laughed.

"Cabins," she said. "That's the best part, so far."

"I'll bet none of your friends has walked 250 miles," said Adele, "or however far it's been."

"That's for sure!" Kyra said, with an obvious note of pride.

"Kyra's gonna make it to Maine," said Al K.

"Yaaaaayyyy," cheered Al S.

We soon sacked out, one by one, on mattresses near the fire and in the loft. It seemed appropriate somehow that we'd come from a candlelight party in the snow at eighteen degrees, and another even colder night camped above six thousand feet, to a warm, comfortable cabin. No one failed to note how our fortunes had improved.

With everyone still asleep next morning, I sorted through the box from "Mission Control." Friends Paul and Fayne Doering in Rochester, New York, had agreed to fill this post, for though we made our own arrangements as we went along, we still needed occasional aid. At towns such as Fontana or Hot Springs, we would send them the estimated date of our arrival in subsequent towns. They would thus have some idea of where we were and could send items from mail we'd had forwarded to them.

They would look after our car when it arrived from Atlanta and handle equipment exchange. When summer came, for example, we would send for warm weather gear stored in the car and mail heavier items for storage until needed again.

Paul also paid our bills and sent us money orders for cash needed on the trail. Walking-around money, as it were. I transferred money by mail between Phoenix and Rochester accounts whenever the bank balance dwindled.

The Doerings' package contained letters from friends, two jars of grape jelly, and a cheery note from Paul.

"The enclosed jellies are from the personal jelly-cellars of the Mobil Oil Company," he explained, "which gave them away with every eight gallons of gas. I tried them, but they just gummed up the carburetor. I'll send you more from your supplies when they get here (with the car), and they'll be waiting at your next postal stop."

Hikers stirred downstairs before long. Al and Al planned to cover sixteen miles that day so were packing to leave. Adele and John thought they'd write a few letters before departing. We were headed for town.

"Wash day," I told Al Sax. "The only clean clothes we have are a pair of socks apiece, spare shorts, and down jackets."

"Sounds excessive to me," he replied. "At the laundry, the well-dressed hiker wears only rain chaps and a cigar."

"We probably won't see you again," I said. "You'll be gone when we get back."

"Guess so," he said. "Do you think Jerri would take our picture? With Kyra?"

They boosted Kyra onto their shoulders.

"The popcorn," Jerri said; "get the popcorn."

And riding high on the shoulders of one Al from Pennsylvania and another Al from Massachusetts, Kyra held the popcorn aloft as Jerri took the picture.

We said goodbye and walked into town. We couldn't know then how final the farewell would be. We heard first from other hikers. Later, an almost painfully sad letter from Al Sax told how the Al^2 hike to Maine came to an abrupt end three weeks out of Hot Springs.

Writing "Dear Lowthers[3]" he explained how Al Kesselheim broke a bone in his foot outside Pearisburg, Virginia, forcing them to leave the AT until at least the following summer. Saying that he found himself checking maps at times to see where they might have been, he signed off poignantly, "Al[1]."

Adele and John were leaving when we returned. They had summer jobs with the Appalachian Mountain Club in New Hampshire and were "strolling off a bit of the southern part of the trail" before reporting to work.

"Be sure to look us up when you reach the White Mountains," said John, as they walked back to the trail.

We would, we said. But that was fourteen hundred miles away....

Shopping, repairs, and miscellaneous errands consumed the rest of the day. Kyra joined me on one trip to town.

"Where to?" she asked.

"The hardware store." For a quarter, I bought a spool of thin wire and cleared the stove's clogged passageways.

"That was easy. Now where?"

"Variety store." For a dollar, I bought a two-section cane fishing pole. "Here's your new walking stick," I said, handing her the bottom half. "Now, about this 'town list' of yours."

Marked "Special Delivery ... Fragile ... Air Mail ... Important! ... Special Handling," the folded letter with stamps drawn on it had arrived in Davenport Gap Shelter. It listed thirteen things she wanted in town.

"'6. Bed in motel (real).' I think we can mark that off, along with these cake and ice cream entries."

"Uh-huh. How about 3?"

"Hmmm, '3. Sundae (and/or parfait)'. You want that, too?"

"Sure. This is town, right?"

"Okay ... we'll look around. Here, '7. M&Ms (doesn't *have* to be a one-pound bag)'; I got those...."

And we wandered about Hot Springs accumulating gum, doughnuts, cookies, a chocolate Easter bunny, until the entire list had been satisfied.

"How do you like the AT now?" I asked. "You've been keeping up pretty well."

"Oh, it's better. But I still don't like uphill."

"Me, either. I wish you'd stay within sight of us, though, and
not get too far behind going up, or ahead going down."

"You guys are always talking. I like to be by myself so I can
think."

"What do you think about?"

"I've been building a house."

"Where?"

"On an island. It has a big yard and lots of trees all around."

"Are there other houses on the island?"

"No, just mine."

"Sounds nice. You have a big garden, I suppose."

"Yes, and a pond. I can go swimming in the summer and
skating in the winter."

"Do you have a phone?"

"No," she said.

"How about electricity?"

"I get it from the waves somehow, but I don't know how it
works. The house is heated and cooled by the sun."

"Do people come to visit you?"

"Sometimes. I visit them, too."

"How?"

"I have a boat."

"Pedal-powered, no doubt, like those on the duck ponds in
Phoenix."

"No, it has a big wind-up propeller."

"Um ... okay. Just don't get too far from land."

"Sure," she said, giggling.

"And when you're so busy thinking, be careful to watch for
blazes. I wouldn't want you to get lost."

"I won't get lost."

"You're sure."

"Uh-huh."

We walked out of town with our haul and headed toward the cabin.

"I *was* going to run away once," Kyra went on.

"When?" I asked, trying not to seem surprised.

"Back before Charlies Bunion when Mom got so mad."

"How would you have done that?"

"By dropping farther and farther behind. I thought I'd follow a valley down to a road and then walk to a town."

'Then what?"

"I never figured that out. I just knew it wouldn't work. I mean, I'd have no money and no place to go, and nothing to eat in my pack but marshmallows. I think I'd get pretty tired of marshmallows...."

We carried load after backpack load of groceries back to the cabin all during the day. I'd hoped to get underway by early afternoon, but trail-food packaging took every available hour. We paused only for gigantic meals as if it might be months before we again got to town.

I described them in detail in the log. I thought news that we ate seven hamburgers and several pounds of fried potatoes, a whole chicken plus a paragraph's worth of trimmings important somehow. Food was on our minds. Cold weather and continuous exercise left us constantly hungry. We packed more food for fewer days in the miles ahead, and would likely still stop at every remote country store or gas station for soda pop, candy bars, or our favorite snack — individual fruit pies. We ate like never before in our lives and still lost weight.

I met Ken Bailey on one trip to town. Ken was headed for Maine also; we'd met him a couple times before.

"Know of any place to stay?" he asked.

"Remember the cabin where the trail comes out of the woods?"

"Yeah, I passed it earlier today."

"There were seven of us there last night. You can join us to-night. Knock on the door and Jerri will let you in."

I found him there when I returned and we set another place for dinner.

Jerri seemed almost grateful that work remaining had extended our stay. She still felt miserable from her cold and hoped a day or so out of the rain would help. Her condition didn't affect her sense of humor, however.

"I stopped at a shoe store to look in the window," she said during dinner. "I noticed a beautiful pair of high-heeled, fancy dress sandals. 'What lovely shoes,' I said to myself. 'I should buy a pair and send them home to have when we're done.'

"Then I remembered summer would be over before we finished. A whole summer would be gone and I'd have no use for 'girl shoes.' I'd wear nothing but clumpy boots the whole time."

CHAPTER 8

The Ten-Year-Old
Earns Her Stripes

*Gorp is a trail snack which consists of peanuts,
M&Ms, and raisins. Try it sometime, but I'd skip
the raisins if I were you.*

- KYRA'S DIARY

THE TRAIL LED BACK to three- and four-thousand-foot levels in a
region of rolling hills and farms. Weather and scenery improved, bringing us warm, sunny days for Easter weekend. We
walked through quiet woods and across cleared ridges, looking
into Tennessee on our left, North Carolina on our right. Trees
had leafed out part way up mountain slopes but we saw no
leaves on top. Views would be obscured when they did arrive;
perhaps we weren't in any rush.

Flowers for flower-watchers were abundant meanwhile and
Jerri reliably pointed them out — fire pinks, blue flags, bloodroot, acres of spring beauties. Much like us, each showed a
hopeful face to the sun.

A day out of Hot Springs, the trail emerged from the woods

in Allen Gap where Tennessee Highway 70 met North Carolina 208. We stopped, lured by a gas-station grocery. The two women running the place recognized us right away; they'd been hearing about Kyra from other hikers for days. News of a little girl on the trail seemed to be moving right along.

"The rest of the day we rested every eight minutes." So I complained in my journal as the suddenly hot and muggy afternoon slowed us down. The going was easy though; we walked eleven miles before setting down packs for the night. Jerri cooked strange, dehydrated things for dinner, reconstituting cabbage flakes and yam flakes, adding marshmallows and ham-flavored soy protein. I wrote in the log that it was all very good. I said that about everything. The cook read the log, you see.

Jerri served oatmeal with mincemeat and prunes for Easter Sunday breakfast.

"Horrible," Kyra pronounced it, turning up her nose at unpitted prunes. "This is dog food." Even the smiley face of M&Ms on top failed to catch her interest.

"That's all we have today," Jerri said. "You'll starve before lunch if you don't eat it."

Kyra said she'd rather and continued to stare with disgust at the dark brown porridge. Digging through her pack for something to disguise the flavor, she discovered a mouse had nibbled into her personal candy bag. Her grumbling increased.

"First I get moused, then you give me dog food. I think I'll stay in bed today."

Nearly everyone we met asked about Kyra. How did she like the walk? they wanted to know. How had she gotten out of school? Didn't she miss her friends? She'd traveled with us some before, we would say....

Born in Minneapolis, she'd accompanied us to New York at age three months so Jerri could study photography at Rochester Institute of Technology. She'd come along on trips in the years that followed, camping throughout New York and New England on weekends and vacations. Kyra had slept in rain-soaked tents before her first birthday.

We moved to Phoenix when Kyra was five, taking a round-about, seven-thousand-mile route via Acadia National Park, Cape Hatteras, and Key West. By the time we'd driven the straight-line distance to Phoenix, we were farther away than when we began. Kyra saw western states thereafter — by car through California, Nevada, and Arizona; on foot into Grand Canyon, the Superstitions, and other remote places.

We took her backpacking into Yosemite on her ninth birthday and there she met a bear. It approached our back-country campsite near where Kyra stood at the fire. Neither Jerri nor I were nearby. Kyra knew she should be strong and not show she was afraid. She wanted to call out but didn't know whether the bear could understand English. Closer and closer it came as she tried to decide what to do. She finally yelled when the bear was ten feet away. I'd heard her, charged the intruder, and chased it away.

We traveled by raft down three hundred miles of the Colorado River that same summer. The West thus added to her collection of experiences — getting lost before breakfast on a hot desert hike, exploring Death Valley ghost towns in Christmas snow. And eating peanut butter, salami, and M&M sandwiches on white bread, the most concentrated form of junk food she could imagine, on Colorado River beaches with the roar of rapids nearby.

Kyra had been around, we said when people inquired; hiking the Appalachian Trail was just a longer trip.

Jerri broke news of our hike to Leigh Hanks, Kyra's sixth grade teacher, a few months after the river trip. She reacted with interest and accelerated Kyra's studies so she could miss two months of sixth grade and two of seventh without problem. On departure day, she asked only that Kyra keep a daily diary of interesting events and send her copies once a month.

Kyra's journal contained many similar entries so far, like, "We woke up and it was raining ..." but Mrs. Hanks would be sure to read them with a smile. Recovering from her trials Easter morning, Kyra wrote, "That night a dangerous mouse stole a whole M&M from my very own private supply. Horrors!"

Oatmeal and prunes for breakfast again next morning: Kyra pretended to be asleep.

"Wake up, Fido," Jerri said. "Time for your dog food."

The ensuing scene reached comic heights of distress. To capture Kyra's mood, I later wrote a poem for her in the style of a Dr. Seuss story I'd read to her years before:

> Will you eat oatmeal and prunes?
>> I cannot stand oatmeal and prunes.
> Would you eat them in a car?
> Or when lunching with a Czar?
> Topped with dabs of caviar?
>> This mess just isn't up to par.
>> Why must you make things so bizarre?
> Not even in the month of June?
> Or if I sang a little tune?
> Maybe up in a balloon?
>> It will contaminate my spoon.
>> And I'm too young to be immune.
> Could you eat them with a fox?
> Or while sitting in a box?
> Maybe climbing over rocks?
>> I think I'll put some in your socks.
>> You'll see! You'll break out in a pox!
> Perhaps you'd eat them on a train
> Or while walking in the rain.
> And surely on your way to Maine!
>> You'd better pour them down the drain.
>> Quick, before I get ptomaine!

Oh, would you eat them with a frog?
Or if balanced on a log?
Your insides they will soon unclog.
　　It's food fit only for a dog,
　　So kindly end this dialogue.
Oh, will you eat oatmeal and prunes?
　　I just detest oatmeal and prunes!

We reached Devil Fork Gap an hour after breakfast. The walk through high, peaceful farmland was deceptively pleasant. We watched people hoe gardens in the distance and talked to residents where the trail passed near houses or yards. We were all set for a fast easy day. No such luck. Devil Fork Gap marked the start of nineteen miles of trail we would remember in great detail.

Billed as "numerous steep grades" in the guide, the trail crossed every fence in five counties and led us scrambling straight up and down every elevated piece of ground within range. We gasped along amid growing frustration, stopping more often than usual. I counted "steeply" twenty-two times in the directions before finding any sign of relief.

A patch of trout lilies and larkspur mercifully rescued us for a lunchtime photo session, then climbing and complaining resumed. Exhausted at day's end, we pitched our tent near a stream — and next morning began again.

Not until the top of 5,516-foot Big Bald did we find a scene of interest. Curiously twisted trees dotted the weedy summit and followed meadow-like ridge to the next peak. Bent and shaped by the wind, clutching at rocky soil, the widely spaced trees stood black and silent against low-hanging clouds. We passed through them slowly, now and then stopping to look back.

We were frothing again by mid-afternoon.

"The section between Whistling Gap and Spivey Gap proved to be totally absurd," I wrote in my journal. "They run you straight up a hill to see 'splendid views' of the same damn mountains you've seen all week, then dump you over the side for a descent so steep it's barely possible to stand up. The climb over High Rocks was unnecessary and pointless. We were all fairly sputtering...."

Fortunately, relief wasn't far away. The cursed nineteen miles ended as the trail crossed U.S. 19W and leveled off for a quick run to shelter. We camped alone. Kyra gathered wood and helped lay out bags and find places to hang the packs. Jerri topped off the evening by baking a peach and apricot upside-down cake. It was easily the high point of the day.

I paged through the guide, noting by flashlight we'd covered nearly forty miles in three days. Climbing had been difficult, even ridiculous, at times, yet we were doing the daily miles and more. We were getting tougher. Persistence was paying off ... perhaps we'd soon be a match for these mountains.

We reached the road to Erwin, Tennessee, the next day around noon. I chose the service road over the high-speed Asheville Highway and thumbed one car. I stood in the Post Office ten minutes later. The closed Post Office: it was Wednesday afternoon.

I banged on a door marked Private. The janitor answered and said everyone had gone to lunch — come back in half an hour. I asked directions to a grocery store: a mile and a half out of town. And I couldn't remember how to get back to the trail. Great planning. I went for a walk.

We'd changed our food supply system in Hot Springs. Instead of loading on ten days' food, walking as far as it would take us, then trying to fill in from stores along the way, we had turned to a more calculated approach.

We'd purchased food for 17 days, enough for 165 miles to Damascus, Virginia. After putting six days' worth in the pack, we'd mailed another six to Erwin and five more to Hampton, Tennessee. Assuming we could arrive during Post Office hours, we could resupply more easily and walk farther with lighter packs between stops.

No one else did it this way. Hikers traveling alone and walking fifteen to twenty miles a day carried food for several hundred miles. They would buy enough in Hot Springs, for example, to last till Damascus.

Some hikers purchased most of their food in advance or had mothers or friends to do their shopping. Their packages were mailed to them along the way; they only had to find the Post Office, load their packs, and move on.

I banged on Private again thirty minutes later and a genuine postal clerk answered. He regarded me with considerable distaste but retrieved the box. I loaded prepackaged food into my pack, then walked in the rain the mile and a half to Erwin's discount supermarket. We hadn't mailed common items so I bought peanut butter, honey, gorp ingredients, and the like to complete our inventory.

I looked around, wondering what to do next. Damn ... the whole afternoon was wasting away. Where was the trail?

The road across the field from the store looked familiar. I walked to it and thumbed a ride. The driver took me to where Jerri and Kyra sat under the tied-up rain fly.

"So much for our easy resupply," I said to Jerri.

"What's the problem?"

"The Post Office was closed and I wandered all over looking for a store."

"You got everything, didn't you?"

"Sure, but it took more than three hours."

"We have all day," she said. "Besides, we had a nice time writing letters."

"I hope the next stops go better."

"Such a rush you're in lately."

The trail followed the Nolichucky River bank for a mile and a half, then led an equal distance along a jeep road through hemlock and rhododendron forest. We made excellent time. With an hour of light remaining, I figured we'd easily finish the mile uphill to Curley Maple Gap Lean-to before dinner. Then the rain began. Mild showers had come and gone all day so we left rain gear tucked away and started to climb.

The sky grew grimly dark in a very short time. Rain measurably increased before we'd gone a quarter of the way. We wordlessly picked up the pace. Dark clouds loomed above and rain began to pound the forest, pouring off leaves and branches to the ground. We broke into a run but were soaked within minutes. We'd waited too long with the rain gear again.

Water drenched us, splashed us, ran from our packs and clothes. Floppy rhododendron leaves hanging in clumps slapped our faces, arms, and bare legs and dumped icy showers at the slightest touch. We looked anxiously around every bend in the trail but caught no sign of the shelter. Only wet, darkening forest lay ahead. And behind, in thickening gloom, Kyra had dropped from sight.

The torrent kept on under blackening sky. We walked and ran as fast as we knew how. Every turn in the trail revealed the same disheartening scene: dark forest and winding, muddy path. No shelter ahead. No Kyra behind.

"Let's stop and wait for her," I shouted at Jerri, some distance ahead. "We won't get any wetter."

"It can't be much farther," she yelled back. "Drop your pack at the shelter when we get there and go back for hers."

We kept on, seeing nothing ahead or behind.

I raced into the shelter at last, tossed my pack aside and turned to go back. Kyra came gasping in at a dead run before I could take a step. Only one bend behind, she'd kept up all the way and caught us at the end, but was barely holding back tears.

I whisked off her pack and found her dry clothes. Warm down booties quickly replaced wet boots and socks, and a dry down jacket supplanted soaking shirts and jeans. With hugs and glowing praise, we zipped her into her bag.

"I'm sure tired of rain," I said, "and mud and wet clothes and droopy wet bushes beating me in the face."

"Do you think we should quit?" Jerri asked.

"Sometimes I wonder on days like this."

"What do you think, Kyra?" Jerri asked.

Kyra's tears retreated and a brave smile returned. "Let's go to a warm motel and think it over."

Rain pounded ever harder on the leaky tin roof, then came thunder, lightning, and hail. It was a good night to be inside.

Morning brought the final installment of the oatmeal-and-prunes experiment. Kyra, trying a more polite approach, asked to be exempted. Jerri cooked a special chocolate batch on the side and brightened Kyra's morning as much as breakfast in town.

By mid-afternoon we were on the run in the rain again. Five and a half miles separated us from shelter — up, over, and far down the other side of 5,180-foot Unaka Mountain. We took only a moment to decide we could make it. But this time, we put on rain gear.

We climbed quickly on a Forest Service road as rain held to a steady drizzle. We reached the mountain's crest and plunged into dense forest on a zigzagging path. The trail wove sharply in and out of narrow openings between close-packed trees. Light dimmed to near-dark as branches merged thickly about us. Rain dripped, misted, showered. Wind swirled fog through the trees and across our path.

I slowed my pace and looked about in eerie silence. Sky and mountain disappeared; trees and fog remained. Mountaintop syndrome again, but different. No rapturous "see the whole world" view ... there was no world ... only darkened tree trunks, tangled branches, wispy fog. Strange. Striking. Perhaps even ... beautiful.

The interlude ended just across the crest and we began a long descent. Rain turned long sections of the trail to squishy, boot-slopping mud before we'd gone far. I followed Jerri at a considerable distance and wondered about Kyra, asking again questions that always came at such times.

Was she all right? Would she keep on, day after day, no matter what the weather? She'd dropped behind again and I stopped to look back. No ten-year-old cared to be seen with parents day after day, she'd said. She hiked behind us so she could be Kyra Through-Hiker walking alone. So she could be Walking from Georgia to Maine, not just tagging along.

I felt a stab of conscience as I watched the small figure bob along in shorts, orange rain jacket, and big red pack. Mud streaked and splattered her bare legs. I knew she must be freezing in cold gusts of wind. Why was she still doing this? Because we bribed her with chocolate bars? Hardly. Because other through-hikers treated her as one of them? Perhaps. Even so, was it worth it? Was slopping through the mud today any more fun than yesterday? As she approached, I started to ask....

"Isn't that pretty?" she said, pointing out a red trillium blossoming near the trail. "And look at those Dutchman's breeches — they're getting all wet!"

Her eyes gleamed with the light of a child's discovery. She bent down to touch delicate white blossoms sprinkled with rain.

"That's what happens when you hang out laundry on a rainy day," I replied.

She looked up and smiled, then led the way down the trail.

CHAPTER 9

Gotta Get to Maine

The man who goes alone can start today; but he who travels with another must wait till that other is ready.

                                                    - THOREAU

I COULDN'T BELIEVE IT: an inch of snow blanketed the ground in supposedly sunny Tennessee on April 28, the thirty-ninth day of spring. I thought perhaps I'd dreamed it, or that sunlight played tricks in heavy morning dew. Frozen boots and dull gray sky told me no. I clumped around outside the tent a while to make sure.

We'd pitched the tent in a collapsing shed a quarter-mile off the trail on the Tennessee side. Three walls of the structure remained and its roof sagged to touch the ground on the open side. It had offered the only protection from wind and rain the night before.

We'd turned off the trail to find a cabin mentioned in the guide, but that had burned down long before. Clearing the shed of trash and leveling its lumpy dirt floor, we'd moved in. Tent walls drooped to fit the confining interior. Guy lines ran through cracks in walls to pegs driven into the ground outside. Everything seemed fine from inside our bags, however. Jerri even made popcorn, immediately alerting the mice.

But not snow, I complained to a soundless white morning. When would this end?

Kyra, up early and also tramping about, left her opinion written in snow on the shed roof: "Kyra was miserable here!"

The sun burned through fog by the time we started back to the trail and revealed perfect blue sky. We walked again in winter post-card scenes, over Little Rock Knob and up Roan Mountain. Jerri pointed out details of the spectacular, off-season show dazzling us from every side — sunlit tree branches finely traced with white, snow-heaped small plants with frost-edged leaves, snow reaching down from white-capped peaks to meet leafy green coming up from below.

Snow deepened as we climbed Roan Mountain. We plowed steeply and steadily on, occasionally through knee-deep drifts. Jerri stopped often for photographs. I wrote messages to Kyra in the snow with my walking stick — "Hi, Kyra," "C'mon, pokey bug" — so she'd find them as she followed along. She caught us at the summit and charged ahead to where wind had blown snow cover thin in a grassy clearing. She planted her walking stick with flapping red bandana attached to claim the 6,150-foot peak.

Several peaks over we climbed Grassy Ridge. The trail led around the summit just below its full 6,189 feet. Hardly disappointed, we walked on to the concrete-block shelter on the mountain's north slope. Its open side faced the wind, its screen bunks were badly ripped up, but we had no thought of going on. We cleared out blown-in snow and joined Doug Wilson, a through-hiker from Santa Barbara who'd passed us climbing Roan Mountain. Already bundled in his bag, wearing puffy down mittens that extended halfway up his arms, Doug had a head start on the night's big project: keeping warm.

90

We noticed ramps in profusion poking out of the snow. We'd been looking for these onion-like plants to add to our evening meal. Under the circumstances, we left the experiment for another time.

I pitched the tent fly across the shelter opening to block the wind. Jerri and Kyra got into their bags at once; I followed soon after. I watched the night grow dark, saw stars brighten in a clear sky, and tossed about on the sagging screen bunk to find a comfortable position. Sleep came fitfully. I woke every time I turned over, only to realize that morning lay a long way off. Cold seeped into my bag, through down pants, down jacket, down hood. Through two pair of socks on my feet. We had no gloves so wore socks on our hands in the cold. No class next to those big orange mittens of Doug's....

Thirty-nine days we'd been walking. Here we were, still freezing. If I felt this cold, what condition must Jerri and Kyra be in? Thirty-nine days ... Robert E. Peary sledged 475 miles to the North Pole in 37 days, in "distinctly crisp" weather some-times reaching minus 59 degrees. Considerably more cold and miserable than Grassy Ridge, I supposed, turning over again. The thought failed to cheer me.

Next morning, we walked down the mountain into spring. The snow's grip weakened as we descended. Green grass and flowers began to show, then took hold. Looking back, we saw the dividing line above us, white turning to green. The sun shone. The air felt warm. There were no more 6,000-foot peaks until New Hampshire: this was it − spring! And this time, we knew it would stay.

Walking became easier and easier. Rain, snow, ice, high winds, and even steep trail were gone for a time, leaving a smooth path that wound across greening fields and invited us to follow. It seemed filled with promise, no less than if paved with yellow brick.

We walked in single file, Kyra in the middle for the moment.

Jerri stopped to look at a flower from time to time, or to stand with her face in the sun, then we moved on. Kyra asked for names of flowers that stood above ankle-deep grass, and those just a touch of color in the green. Jerri supplied them, often with distinguishing marks and family names. I walked behind. My attention wandered....

We had done well. Given the weather, the terrain, the conditioning we'd needed, we had done well. Counting mileage off the trail, thirty-five miscellaneous miles to towns and such, we'd averaged ten miles a day. Exactly according to plan....

Rest stop. Jerri laid down in the sun and Kyra pulled out the canteen of lemonade. Ten minutes stretched to fifteen.

"Let's go," I said.

"Well, okay," Jerri replied.

Ten miles a day. Short days, too. Daylight lasted longer now ... and nearly six weeks of walking had toughened us. We'd have no trouble making ten miles ... or twelve ... maybe fifteen....

Jerri stopped. Something puzzled her.

"Get me the flower book, will you?" she asked. "I don't recognize that one."

I dug it out of her pack. Better keep it on top....

"It's not in here, either," she said. "I'll get its picture and we'll look it up another time."

We moved on. Jerri walked slowly looking from side to side. Kyra followed closely.

Figure twelve ... no reason why not. We were in shape. Walking would get easier through Virginia. We could really chalk up miles over summer....

Then it hit me, something I hadn't quite seen. A walking distance measured in thousands of miles had always been absurd. Even a few hundred miles once seemed beyond reach. We'd covered four hundred miles now and conditions were improving. If we kept going ... if we kept doing as well as we had....

And there, two miles into spring, I knew Mount Katahdin stood within our grasp. If we kept moving, if we stuck to our plan, we could make it. *We could really walk to Maine!*

Jerri stopped again. She began to joke with Kyra and they laughed and jostled each other for a moment. We walked on, lurching to a stop each time they noticed something new. An hour passed. We dawdled through less than a mile. Another rest stop dragged. Resting ... from what? Jerri set down her pack again after walking ten minutes more.

"What now?" I asked, exasperation setting in.

"There are things here I want to photograph."

I stood around, waiting, stewing.

"Are we going to walk today?" I asked.

"Sure," she said. "Why?"

"We'll have three miles by nightfall at the rate we're going."

"We'll do better than that. But so what if we don't?"

"We finally have a nice day and easy trail. I'd like to cover some ground."

"These are the things I came to see," Jerri said. "I'm not going to race past them just to make miles."

"We're not *racing* past anything. We're poking along."

"But it's warm and sunny at last and there's new, growing things about. This is what it's all about as far as I'm concerned. Why don't you enjoy it? Breathe the spring air, lay in the sun, run your fingers through the grass. We've earned it!"

"I've been doing that every ten minutes."

"Don't be in such a rush. It's a good day to rest after what we've been through."

She took out her camera and focused on a cluster of purple violets. Kyra shed her pack and joined her. Bristling with irritation, I walked on, stomping away at top speed until Jerri and Kyra had fallen far behind.

I wasn't asking much ... just a reasonable pace and a reasonable number of miles. I didn't mind stopping ... I liked to see things, too. But why every ten feet? Was every flower that special?

I covered flat trail in a rush, feeling some urgent need to put miles behind. Feeling the freedom to walk, to go for miles and miles without being slowed by weather. Behind me, Jerri and Kyra felt new freedom, too — to stop and rest and loll in the sun-warmed grass.

After an hour I waited, sitting atop a fence and looking back over a wide meadow I'd crossed. Two figures appeared after a long while, moving slowly, seeming very small on a distant ridge. What would I say? I needed time by myself, perhaps. No ... that was Kyra's line. I started to laugh: forty days in the wilderness and he wants to be alone.

Jerri and Kyra arrived.

"Were you hoping to get to Maine today?" Jerri asked.

"I just wanted to walk," I said, "and not poke."

"We'll get there," she replied, as I helped her over the fence. "But if we can't enjoy what we're passing through, I don't want to go."

We met Ken Bailey once more on our way up Big Yellow Mountain. I asked him how we kept catching up.

"I got rained out again," he said. "And last night I followed those misplaced guidebook directions to the Trivett House in Elk Park. I got there, but only after walking nine miles and hitchhiking some. It was worth the trouble, though. Room, shower, breakfast — all for $3.50. The biscuits alone are worth that!"

We crossed Big Yellow and walked over and down Hump Mountain, last of five grassy balds in that section of trail, last of even the 5,000-foot peaks for a time. A convenient ride took us the mile and a half to Elk Park, North Carolina, where we found the Trivett House and checked in. Mrs. Trivett showed us to rooms upstairs and invited us to make ourselves at home. We'd read about "Granny" Trivett. She was seventy-seven.

94

"Where do you find energy to run a rooming house?" Jerri asked. "Others years younger than you can barely make it to their rocking chairs."

"Oh, I keep busy, all right," Mrs. Trivett replied, "cooking and keeping rooms neat and tidy. I guess I don't have time to get old."

We'd heard good things about that cooking, I said.

"Breakfast is at seven," she said with a wink. "Don't forget."

Five of us assembled promptly at seven next morning. Doug Wilson had followed the news to town, along with Jeff Menzer, a through-hiker from Ohio. We sat down to white plates and a clean, white tablecloth, and ample servings of eggs, bacon, grits, juice, and coffee.

Sam Trivett, eighty-three, brought the biscuits. The basket of soft, oven-fresh creations emptied in one pass around the table. Topped with butter and homemade jam, enhanced by the aroma of more baking in the kitchen, Granny Trivett's biscuits put everyone's plans to hit the trail on hold. Another full, steaming basket replaced the empty, then another. Little wonder the Trivett House came so highly recommended.

"These are suuure good biscuits!" Doug said, as Mrs. Trivett brought another basket.

"The best I ever ate!" added Jeff.

"Excellent...."

"*Fantastic*...."

"Thank you all," Granny said with a smile. "Like I always say, it's the biscuits brings the boys in."

"I'd never tasted grits," I told her. "They're pretty good."

"I don't really care for them myself," she replied. "But most folks in the South expect them. Farther north you get into toast country. Then you get hash browns instead."

I signed the guest book as we left and noticed Peter Home Douglas, the lad with the jelly stain on his sleeping bag, had signed in three days before. He was taking two weeks off to rest a bad foot, he'd noted. Fifteen miles a day, he'd told us at Big Stamp....

We walked that day under bright, sunny sky through rolling fields and apple orchards in full bloom. The countryside seemed restful; we moved along even more slowly than usual. We left the state line and North Carolina behind after an hour or two and put both feet into Tennessee. Two states had passed; we had twelve to go.

We ate our first lunch resting on pasture grass, saw a bluebird and patted a horse on the nose, and later stopped under fragrant apple blossoms for the day's second lunch. Looking back, we saw peaks from the previous two days: Little Rock Knob, Roan Mountain, Grassy Ridge, Big Yellow, and Hump Mountain. Ahead, more of the same — mountains we had yet to meet.

A pickup truck stopped nearby and the land owner walked over to us.

"AT hikers, I see," he said. "It's a good day for it."

"That's for sure," I said.

"Be sure to close any gates you go through," he went on. "Someone left one open the other day and fifty head of cattle wandered into the wrong field."

"'Leave gates as you find them.' That's the rule, isn't it?" I asked.

"Yup," he answered. "And if everyone would, I'd be happy to have the trail cross my land. But I can't be roundin' up cattle all the time."

We ended the day at Moreland Gap Shelter. Jerri cooked stew and the wintercress she'd picked. Kyra roasted marshmallows and made s'mores. Jeff joined us. In the campfire's warm circle, we traded stories of the trail since Georgia. We didn't often build a fire, but on a long evening it made for pleasant companionship as the night turned cool.

The trail led next morning through sterile woods with hardly a sign of a white blaze. We walked over stony ground, negotiating carefully among intersecting paths and roads. Scenery looked dull, both near and far. A good stretch to cover quickly, it seemed to me, but uncertainty about where we were going slowed us down. Surroundings had been pleasant the day before; I'd been content to mosey and take it all in. Now, with nothing of interest in sight, I wanted to move on.

We reached White Rocks Mountain Firetower about half past ten. Kyra had dropped behind again and was nowhere in sight. Ten minutes passed, then fifteen. She didn't appear. Suddenly angry, I started down the long hill to find her.

I found her a quarter-mile back, crying as she climbed slowly toward the tower.

"Where have you been?" I demanded.

"I ... I got off ... the trail," she sobbed.

"If you'd keep up like you're supposed to you wouldn't have that problem. What happened? Why are you crying?"

"I didn't ... get lost really," she went on, her voice shaken by sobs. "But I ... I thought I had."

"Give me that pack and let's get moving."

I slung her pack over my shoulder and set a brisk pace. She lagged just behind, still crying and seeking to explain.

"I got halfway ... up this hill and thought it was wrong ... so I went back down. At the bottom, I looked around ... and decided I must have been right after all. But I still wasn't sure ... and I didn't want to ... to climb all the way up again for nothing...."

"I thought this would happen sooner or later. You walk in the middle from now on."

"I'm *sorry*, Dad. I ... was *being* careful...."

"What's the matter?" Jerri asked as we neared the crest of the hill.

"Miss Pathfinder here got confused and thought she'd lost the trail."

"Is she okay? Why are you carrying her pack?"

"Just to get her up this hill. She's not hurt."

"Tell me what happened," Jerri said, putting her arm around Kyra and leading her to the firetower steps.

Kyra sat down and haltingly explained.

"It's all because she keeps dropping behind," I burst in before she'd finished.

"Maybe," Jerri said. "But don't be so harsh. She's scared and upset."

"If she'd keep us in sight she wouldn't *be* upset!"

"I know, but she needs comforting, not yelling."

"She'll walk in the middle now, that's for sure."

"SIMMER DOWN, will you?"

"Dammit, I don't know how we're going to get anywhere. We go slow when it's nice. We go slow when it's boring. Delay after delay. We'll still be poking through Virginia in *December*, if we ever *get* there...."

"Hi," said a voice above us. I looked to the top of the tower stairs and saw Jeff. He'd been visiting the ranger on duty and could not have missed the disquieting scene below.

"I brought you a present," he said. He bounded down the steps and handed Jerri a bouquet of ramps he'd dug and cleaned.

"Happy May Day," he said with a smile.

I felt foolish and at a loss to explain. Jerri said something to Jeff, then we put on our packs and headed up the trail in silence. Kyra walked in the middle. I followed some distance behind. An hour passed. The scenery did not improve. Later, at our lunch stop, Jerri sought to describe the problem.

"We have different goals for this walk, it appears," she said, gently. "It wasn't obvious till the days got longer and nicer."

"What do you mean?" I asked.

"When the weather was so bad, we all worked together. We did our best and didn't worry about how long it took. Walking is getting easier and more interesting now. The things I came to see are growing and blooming all around, and I want to stop and see them. But you want to go, go, go."

"I don't mind stopping to see things." I said. "If we do our ten miles like we agreed, and maybe some extra to fill in short days, you can stop all you like."

"But that's the problem, don't you see?" Jerri said. "You're on a schedule: ten miles a day, seventy miles a week, three hundred miles a month. You're hiking to *Maine*, not to see what's here. I want to enjoy each day as it comes, watch the birds, smell and touch the flowers. You're turning this into a quest. *Gotta-Get-to-Maine*, that's what you've got!"

"If we plan a section for six days, and we bring six days' food, then we should try to do it in six days, right?"

"Sure, and we're doing that. But why get there early? Why carry food to town? Shouldn't we take time when we have it?"

"I guess so," I replied. "But we've been trying to get to shelters when we could. They'll be more crowded in the summer and we won't find space if we take all day getting there."

"Shelters are handy," Jerri said. "We can sometimes stretch a bit to reach one instead of putting up the tent. But why get there at three in the afternoon? Did we come to the woods to see shelters?"

"No, but that's where water usually is, and I'm tired of nights in a wet tent."

"What you're really worried about, I think, is winter hitting Maine before you get there."

"Baxter Park closes October 15," I said. "Two thousand miles in two hundred days puts us there October 6. Add a week because the trail's longer than that, and because we're a little behind ... it doesn't leave much room."

"What are you going to do when you get there?"

"Well, when we finish the trail we can take our time driving home."

"What!"

"What I meant was...."

"You have everything backwards. It's spring — the beginning. Flowers are growing, the sun is warm, and we can finally do what we came to do. You're thinking about the end. You want to rush through everything to be sure to be there for the *end!*"

"That isn't what I said...."

"Isn't this a little early to be concerned about that? And does it really matter? Didn't every hiker's story we read say 'I wish I'd taken more time'?"

"I suppose."

"Look, I want to get to Maine, too," she said. "It's too beautiful to miss, especially in the fall. But I want to live this whole experience and get there the last possible day. If snow starts to fall as we come off Katahdin, that will be perfect."

Jerri was ready for any argument so I took my medicine and agreed to be more patient. Sure, I wanted to go, go, go. Sure, I wanted to reach Katahdin and finish before winter shut the mountain down. Was that so unusual? What I'd tried to say was just what she was saying: let's enjoy the experience; let's reach the goal in time. But it came out different when I said it, like I wanted to race through the hike and relax when it was over. That wasn't what I'd meant. This was simply my approach to problems — set goals; work toward them at a regular pace. It had always worked before....

The moment was lost, in any case. It seemed prudent to be more accommodating for a while. Perhaps we'd make better time as months went on. We'd kept to the plan so far; maybe everything would work out. I'd just have to wait and see. Meanwhile, I guess I could claim one distinction. I had possibly the earliest reported case: Katahdin Fever in Tennessee.

We walked on to the entrance to Laurel Fork Gorge. The three miles through the gorge were the prettiest on the entire AT, some thought. Jerri was pleased that we'd arrived on a nice day. While we rested and snacked, Kyra sat on the stream bank dunking a canteen in the water, holding its two-foot cord. I watched her lift the canteen, drop it, let it drift, lift, splash, let it drift — and saw a snake coming directly toward her.

It was three feet long. It swam with the current to where Kyra played and slid onto the bobbing canteen. She screamed and jumped back, yanking the canteen from the water. The snake darted under a rock. I flushed it again with my walking stick as we all crowded around the bank. It struck, fell with a splash, then exited quickly downstream.

Kyra shuddered from the encounter.

"What kind was that, Mom?" she asked. "It sure was big!"

"I don't know," Jerri said. "I didn't see it very well. It might have been a moccasin or a plain water snake."

"I didn't like it, whatever it was. Do you know, Dad?"

"A canteen snake," I replied. "They bite canteens looking for Gatorade. You jumped away just in time."

"Sure, Dad," she said with a faint smile.

The trail followed a railroad grade into the gorge, then descended abruptly along Laurel Fork Stream. Creeks plunged into the gorge at points along steep, wooded slopes. Bright sunshine gave sparkle and shadow to trees and fast-moving water. White flowering dogwood and brilliant new green leaves added color to the scene. Rhododendrons bloomed — huge blossoms in many shades of pink brightened the path at every turn. Jerri and Kyra stopped often to sniff them. So did I.

We took an off-trail left to Potato Top for the recommended overall view, talked to an older gentleman out gathering wild bees, then continued down to Laurel Falls. Late-afternoon sun flooded the frothy, forty-foot cascade and our heads filled with the rumble of rushing water. Jerri hurried to get it all photographed while light remained. We watched till the falls and the trees beyond completely darkened in shade.

We passed one-at-a-time and hand-holding-hand along the

base of a rocky cliff, high water lapping at our boots, then began climbing back out of the gorge. We camped near the top, then walked the last few miles to Tennessee Highway 67. Jerri lingered again over dogwood trees and bursts of rhododendron. She stopped for fire pinks and red columbine, and a patch of pink lady slippers, the first she had ever seen.

The Hampton resupply stop hit new highs in efficiency. I started walking the mile to town, thumbed a car I heard coming behind, and stood in the Post Office moments later. I retrieved our supply box, loaded my pack, and departed just as the Post Office closed. Wednesday again, but my timing had improved.

"An hour and a half," Jerri noted when I returned, "you're getting better."

"Five minutes later and the Post Office would have been closed."

"The South may rise again," she said, "but it won't be on Wednesday."

Rain followed us all afternoon as we walked through mountains of the Cherokee National Forest. We passed a shelter too early to stop, then found the going too difficult to reach the next one. By the time we'd climbed over, under, and around a quarter-mile of blown-down trees, we felt ready to camp anywhere. I found no tent-sized piece of ground that didn't slope, so finally pitched the tent in the trail.

We roasted brown-and-serve rolls on sticks over the fire after dinner, then lay back listening to the ceaseless call of a whippoorwill. "Whip-poor-will, whip-poor-will," repeated without pause, had been counted beyond a thousand by others with more patient ears. I kept no tally. Sleep seemed a better idea.

We crossed Tennessee Highway 91 Friday noon, May 4, our forty-fifth day on the trail. We would hit Damascus, Virginia, in twenty-two miles, but unless we walked all night, we'd find the Post Office closed for the weekend. Leapfrogging supplies would be locked away once more.

The highway led fifteen miles to town. I had time to hitch-hike there, we decided, to make arrangements and return before dark. Jerri and Kyra walked on to Rich Knob Shelter while I stood at the roadside and waited.

And waited. No cars passed in either direction in the first half-hour. I noticed how quiet everything was, just standing there. Birds twittered, wind stirred the trees — precisely when I would have welcomed the sound of car or truck, I'd found peace: no unnatural sound. Another half-hour saw two cars pass. Neither stopped. Patience is the thing ... I'd hitchhiked nearly forty thousand miles over the years and certainly learned that.

The third car stopped.

"We'll take you right to Damascus," the driver said. Tim and Ron from Elizabethton, Tennessee, were just driving around and had nothing else to do. I explained my mission and asked about their plans after Damascus.

"We're coming back this way," said Tim. "We'll wait and give you a lift."

I met a party of day-hikers in the Post Office.

"There sure are a lot of backpackers out this year," one said.

"I've seen six Georgia-to-Maine hikers in the last three days," added another.

"Say hello to number seven," I said. "Eight and nine, my wife and daughter, are back at camp."

"You're the father of the ten-year-old girl going to Maine?" said a couple of them at once.

I answered yes, unleashing a barrage of questions. I tried to reply as I retrieved boxes sent from Hot Springs. Gus Crews introduced himself.

"The AT runs through the center of town here so people are very interested in hikers. We've been hearing about you and the ten-year-old for days."

Mr. Crews had completed his end-to-end hike by walking

various sections over a period of seventeen years. I asked about a good place to stay.

"Mrs. McQueen takes in hikers," he said.

"It's the big white house up the street," said someone else.

My chauffeurs drove me to the big white house.

"Sunday night is open so far," said tall, white-haired Mrs. McQueen. "I'll put you down for the big room at the end of the hall."

I stored packages in a closet at her direction, returned to the trail with Tim and Ron, then set off for the shelter.

For three miles I walked alone. Jerri had kept the guidebook and my watch had stopped, so I traveled in complete detachment — and at my own pace. White blazes plainly marked the trail and I had a sense of when a mile had passed. Otherwise, I didn't know a thing — not where I was, how far to go, what time of day. For three miles the world about me had no names or numbers. Trees were just trees, mountains just mountains. Knowing a poplar from an elm, Rich Knob from Door Knob, or a splendid view from a magnificent panorama hardly mattered.

Three miles: I'd do it in an hour. Let's see ... figure fifteen-mile days ... Katahdin by mid-August. Wait a minute ... try to see what's here, Jerri said.

What *was* here? Trees, mountains, creeks ... uphill and down, right turn, then left ... just like any other day. Was that all? Guess so. Oh, add sky and clouds and creatures ... that rounded things out. Maybe hikers. What else? Was there anything else?

Yes. Something was different. I'd once thought the woods a foreign place. One went there to visit, toured the sights, then returned to safety at home. Today the woods seemed ... friendly. Today, being here seemed different.

I began to sense something. Like ... take the guidebook away, the watch away, the names, the mileages, the measurements away that made the trail like the world we'd left

104

behind ... take this place for itself.... I couldn't quite define it. The woods seemed more comfortable than they had our first day; that was all I could say....

My thoughts turned to Tim and Ron. We'd met many helpful people along the way — fishermen in Wesser, Mrs. Stewart at Fontana, Father Carmody at Hot Springs, two teenagers on a day off from work. They'd been positive, friendly people, helping when we needed it most. I felt heartened that we could walk across the land and meet them. It brought a dimension to the hike I hadn't considered. Nobody had been negative. How far would we go before finding that?

Not far, it turned out; he was waiting at the shelter.

Frank was not unsavory, violent, or even threatening. He just bitched, non-stop. He'd been at it for some time when I arrived and he kept it up all evening. Errors in the rotten guidebook, lousy stinking weather, developers and strip-miners destroying the world — nothing escaped his wrath. I couldn't see why someone with such a disposition would hike the trail, yet there sat Frank, personally tormented by the same conditions that affected us all, apparently restraining his full fury in the presence of ladies.

He resumed his tirade at first light and finally departed after a week-long half-hour. A good day to take it easy, we decided. Let Frank push on and build up a real good lead.

We crossed into Virginia at noon the following day. After ten days in Georgia and thirty-six in North Carolina and Tennessee, I finally began to think we were getting somewhere. The Virginia line was gateway — to summer in the mountains, to the confidence we could keep on going.

Kyra and I made an arch of walking sticks at the signpost, "Ta-da!" and welcomed Jerri into our fourth state. Four hundred fifty miles of Appalachian Trail led across Virginia, more than we had walked so far. We would be there quite some time.

Mrs. McQueen took us in like old friends. She seemed

especially happy to have Jerri and Kyra to talk with; the usual hiking trade brought few ladies to stay.

She'd also rented the other upstairs room, to Frank. He'd arrived the night before and stayed an extra day. I learned a disheartening fact from him later that evening. The trail had been relocated outside Damascus. Twenty new miles now included traverse of Mount Rogers and Whitetop Mountain. Unaware of this, we'd planned a nineteen-day walk to Cloverdale, Virginia, and had arranged to meet friends the sixth day. The new trail added two days to both.

"Now we have to rearrange our plans," I complained to Jerri as I passed along the news.

"Let's go the old way," she said, studying the guide. "It shouldn't be hard to find. Besides, the new trail is high and the old one is low. I'd rather stay low with spring."

"Shouldn't we stay on the AT?"

"That was the official trail last year," she said. "Does anyone care where we go? Whose trip is this anyway?"

The logic of the obvious prevailed.

For two rainy days we restocked, repackaged, and repaired. Chores kept us up past two o'clock each night, and with only two twin beds in our room, we took turns sleeping on the floor. As tired as I was, I could have slept on the stairs.

The Doerings had sent a box of items we'd requested, including a book of folk songs for the alto recorder Kyra carried. Paul's letter listed interpretations for some of the songs therein. On page 77 we learned the fate of a hiker who bought cheap boots: "Man of Constant Sorrow." Page 104 showed a picture of the Lowthers seeking a lean-to after dark: "Three Blind Mice." The question to ask after misplacing guidebook number six appeared on page 13: "Do You Know the Way to San Jose?"

We found time to visit with Mrs. McQueen. Her husband had died years before. She'd found the empty house too lonely then, so spent nights across the street with her cousin, Mrs.

Keebler. Eventually she'd moved in there for the winters. When Mrs. Keebler's husband died, Mrs. McQueen settled in permanently. The two women shared a happy life for nearly fifteen years.

Left alone again when her cousin passed on, Mrs. McQueen reopened her big white house and moved back across the street. She'd started renting rooms as Mrs. Keebler had once done; travelers brought company and a variety of stories to tell. Hikers were the most frequent guests, she said. She recounted for us first-hand impressions of some of them, especially "all the famous ones," as she put it, authors of the books we'd read. Her friends often asked why she wasn't afraid to open her home to strangers.

"Why should I be afraid?" she'd tell them. "These are nice people, and it keeps life interesting."

Rain finally ended on the morning of our departure, though a cold wind blew suspicious clouds in several directions. The storekeeper called it "clearing." We called such conditions "not actually raining." Donning our packs and waving final thanks and good-byes, we headed again for the AT. Mrs. McQueen smiled and wished us well.

Fully loaded packs came immediately to our attention as we walked through town. Mine weighed fifty-six pounds, the bathroom scale had said, but it felt like five times that. Paul Doering's letter had mentioned a "suggested diet for hikers," as a cure for heavy packs. It appeared on page 30 of our songbook: "Sunshine, Lollipops, and Rainbows."

CHAPTER 10

Bouquets and Symphonies

I will be the gladdest thing
under the sun!
I will touch a hundred flowers
and not pick one.
- EDNA ST. VINCENT MILLAY

TWO PATHS DIVERGED AHEAD. White blazes marked the right-hand trail leading to Whitetop Mountain. Yellow marked the old route to the left, renamed the Iron Mountain Trail. We turned left. An oriole darted ahead as we walked the easy path. A scarlet tanager burst through leaves in a flash of black and blazing red. We followed quietly to get a closer look.

The trail led again to the three-thousand-foot level, this time in Jefferson National Forest. We walked through a nearly flat region of alternating brushy clearings and mixed forest growth, along old woodland roads some of the time, down well-worn dirt path the rest of the way. Lookout points and open stretches of trail afforded frequent views — *of* the Mount Rogers area. Had we gone the official route, following those new uphill miles, we'd have been up there looking down. We met no one. After twelve peaceful miles we made camp at Straight Branch Lean-to in late afternoon.

Carl Windle hurried by at dusk. We thought he might join us but he said he had to keep on, most likely until after dark. We'd met him in Damascus the previous day. What little he'd had time to tell us between his multitude of errands added up to quite a story.

Carl, a policeman from Swansea, Massachusetts, was walking the trail for the Heart Fund. Folks back home had pledged to contribute money for each mile he walked. To widen the project's appeal, Carl gave his story to local newspapers and radio stations as he went along, and talked about it with people he met — when he could spare the time.

He'd arrived in Damascus behind schedule. He had to stay the night, he said, for his pack shoulder strap was broken, his boots needed repair, and his partial dental plate had fallen out. He also needed to restock food. His face betrayed weariness but the stop seemed to him just another frustrating delay. He had only a short leave from his job and had to maintain a steady pace to finish. He felt obliged to get back on the trail quickly to cover more miles.

We'd taken fifty days to reach our camp at Straight Branch; Carl had walked it in twenty-seven. He appeared rested and recharged by the stop for repairs and a night's sleep, yet he was determined to make up lost time.

"Are you enjoying the hike?" Jerri asked.

"No," he said. "But it's something I've decided to do."

He waved and walked on down the trail. A large, red heart sewn on a blue backpack was the last we ever saw of Carlton E. Windle II. But it wouldn't be the last we'd hear. Stories of Carl the hiking policeman would fill conversations and trail registers all summer.

A whippoorwill woke me early next morning. I saw it sitting on a log twenty feet away, its musical, repetitive call shattering predawn silence. I woke Jerri; neither of us had seen one so close before. Sunrise turned the sky orange as we watched and listened to "whip-poor-will, whip-poor-will," repeated without pause. Movement in the shelter finally sent the bird flying.

Three days before, about fifty miles back in Tennessee, Carl had reached Vanderventer Lean-to after dark. Three other hikers there had already bedded down. A whippoorwill sitting in a tree directly outside fired up some time later, calling "whip-poor-will" over, and over, and over. Sound reverberated through the shelter as if from full-blast loudspeakers. Sleeping hikers began to toss and turn. Once awakened, Carl could not get back to sleep.

Tossing, rolling, driven to the end of his patience, he finally erupted from his bag bellowing, "SHUT UP, GODDAMMIT, SHUT UP!" The whippoorwill flew off. The other hikers thought they might do the same.

Jerri made many new discoveries as we continued along the yellow-blazed trail. The first appeared to be seventeen tiny red turkey heads whirling in the breeze on a single stem.

"Pedicularis," Jerri identified instantly.

"Ridicularis," said I.

Two dangling purple arms greeted us next, hanging below a small, green, open-mouthed face with white chin whiskers. A curved purple tail arched high over its head.

"A whorled pogonia!" cried the walking Peterson field guide.

"Balonia," giggled Kyra.

"Hey, have some respect," Jerri said. "That's no way to talk about an orchid. Besides, it's supposed to be very rare."

"What are those white flowers?" Kyra later asked.

"Anemone," Jerri answered without hesitation.

"How do you remember all these names?" I said.

"I've seen their names and pictures in flower books ever since I could read. Plants are interesting. Once you recognize family traits, many of them are easy to remember."

110

Next we stopped for just-unrolling ferns. A bunch of them stood about as if chatting at a party, looking like spindly characters penned by Dr. Seuss.

"With ferns like this," said Kyra, straight-faced, "who needs anemones."

When we rejoined the AT in the afternoon, a Jack-in-the-pulpit caught Jerri's eye. She paused to show us a black "Jack" preaching under a green-and-white striped canopy.

Toward evening Kyra made the prettiest find of all: bi-color birdfoot violets. Five-petaled flowers — with three petals in shades of white and lavender, and two of deeper purple — grew in clumps of eight or ten against dark green bursts of deeply notched leaves. Rain clouds gathered then. We hurried the last two miles to Raccoon Branch Shelter.

We arrived near dark and met Bill Rombin from Gettysburg. He reported on views *from* Mount Rogers (nice), and related trail news during dinner. I lit our candle lantern as stories went on and thumb-tacked its long cord to a shelter roof joist. I could thus sit up in my bag, lean against my pack, and have enough light to write the day's log.

Based on distances shown in the guidebook, I computed mileage for the day at 16.5, our longest walk so far. I added this to my notes, then reached to extinguish the lantern. Disaster. The tack holding the cord popped out and skittered across the floor. The hot lantern fell into my hand and burned; I couldn't hold on. It dropped to my bag and rolled to the floor.

I looked for any sign of fire; the candle had gone out. I grabbed a canteen to soothe my hand. *My thumb tack — where was my thumb tack?* I'd checked shelter walls and outhouse doors for days looking for one so I could hang the lantern wherever I wanted.

Bill and I scrabbled about on hands and knees probing the darkened shelter with flashlights.

"I don't see it, Mickey," Bill said.

"It probably fell down through a crack between floorboards," I answered.

"We'll look again in the morning. Or maybe someone will roll over on it and find it even sooner."

I checked under my bag, then shut off the light and lay down. Phooey ... the thumb tack had been such a good idea.

Shelters in the Jefferson National Forest were the best of any we'd seen. Sturdy frame walls, waterproof shingle roof, and elevated wood plank floor protected us from wind and rain, and the open, roomy interior imparted no feelings of confining gloom.

I heard pattering of rain and gentle stirring of wind as I lay in the quiet. Appreciate what was here, Jerri said. Okay, what about a storm? It had size and power. It could begin with a hush and grow quickly to Wagnerian dimensions. I watched and listened. Sounds were soft and remote at first, then they swelled as the storm approached. I tried to pick out each element as it grew and descended upon us....

Droplets bounced off leaves, thumped on branches and tree trunks and the roof of the shelter, and drummed to the ground in a muffled, expanding tattoo. Wind swayed the trees. Limbs creaked. The season's new leaves fluttered and sighed. Branches raked the shelter, the roof, the walls and the shelter groaned in stiffening gusts. Thunder boomed and growled and lightning flashed the scene.

Bursts of wind-blown rain lashed the forest. Puddles formed and widened. Water splattered and splashed and fell from saturated trees. Rain blew in sheets before wind that whispered, whistled, shrieked through branches and leaves. Thunder crashed. Lightning streaked the sky once more as rain hammered the shelter. And into the night the storm blustered and sang as its sounds dominated and blended in turn. I fell asleep surrounded, bombarded, then woke again later to silence — safe and still dry.

In the morning (without the thumb tack), we set off to change mountains. We'd followed the crest of Iron Mountain from Damascus; it was time to trade it in for the next in line. Unlike jumbled peaks of Georgia and North Carolina, mountains in southern Virginia lay in long rows nearly side by side and end to end. High viewpoints revealed what looked like giant, fuzzy caterpillars all waiting in line. The trail led up the side of one, along its flat crest for a day or more, then down through a valley to another.

The trail's route through the regular, topographical lines on our maps showed this pattern continuing all the way to Cloverdale. With nearly ninety more minutes of daylight than when we began, it looked like we could log some quick miles.

Why, I got to wondering as we plodded along, was Chunky Gal Mountain so near Big Kitchens Knob? We'd passed those points long before but the names lingered. What grew in Devils Tater Patch? What happened at Lordamercy Cove? Unusual place names posed unanswered questions, especially for someone with time to spare.

Lost Spectacles Gap: that was easy, but for whom was the French Broad River named, and who were the victims at Lowly Martyr Gap? Who lived in Upper Pigeonroost? Could I take the Tweetsie Railroad and find out? Maybe I could walk there on Pickens Nose Trail.

"Store stop coming up," I said. We were descending to the village of Teas.

"Picture stops, too," Jerri said. We passed cows in sunny pastures and houses with well-tended lawns.

A two-story log home, elegantly posed with ivy-covered chimney against a puffy, white-cloud sky, required photographs from several angles.

Three painted roosters adorned the side of one farm's chicken coop. Another building pictured sheep and goats in a fenced, grassy yard. We stopped for those, too.

"Are you surviving all this?" Jerri asked.

"I'm doing fine," I said. She probably thought I was itching to pour on the coals. To cover more miles ... to get to Maine ... to conquer the Appalachian Trail. Not true. When scenery was interesting, or at least marginally so, and we weren't wasting time, I was content no matter what the pace. And patient: I held lenses while Jerri took the pictures, I entered in the log each night the name of every plant she'd seen that day, and I dutifully saved Betty Crocker coupons from every such package purchased on the way. Macho trip? Me?

"Where's the store?" Kyra wanted to know.

I found it. It had gone out of business.

The climb back out of the valley led first through a manganese mine — barren, reddish-brown flats that radiated waves of heat in the mid-day sun. We crossed the wide expanse as if plodding though a desert. Streaks of purple, white, tan, magenta, and pink were noticeable in the sandy soil in the operation's more desolate reaches.

"Area resembles the Badlands of South Dakota," advised the guide. Perhaps. I thought it looked like the average sand and gravel pit.

Thinking again ... mind wandering on problems of no consequence. Lots of time to do that in two thousand miles. We'd passed Deep Gap the day before. I'd counted six Deep Gaps, six Low Gaps, and five Rocky mountains and knobs in trail guides so far. Other places had no names at all. This seemed fitting mind-wandering material. I began making up new names, and corresponding guidebook directions....

From road through Spark Plug Gap (3,527 ft., 0.0 m.) ascend steeply on ungraded trail. Turn northwest in dense forest growth at 0.9 m.; reach summit of Dash Board Knob at 1.5 m. (Views obscured.) Descend gradually, then resume ascent ahead.

Attain high point in Pretty Pass (6,329 ft., 2.1 m.). Blue-blazed side trail leads 27.4 miles to wooded summit of Two-Hand Pinnacle (4,526 ft.), no water or shelter. Main trail descends steeply ahead. Enter Cold Water Flat at 3.4 m. (*Water* at Inner Spring 200 yds. to left, quality uncertain. Concrete block Animal Shelter 100 yds. farther, wire bunks for six.)

Turn north at 3.7 m. and ascend somewhat. At 4.1 m. ascend a great deal. Pass Truor Falls at 4.4 m. (32 ft. drop of Back Door Creek. Forest Service campground 1/4 m. to right.) Continue climb hand-over-hand ahead. Reach top of Don't Peak (5,871 ft., 4.9 m.) and cross open summit to Get-To-The Point at 5.0 m. Here are spectacular panoramic views of the Lolobrigidian Hills, Hob Knob, and Billiard Bald.

The hot afternoon walk proved uneventful. Forty miles in three days had caused Jerri no new blisters since she'd at last removed her bandages in Damascus, but we took it easy just the same. Even when the going got rougher and we had to work for each mile we didn't hurry. We had plenty of time to reach Killinger Creek Lean-to before the Friday-night crowd. We found the place at five o'clock, exactly as planned. But the lean-to wasn't there.

We kept going, figuring it lay farther on. The trail led immediately through a long stretch of loose rocks and we slowed our pace even more. The shelter lay in a gap, I read, yet we tiptoed through gap after likely gap and found nothing. We spent an hour covering half a mile, then the trail left the rocks and headed back up the mountain. The only water was near the shelter; we would have to find it. I sat down to read directions again.

"We are clearly beyond where this wonderful book thinks it is," I said. "See, this ascent we're starting is after the shelter."

Jerri took over, reading what I'd pointed out.

"You're right," she said. "Have you checked north-to-south?"

"No."

She turned to the front of the book and began reading north-to-south directions for the same area backwards.

"Aha!" she exclaimed; "the book is wrong. North-to-south puts the lean-to in the next paragraph."

"How far to the next paragraph?"

'Three-quarters of a mile."

We didn't beat the crowd. Eight of us plus a sheep dog claimed space in the shelter and rolled-out mummy bags soon filled the space like an Egyptian tomb.

"We start early on a supposedly easy day and still manage to drag in near dark," I wrote. "Parkinson's Law has universal applications."

"Mickey, you'll never believe what I found!" I heard Bill Rombin shouting next morning.

"I give up — a thumb tack."

"*The* thumb tack."

It had rolled under his sleeping bag and stuck there for a day and two nights. I gravely accepted its return.

"A fantastic sunrise going on outside," Bill observed, "and the biggest event of the morning is finding a thumb tack."

Guidebook directions remained a puzzle that day, so we continued to follow north-to-south backwards. When I'd first obtained the guides back in Phoenix, I'd decided to remove sections we wouldn't need. Get rid of north-to-south, several authors advised. The ten books come in loose-leaf, post-binder form; put the south-to-north part in five binders instead of ten. Save time. Save weight!

So there I was, pages scattered over the living room floor, discovering in my haste: three guides in spiral binders, one in paperback, and six in post-binders with varying theories on how far apart post holes should be.

"What are you doing?" Jerri had asked.

"Cutting the guides down to five books," I'd said.

"What for?"

"We're walking north. Why carry directions for going south?"

"The books won't be any lighter each," she'd observed, in her usual penetrating way. "There will just be half as many."

"Hmmm," I'd demurred.

"We'll only be carrying them one at a time," she'd gone on, "so it won't make any difference. Besides, we might need the north-south part."

We reached the village of Groseclose near Interstate 81 by noon. We called our friend, Mary Cox, in Draper, Virginia, and arranged a meeting at Big Walker Lookout for two o'clock the next afternoon. She'd bring the family, she said, and some fried chicken. We'd have a Sunday afternoon picnic on Mother's Day.

We passed several hours of roads, brushy back lots, and scrub forest, then started up Walker Mountain for the final two miles of a fourteen-mile day. Kyra noted pink azaleas and the first flame azaleas. Whole hillsides would explode with them soon, filling the woods with bursts of yellow, orange, and red.

John Laming, a nineteen-year-old Englishman, joined us for the climb. He walked ahead with Jerri and talked nonstop all the way. As part of his outdoor training in England, he said, he'd had to climb a three-thousand-foot peak and maintain a conversation without running short of breath. He'd learned his lesson well.

"It was wonderful," Jerri said. "All my senses went numb and I climbed the whole two miles feeling no pain whatever. I only had to gasp 'Uh-huh' once in a while."

Walker Mountain Shelter and its surrounding area was overrun with Girl Scouts. We walked quickly on, searching for a flat area out of earshot. Passing the nearby firetower, we heard a call from aloft:

"C'mon up. *Great* campsite."

It was Bill. John and his companion, Jim Wilson from Buffalo, climbed up as well. Six of us scraped aside litter in the one-room penthouse, fifty feet in the air, and rolled out bags. Kyra helped at every opportunity. She had no time for Girl Scouts; she wanted to be with hikers.

Strong winds rocked the tower all evening, adding a sense of minor drama to the panoramic view. I watched as sunset lingered. Blue-gray clouds turned orange and glowing red, then began to fade. Tiny lights winked on in the valley and grew in brightness as the sky turned dark. I stared out the tower windows as day became night, as mountains vanished in blackness, as a room filled with chatty hikers fell to quiet.

Sunny weather made for pleasant walking again next day and we arrived ten minutes early for our appointment.

"How did you know when you'd get here?" Mary asked, surprised. "We were prepared for a wait."

We walked a mile and a half an hour, I explained, and the eight miles from the tower to Big Walker Lookout were fairly routine. Mary and Tom Cox, with daughter Donna and twin sons Gary and Barry, took us by car down the mountain to a local picnic area. Though we were meeting for the first time, I'd corresponded with Mary to keep in touch with her roving brother, Lloyd Sumner, as he bicycled around the world.

Mary's idea of lunch filled a whole picnic table. She'd brought fried chicken, baked beans, fried apples, potato salad, biscuits, and an accompanying list of ingredients that filled four lines in my log. How three slightly seedy hikers just out of the woods rated such treatment was a bit puzzling, but we didn't protest. We filled our plates and filled them again. Our Southern friends really knew how to pack a lunch.

They invited us to stay a day or so. The lure of hot showers and such home cooking was hard to decline, yet the promise of sunny weather ahead drew us on.

Back at the trail, Tom gave me the supply box I'd mailed him and I loaded my pack. We shook hands, promised post cards, and staggered up the trail amid a chorus of goodbyes. The eight days' food jammed on top of that already on hand made my pack the heaviest ever. I wondered how we could ever need it. After Mary's lunch, I didn't think we'd be hungry again for days.

Four miles on we awoke to clear sky, soft grass, and a view of distant mountains. Kyra thought the setting far too peaceful even to consider getting up. She ordered breakfast in bed. I wanted to take down the tent. I dragged her out, tossed her over my shoulder, and carried her bed to breakfast.

"Good morning, Kyra-in-the-pulpit," said Jerri, noting the sleeping bag hood flopped over Kyra's head.

"G'morning," Kyra said, giggling.

Later, with bags stuffed and tent and kitchen gear stowed away, we started up the trail. Jerri would remember May 14 for years to come, as the day we saw ten miles of flowers.

It was obvious, even to me, just how differently Jerri viewed the world than I did. I saw the grand and the magnificent. I had to reach for smaller things, have them called to my attention, as if some interest threshold had first to be crossed.

Jerri had no such threshold. The color of reflections in a puddle, the touch of light and shadow on a tree, might captivate her as much as a waterfall or superb mountain view. The natural world held her attention and she found everything in it of interest.

She'd paged through every flower book, bird book, or other field guide she could find as a child and was still doing so. She had great respect and appreciation for the land and the beauty it provided, and wanted to know all she could about it. That's why she stopped to follow birds and listen to their songs, she said. And why each familiar flower that jumped from the pages of her mind to appear suddenly at her feet made her want to stop — to see and touch and smell it, to remember it forever.

I had already logged more than fifty different flowers she'd seen. I'd entered common things — daffodils, buttercups, even dandelions — on up to the exotic whorled pogonia, the few known locations of which were kept purposely vague. She'd stopped for every violet since Georgia, I was sure, and those with beaded raindrops nearly guaranteed a stop for pictures. She'd photographed a false hellebore for an hour one morning, intrigued by patterns in its leaves. She felt no forward-driving urge to see something bigger, grander, more spectacular around the bend. The daisy or rhododendron leaf at hand was enjoyment enough. She seemed content with such things. As she put it, watching and seeing was what she did.

She walked into a bonanza after lunch at Turkey Gap. It started quite innocently with trilliums, the large-flowered kind. Off came her pack and out came the Nikon. We followed from flower to flower as she photographed delicate white blossoms that did everything in threes. Back on our way, we got maybe ten feet. She found more white trilliums and some in every shade of pink, lining the trail as far as we could see. We stopped again and again.

Lily of the valley joined in, then azaleas, yellow, pink, and orange. We all but crawled through a constant barrage of color that made those bleak, snowy days seem part of some other trip, so long before.

"Yellow lady slippers!" Jerri cried as we passed around another bend. She shed her pack again and got down on hands and knees to watch dozens of bobbing yellow slippers wave in the faintest breeze.

They were too lovely merely to be glanced at, Jerri said between pictures. We should admire each one for itself.

Kyra knelt down and lightly touched each blossom, saying, "You are beautiful ... you are beautiful ... you are beautiful...."

"And look," Jerri said, pointing to one delicate bud bursting into bloom, "this one is just being born. Today is its birthday."

Kyra smiled and began to sing, "Happy birthday to you...."

CHAPTER 11

Annie Dillard,
Won't You Please Come Home

*I'd trade a dozen ascents of Clingmans Dome for
an afternoon with a red eft.*

- JERRI

WE MARKED THE FIVE-HUNDRED-MILE POINT at Crandon, Virginia,
where the trail wound down off Walker Mountain to cross Virginia Highway 42. We'd walked farther than that, but it made
little difference. Significant mileposts were celebrated near
something to eat. We marched directly to the Crandon Grocery,
bought lunch, and settled down on the back steps to whole
cherry pie a la mode.

We already knew the next five hundred miles would be different. Weather had improved and soon school would let out.
That meant more people on the trail.

We'd seen rain or snow on twenty-five of our first fifty-six
days and never doubted we'd find water in creeks and springs.
Sources would be less reliable in summer.

We noticed another difference also: hard-surface roads. The

trail followed eight miles of asphalt and gravel out of Crandon, and by the time our jarring bootsteps had taken us through Dismal Creek Valley, down Dismal Creek Road, to Dismal Creek Falls, we thought the area perhaps well-named. We welcomed easy walks along backwoods dirt roads. But pavement, honking horns, and diesel fumes added nothing to the day.

Newly relocated trail took over at the eight-mile point and led into the woods. The road continued ahead but we happily took shady trail, thinking it merely a parallel route for the short jaunt to Wapiti shelter. Two hours later the meandering path still led us on, far beyond any indication of where we might be. Several times we entered clearings maintained as grazing plots for deer and thought we'd see a sign. The fresh-cut trail offered only white blazes and continuing twists and turns.

A marker finally pointed to the left. We walked a half mile back to the road, then up a hill to the shelter. In three or more miles of trail we'd avoided a mile and a half of road. The wisdom of it all remained unclear.

Ned Barr from North Carolina joined us soon after. He'd started April 1 on Springer Mountain and in his casual, strolling way, had handily eclipsed our eleven-day lead. He would "get into this trucking thing" occasionally, he said, and really put away the miles. The rest of the time he just ambled along. He'd hiked some of the trail before. This time he wanted to see it all in one trip. We talked of Joseph, a southbound hiker who had crossed our paths on Walker Mountain.

Joseph and his dog, Charlie, had been "just driftin' south, maybe to Asheville." They'd hitchhiked from Washington, D.C. and walked the AT for about three hundred miles. Joseph didn't remember exactly when they'd left, only that he'd felt like moving on. Walking seemed a good way to figure out where to go and what to do next.

Charlie looked like a German shepherd but was half coyote, Joseph said. The dog carried its own food in a pack and hauled in a woodchuck now and then to add to their supplies. Joseph cooked and shared these with Charlie and anyone else willing.

We'd met Joseph in High Rocks Shelter the night before and watched him cook more standard fare. He carried corn meal, brown sugar, powdered milk, Alpen cereal, and raisins mixed dry in a paper bag. Multiple meal choices was too much bother, he said. He cooked the same thing three times a day. He added other ingredients if he had any but liked it plain just as well. One bag of food made things simple, Joseph said; he could stir leftovers in with the next meal or eat them cold out of the pot.

Ned had run into Joseph that morning on the trail from Turkey Gap. Both walked along absorbed in surroundings, neither noticing the other on the trail ahead. Closer and closer they'd approached, one going north, one going south, minds wandering elsewhere in space and time. Inches from collision, each jumped aside with a sudden start.

"... um, sorry," Joseph said, by way of explanation. "I was in Long Beach in 1964."

We continued along the new trail next morning. The sun quickly dispelled the night's freezing temperatures, and as wet grass dried and cold air turned soggy-humid, our eighth consecutive bright blue day very soon felt hot. The trail joined an old jeep road and a passing Virginia Game Commission work crew offered us a ride in their truck.

"Take the packs," Jerri said. "Walking without them for a couple miles will be even better than a ride."

We caught up with them again on Sugar Run Mountain and asked about the trail we'd been following.

"It's been rerouted all the way to Pearisburg," the driver said. "Takes twenty miles to get there now instead of fifteen."

Had we looked more carefully that morning, I later learned from a note left by Ned, we'd have noticed the old route's faint blazes behind the shelter. He found them after we'd gone and walked all the way to Pearisburg by mid-afternoon.

We stopped at a rocky overlook beyond Sugar Run for a look at our next few days' walk. Pearis Mountain, the next day's program, presented a long, level crest one valley over. It would drop us in Pearisburg on a Thursday afternoon. Peters Mountain, a distant lump in the haze farther on, would keep us busy the day after. Nothing ahead seemed unusual or formidable ... just another selection of ups and downs. Trees had leafed out nearly all the way up the mountain slopes. Only summits and ridge crests had yet to be covered in green.

Many hot and perplexing miles followed. We stuck with the new trail but confusion between old trail, new trail, and segments of former trail scattered other hikers like dandelion fluff before the wind. We directed the lost and bewildered as though we really knew the way, but we were never quite sure.

A sign alleged Docs Knob Shelter to be 6.3 miles ahead. We walked more than ten miles and didn't find it. The five new miles had been inserted between the sign and the shelter, we concluded, but when evening came and the trail left the valley to take us up Pearis Mountain, we decided we'd had enough. We put up the tent and called it a day.

A car drove up at dusk and parked nearby. Two high-school fellows got out and strapped on backpacks in fading light as if getting ready for a hike. I walked over to say hello.

"We've been looking for Docs Knob Shelter all day," I said. "Is it around here somewhere?"

"Sure," one of the boys replied; "two hundred yards up the hill. We're headed there for the night."

It *had* seemed a strange time of day to start a hike. The news gave us no inclination to move, however.

Navigation problems were common in stories of hiking the AT. More than a third of the accounts published over the years mentioned walking in a circle or hiking the wrong way. Some hikers did so more than once. Others might have preferred not to say. When fog, multiple trails, and lumbered-off blazes made directions a matter of guess, even the most attentive hiker could retrace his own steps. But it would never happen to us.

That there were three of us accounts for this good fortune. Whenever we got off the trail, one would soon notice and we'd fan out to look. Whoever found the brush-covered blaze or not-obvious turn called the others with a whistle and we'd be on our way again. After a few hundred miles, we'd developed a feeling for where the trail would likely go. We found the right way even when markings disappeared altogether.

Our differing orientation methods helped as well. Jerri grew up in the Minnesota woods and learned to find her way as a child. She'd studied the positions of the sun and stars at different times of the year and could relate them to compass points in nearly any locale.

Kyra found her way in a different fashion.

"Where's north, Kyra?" Jerri would ask.

Kyra would look around, think a bit, and point:

"Squaw Peak is over there."

"Squaw Peak is in Phoenix," I might say.

"Uh-huh. And if *we* were in Phoenix, Squaw Peak would be over there, and that's north."

She'd usually be right on the mark.

I grew up in town and didn't know about north. My world went left and right. I could find north with a compass all right, but the significance faded once I put the compass away. I only used the information to get the map pointed right. Astronomy wasn't my strong suit, either. I first noticed the moon up in the daytime when I was nearly thirty years old. I figured it out mathematically one day, then went and looked. And if you asked me what direction I was going as I hiked into the setting sun, I likely wouldn't know.

But I knew left and right. If we came into camp from "this way" (Georgia), we should depart "that way" (Maine); never mind that we were walking due east.

"If this trail's going to get us anywhere," I might say, "it has to turn right pretty soon."

"North," Jerri would reply.

"Toward Squaw Peak," Kyra might add.

Soon the trail would bend to everyone's satisfaction. Seeing things in different ways helped us. We stayed on the trail, moving forward, and would till we sighted the last blaze.

I woke at four next morning and listened. Birds sang in full-moon brightness and the whippoorwill that sang us to sleep had started up again. I dropped easily back to my dreams, wondering why I'd thought it time to get up.

I woke again two hours later with a feeling of urgency. Light on the ground had lost its moonlit quality. Instead of the crisp glint of sun in morning dew, the view out the tent flap seemed dim, gray, featureless.

"The weather will hold till full moon," Joseph had said. "Weather always changes at full moon."

I crawled out and saw new weather directly above us — rain, any minute. We barely got packed up before it began.

The walk along Pearis Mountain proved singularly dull. Rain alternated between mist and drizzle at first, then settled into a steady downpour that kept on until mid-afternoon. We plowed through wet underbrush for hours and reached the end of the ridge at its high point, Angels Rest. We saw no views from View Rock, so headed down the slippery, two-thousand-foot drop into Pearisburg. Rain ended as we hit the bottom.

The trail followed the highway on the edge of town. A constant flow of cars and roaring diesel trucks blasted us with spray as we walked. Jerri and Kyra grimaced at the noise and foul-smelling fumes and both were nearly sick by the time we turned from the road into town.

We climbed into the foothills of Peters Mountain next morning. The trail wove back and forth on exposed gravel roads, rising steadily, dropping, then rising again as if circling to find the best route. The day turned hot as morning became afternoon. We thrashed this way and that for hours, probing toward the summit, gaining elevation and giving it up. Looking back from open areas, we could see again the long crest of Pearis Mountain and beyond to where we'd stood two days before. We'd done a hundred miles in eight days. In two days, we'd walked nearly as far as we could see.

Still the climbing went on. After three miles we'd regained half the two thousand feet lost into Pearisburg but the top remained out of sight far above. Kyra straggled behind, perspiration rolling down her face and soaking her shirt. Jerri strained upward just ahead.

Full packs again ... always full packs for big climbs out of town. Why not have towns on tops of mountains? Resupply would sure be easier.

"Ascent begins here," announced the guide at the four-mile mark. Swell ... what have we been doing till now?

Then the trail turned up, more and more steeply up.

We fell to the ground on top exhausted after five miles in six hours. We'd been walking our bodies into shape for fifty-nine days, but strenuous climbing had yet to become easy or fun. We recovered more quickly though. After a snack, a canteen of lemonade, and long looks at the outstretched world, we felt ready to go again.

"We have a problem," I said. "The trail's flat for a while ..."

"That's not a problem," said Kyra.

"... and there's one waterhole in half a mile and another in nine miles. The first is too close. The other is too far."

"What's in between?" Jerri asked.

"Symms Gap at four and a half miles looks like a good spot to camp. Anyone want to carry water?"

No one did.

"There's an 'untested spring' mentioned near the gap," I said. "We could trust our luck...."

We pushed on. There was enough afternoon left for four and a half miles.

The grassy field where May apples bloomed at Symms Gap made one of the loveliest campsites thus far. We had views of hazy mountains and valleys, the glow of the setting sun, soft meadow grass for sleeping, and quiet — no other person would be found for miles. No rushing or gurgling of water greeted our ears, either. No splashing; not even dripping. No sound even suggested the presence of water.

The spring would be three hundred feet down an old logging road, said the guide. I located the road, walked the approximate distance, looked around. I saw nothing, heard nothing. Tracking from side to side, I checked in hollows, down slopes, behind large rocks. Nothing.

The road itself showed wet streaks, fresher than from recent rain. I traced them uphill for a possible source. A damp spot in the grass off the road seemed likely. Jerri dipped a quarter-cup of gritty water and waited. The depression slowly refilled. Dipping water ounce by ounce and straining it through a bandana, Jerri and Kyra filled a canteen in fifteen minutes. They continued till dark to fill all six.

Noises ... I listened in the dark to crickets ... buzzing insects ... other minor rustlings and chirpings in the brush. Restful sounds for a warm night. I'd been wary of night sounds at first ... tensing up at passing squirrels, falling twigs, whatever they'd been. No problem anymore....

Soft grass ... let's see, I'd slept on sagging bunks, wood planks, lumpy dirt, stony ground. I'd once thought to rank them: motels, then grass, then wooden shelter floors. It hardly mattered now. Five hundred fifty miles had made a difference.

Lightning bugs ... winking lanterns in the dark. And stars that pulsed faintly in clear night sky. It all seemed so pleasant. Soft lights, soft grass, soft sounds. I could get to like it here ... it wasn't really a foreign place....

128

Breakfast at sunrise brought a welcome change. Tired of every cooked cereal the stores had to offer, Jerri began mixing them together, making her own "Joseph's Mix." Joseph would never have recognized it, but bubbling in the pot that morning were equal parts of oatmeal, instant grits, Ralston, powdered milk, and Alpen cereal, plus a handful of mixed dried fruit. It smelled superb. Jerri loaded the cups and called us all to breakfast. Kyra didn't appear. I checked the tent and found her still in her bag.

"I'll have breakfast in bed, as usual," she said.

I tickled her toes through the bottom of her bag, then dragged her out of the tent. Muffled little-girl giggles broke the morning stillness as I rolled the bag over and over downhill. As Kyra sat up to look out, Jerri picked blades of dry grass out of her tousled hair and handed her a cup of steaming cereal.

"Good morning, sleepyhead," Jerri said. "Breakfast in bed it is."

The trail atop Peters Mountain reentered the woods beyond the meadow where we'd camped. Dense growth on the forest floor had turned it a solid, leafy green, and floppy ferns and spreading shrubbery at times obscured the trail. Walking along called for frequent blasts through the bushes to keep going.

Trilliums, lady slippers, and lily of the valley brightened the surroundings meanwhile, and rare white shooting stars brought out Jerri's camera again. Kyra noticed more azaleas, saw a woodchuck dashing for cover, and followed a blue swallowtail butterfly that fluttered across our path. Twenty days had passed since that final bleak night of snow. In that time the woods had come alive.

A trail relocation soon took us touring again. We climbed. We descended. Nothing gave a hint of where we were. Miles passed. Hours passed. I kept checking the guide but found no sign of progress. Our plans for an easy afternoon to Bailey Gap Shelter, and I hoped beyond, slowly slipped from our grasp. I asked southbound hikers what we would find ahead, but they hadn't been paying attention. The route they described bore little resemblance to what we found.

We reached the shelter late and there met Cyrus Musiker of Rhode Island. He'd started March 23 in Georgia and already several curious tales preceded him. Cyrus, word had it, hitch-hiked parts of the trail. He'd skipped a hundred miles, according to purists we'd met, and was viewed with disdain. Cyrus, the AT Hitchhiker, they called him.

We found him friendly and talkative. He carried a hodge-podge of gear, and if he appeared less than certain about how to use some of it, he made a pleasant companion just the same. People could say what they might, he said, confirming the hitchhiking rumors; he would see the trail in his own way. If others didn't like it, too bad.

Cloudy sky continued after a rainy night and we moved on through damp, dimly lit woods. We kept quiet as could be through "wilderness area which until recently was a privately owned game preserve," but the "deer, grouse, and possibly bear" must have had the day off. Nothing moved on the trail and we heard no sounds in the brush.

Several hours of daylight remained when we reached Big Pond Shelter. Water in the pond was known to be stagnant, so we'd carried a full load of our own three miles, thinking it best to be safe. I planned to go on after a brief rest, to stretch a twelve-mile day to fifteen. Jerri discovered an old copy of Newsweek, however, and that ended that. She settled in — for the evening, it appeared — to catch up on news of some long past week.

A melodious colony of frogs was in full serenade at Big Pond itself. Their song diminished as I neared, then tiny splashes rimmed the pond and all became suddenly quiet. I crouched at the water's edge. Tadpoles wriggled by. Wet, green noses protruded from the water and bulging eyes peered cautiously through weeds. I waited. The frogs waited. I heard no sound. As I retreated, the chorus gradually resumed.

Back at the shelter, Jerri reported no urgent news that demanded our immediate return. Apparently, she said, we hadn't even been missed.

By morning the sky had cleared. We left camp early, passed through a dewy, sun-sparkled clearing, then started downhill three miles toward Sinking Creek Valley.

Tall trees closed overhead as we entered the woods. Warm sunlight filtered in, making a patchwork of light and shadow on the trail and forest floor. Jerri pointed to backlit greens and golds shimmering above and around us, to leaves in every spring shade that fluttered and rustled in the breeze.

"I haven't seen such a perfect spring morning in twenty years," she said. "It's like being ten years old again." She bounced along, intrigued anew with each leaf and flower, each sight and sound and smell.

Her enthusiasm spread. I noticed air that smelled crisp and clean, woods that felt fresh and new, and heard birds singing to the rhythm of boots crunching down gently descending trail.

"I'm ten years old ... I'm ten years old ..." Jerri sang as she skipped ahead.

Kyra was mortified.

"Really, Mother," she said. "*I'm* the ten-year-old!"

Jerri laughed and went on, "I'm ten years old, ten years old."

We crossed Virginia Highway 42 again at the bottom of the hill and a mile down the road found Duncan's Grocery. *Hides - Raw Furs - Ginseng bought here* read a weathered sign on the building. Considering the probable volume of trade in such commodities, it came as no surprise that the place was closed.

Hikers come to yellow house if you want in store said a sign in the window. I retrieved the proprietor as directed. He'd obviously had much experience with hikers; his sales pitch began at once. He offered cheese, crackers, peanut butter. He brought out chocolate, raisins, lemonade mix. He described at length the convenience and food value of each, assuring us all the while that every hiker so far had bought these things without hesitation. Our $3.16 worth of purchases was clearly far less than he'd had in mind. Disappointed, but wishing us a good hike nonetheless, he locked the store and returned to the yellow house.

The trail atop Sinking Creek Mountain began to show more of the changing season. Ten miles of hot, open ridge had no available water, and tangled underbrush obscured the path and tore at our clothes and bare legs as we pushed our way through. Azaleas in full bloom scored points for the positive side, as did occasional views and infrequent but welcome shade. We walked quickly and made good time, but slowed to a careful ballet through several miles of broken and overgrown rocks.

My sixty-third day began at 4:00 AM. Someone had put a nickel in the whippoorwill again and its chanting call woke me from a sound sleep. I nodded off, awoke, and slept again. We eventually got up to walk twelve miles, described most adequately in Kyra's journal entry for the day:

"May 22 — We woke up and it wasn't raining. We crossed Trout Creek and I fell in. We went to Trout Creek Shelter and I changed my socks and had lunch. We scared up a woodchuck. We climbed up Dragons Tooth and I would have hated to be its dentist. We saw a green snake. We pitched our tent in Beckners Gap and the mosquitoes ate me alive. It rained all night."

"Look!" whispered Jerri, as we broke camp next morning. I looked, and froze; four deer came leaping over a nearby ridgecrest and down the hill toward us. Halfway down, they noticed us and froze. Standing motionless on the slope, they seemed almost to fade from sight, their protective brown absorbed by the blending background. We regarded each other in silence as rain continued to fall. Then, one by one, each flipped its tail with a flash of white, bounded up the hill and disappeared.

"That brightens the day," I said.

"Weren't they pretty?" said Jerri. "See, even rainy days have treats in store."

The wildlife seemed less bothered by foot-traffic that day and in knee-deep grass we stirred up lots of goings-on. Woodchucks and squirrels rushed about hardly noticing us, and slugs and snails moseyed about their slow-paced affairs. Fat toads hopped when we stepped too near. Turtles ambled down the path unconcerned, or meditated in their black and yellow shells. Jerri spotted our first mountain laurel, spectacular pink and white clusters of small, cup-shaped flowers, and also identified spiderworts and phlox. Then she found a red eft.

We'd seen only one newt or red eft on the AT, a week or so before on another rainy day. Here they were out in force, conspicuous in the damp grass. A few miles away, Annie Dillard was watching them, too, and writing about them in *Pilgrim at Tinker Creek.*

Newts are the most common of salamanders. Their skin is a lighted green, like water in a sunlit pond, and rows of very bright dots line their backs. They have gills as larvae; as they grow they turn a luminescent red, lose their gills, and walk out of the water to spend a few years padding around in damp places on the forest floor. Their feet look like fingered baby hands, and they walk in the same patterns as all four-footed creatures — dogs, mules, and, for that matter, lesser pandas. When they mature fully, they turn green again and stream to the water in droves. A newt can scent its way home from as far as eight miles away. They are altogether excellent creatures, if somewhat moist, but no one pays the least attention to them, except children.

We found more on our way up Tinker Mountain and Kyra picked one up to hold. Sluggish from cool air, it moved slowly at first, then picked up speed as Kyra's hands warmed its tiny feet. It moved faster as Jerri photographed, then scrambled from hand to hand as Kyra juggled to keep it aloft. When she set it down, Jerri followed it for another look. It was her favorite creature, she said. She stopped for all nine we saw that day.

Annie Dillard's story of "exploring the neighborhood" hadn't been published yet. We would have been interested to know, no doubt, that in the book we would come to read again and again, the neighborhood was the mountain on which we stood and the creek just down the slope. Were she at home that day, those few miles down the mountain to Cloverdale and south to Hollins, we could have walked to accept the invitation we'd wait a year to read:

> There are seven or eight categories of phenomena in the world that are worth talking about, and one of them is the weather. Any time you care to get in your car and drive across the country and over the mountains, come into our valley, cross Tinker Creek, drive up the road to the house, walk across the yard, knock on the door and ask to come in and talk about the weather, you'd be welcome. If you came tonight from up north, you'd have a terrific tailwind; between Tinker and Dead Man you'd chute through the orchardy pass like an iceboat. When I let you in, we might not be able to shut the door.

As it happened, we tented in pouring rain in Lamberts Meadow. We crossed the rest of Tinker Mountain and Tinker Creek next day, then got a ride to Cloverdale and a motel for a couple of days.

"Were you looking for Donahoe Shelter?" our driver asked.

134

We had, I said, but gave up and slept in our tent instead.

"Well, I'm Donahoe," he continued, "and you didn't find it because I haven't built it yet. A tractor accident put me in the hospital for six months. But you could have used my porch...."

For two rainy days in a dreary motel we worked out necessary details. Another 125 miles would take us to Waynesboro, Virginia, to the edge of Shenandoah National Park. A food box to Snowden near the halfway point would keep us supplied.

That decided, we shopped, did laundry, took showers. We wrote letters, restocked packs, slept in beds. Boring. We'd welcomed town stops as rescue and refuge at first, to escape the cold and eat town food again. By Cloverdale the experience had lost its thrill. Towns were bleak and noisy compared to the summer woods, we all agreed, and cooking huge meals was a lot of bother. Even in the rain, we would rather have been on the trail.

The stop was not without its moments, however. Looking for the closest laundry, I stopped to ask directions at a gas station.

"It's up the road a piece," the attendant said. Noting I was on foot, he added, "... well, maybe more like a piece and a half."

And as I stood hitchhiking to Hollins for groceries, a Land Rover stopped and I met Margart Adams. She was going shopping, too, she said; if I went to the same store she'd wait and bring me back.

She'd gone on to other errands by the time I'd checked through the cashier, so I set my supplies on the sidewalk outside. *My* neighborhood exploration revealed an ice cream parlor. When I spotted the Land Rover heading my way, I bought two double-dip cones for the ride back.

I thanked Mrs. Adams as she dropped me at my door and added her to the long list of those who wanted to hear more about our hike. If we ever did make it to Katahdin, I knew we'd be pleased to have such nice people to tell.

CHAPTER 12

_____

What Comes Down, Must Go Up

*Thou shalt not tell thy neighbor false tales about
good hiking in the mountains lest in deceiving thy
neighbor, when he returneth through snow with
naught save his rifle, he presenteth thee with the
contents thereof....*
                    - MINER'S NINTH COMMANDMENT

COLOR EXPLODED AROUND US. Stands of rhododendron and
mountain laurel bloomed in full glory. Mountainsides near and
far showed bright splashes of pink, purple, and orange. Towering bushes crowded the winding trail; Jerri paused often to
smell and admire their rain-splattered blossoms. We walked
carefully on fallen leaves and petals that made a fragile carpet
of the path.

Rain and scattered fog continued for days as we walked
northeast to follow the Blue Ridge Parkway. We crossed it many
times. Headlight beams of approaching cars sometimes picked
us out of the mist — three orange blurs emerging from one side
of the roadway, vanishing moments later on the other. Jerri
pointed out honeysuckle, beargrass, wild strawberries and

136

roses, and a tulip tree that soared to the sky, its orange and white blossoms burning like candles on every branch. And to the tune of "Eleanor Rigby," Kyra quietly sang,

"All the rhododendron, where *do* they all come from?"

Wildlife was more evident as well. Woodchucks huffed-and-puffed out of our way; squirrels chattered and scolded as we passed. Walking out front one morning, Kyra startled a wild turkey. It burst from cover in a fury of squawking discontent and sped away. Red efts continued to watch us. Perhaps in our orange rain gear, they saw us as huge distant cousins. Then we found mother grouse.

Whenever we came too near one tending a batch of chicks, we'd hear a sudden cry and see her limp up the trail, flapping one wing and dragging the other. We were to follow, of course, until she judged us far enough off. Then she'd fly a wide, circular route back to the nest. None too soon, either. Grouse chicks weren't very organized on their own. If mother were gone too long they'd soon be milling in all directions. Jerri thought it best to play mama's game and follow along as directed. But before passing by, we'd sneak a glance at cute, fuzzy chicks rushing in all directions.

Then came the tourists. On our first night out of Cloverdale, *we* had intruded in gloomy Wilson Creek Shelter. A couple in bright orange sleeping bags perhaps would have preferred to be left alone. But with little light left that rainy, ten-mile afternoon, we'd moved in uninvited. Another night, we were intruded upon as four weekend-in-the-woods types from New York blundered around the shelter. Nature had a way of keeping things in balance, it appeared.

We marked our turf by spreading a six-by-nine-foot ground sheet in one end of the shelter and confining our activities thereto. We tried not to laugh, groan, or lecture when our companions' fire wouldn't start and stoves wouldn't light. When they washed dishes in the creek, left food strewn about, and injured themselves on their own equipment. But it was painful to watch. I busied myself catching up the log.

Some later, two more fellows arrived — rain-drenched parkway cyclists bouncing bicycles down the long hill to the shelter. The crowd thus swelled to nine and our space diminished. Time started to drag.

Stupid rain ... Jerri had stopped early because of it since the next shelter stood six miles off. Or nine miles, or eight, depending on which source one believed. Maps, signs, and guidebook all disagreed of late. We could have tented alone farther on ... but the woods were wet with five days of rain. Even a wet tent was preferable to this bunch of drips.

"These are the Memorial Day campers," I grumpily wrote in the log. "They've come all the way from New York to be miserable in the rain. What will summer be like with amateurs out in force?"

When they learned we'd walked six hundred miles from Georgia, and intended to go on fourteen hundred more to Maine, they were struck by a certain perplexed awe. We didn't fit the image, it seemed. We didn't look equal to the challenge they assumed imperiled every mile. This eventually led them to ask what weapons we carried.

I pulled out my pocket knife then and watched as they grew more confused. A big hunting dagger or a pistol or two would clearly have made them feel better.

"We each have a knife," I explained, but that didn't help much, either.

"But what about snakes?" one lady asked.

"There isn't much danger in the woods," Jerri said. "Animals mind their own business. So do we. As long as we keep food out of their reach, there's no problem."

But that was too simple, not at all how they'd seen it on TV.

"Actually," I said, beginning to enjoy the exchange, "the biggest danger is from falling down." It happened to be true, but it left them shaking their heads and wondering how experienced we really were.

Rain ended next morning and the sky cleared by early afternoon. Underbrush eventually dried and we traded in rain gear for shorts. Crossing the parkway again, we could actually see from viewpoints. In thick fog on days before, parkway *View* signs had pointed to scenes of uniform gray. Rolling green hills and valleys greeted us with the sun's return, two days' worth wherever we looked. Places we'd been and places we had yet to go, all glowing with color from flowers of the season. We walked north to see what we could see.

We camped at Cove Creek. Trash cans nearby overflowed and littered the grounds, but with the next refuge nine miles off, we stayed. After Sunday night with the mob, having any place alone was a relief. I slept soundly on the wood plank floor....

CLANK....

I woke at once, but saw nothing in the pitch dark. I reached for my glasses and flashlight kept near my head.

CLANK ... RATTLE....

Two huge raccoons atop side-by-side garbage cans froze in the flashlight's beam. Each stared at me briefly, masked eyes reflecting fiery red, then resumed pawing through trash. I shut off the light and lay back down; no need to stay up and watch.

Our packs hung inside from the shelter roof. I'd tied foot-long cord loops to each pack frame to suspend them from any convenient nail. When I couldn't find a nail, I'd throw a separate two-foot cord loop over anything available, such as a roof joist. By collecting loop ends and pack cord in a carabiner, the nightly hang-up ritual was quickly and easily done. This made more room on the shelter floor and left nothing sitting around if mice, skunks, or raccoons sauntered in to join us.

Our seventieth day began easily. We crossed Jennings Creek on a long wooden footbridge, then followed a half-mile gravel road into the woods. Jerri stopped to photograph white-crowned stalks of beargrass and large orange blossoms on a fallen tulip tree branch.

Then the going got complicated. The trail led uphill for five grueling miles and we plowed through dense ferns, waist-high cow parsnip, and other green grabby things obscuring the trail. Long passages through stinging nettles left a burning itch on our bare legs. The day turned hot and humid early and mosquitoes followed in pestering swarms.

The goal of the day's efforts, Thunder Hill Shelter, lay somewhere ahead but information disagreed on precisely where. We followed the blazes, hoping some landmark would suddenly make things clear. No such luck. With ten miles behind by dinnertime, we knew no more than before. A stand of miniature yellow lady slippers at Parker Gap Road set Jerri's camera clicking again. A creek flowed nearby; we decided to quit for the day. I walked ahead, looking for a spot to pitch the tent, and found a sign: *Thunder Hill Shelter 2-1/4.*

I reported the news. Signs had been right lately, Jerri said, when all else had been wrong. Unable to resist, even with 4,244-foot Apple Orchard Mountain directly ahead, we donned packs and headed uphill.

The next mile took us up the mountain to the expected apple orchard, then on a wide swing around a U.S. Army radar installation. We descended another mile to the parkway and found the shelter a short distance on. We cheered and baked a cake to celebrate — we'd find no climb as high as Apple Orchard Mountain until Mount Killington in Vermont.

"I saw a mouse in the john," said Kyra, returning from the outhouse after dark. "It was there when I opened the door."

"What did you do?" I asked.

"I shined the light on it thinking it would go away, but it crept into a corner instead. After I'd looked at it all I wanted to, I went in and tried to shoo it out."

"Did it run away?" asked Jerri.

"No, it stopped just outside. The door stood open a bit and the mouse's tail curled inside through the opening. I reached down to touch it, just to find out what a mouse felt like. That scared it off. Oh, it was the *cutest* mouse!"

The next night we camped with five pleasant young folks, drinking their beer and weatherproofing boots with a vigor that spread from Jerri to everyone in camp. The day had begun with loudspeakers booming across hillsides from the radar facility:

"Your attention, please. All supervisors are reminded to meet in Building 14 at 0800 hours."

On that awakening note, we'd gone through miles of nettles, more flooded trail, and had hopped rocks, dodged brush, and scratched arms and legs through a very busy morning. Other hikers passed us in the heat, walking south, sweating and dragging under bulging rucksacks. They'd asked about the trail ahead, hoping for encouraging words like "downhill" or "flat."

Looking down from Hickory Stand, we saw the James River running muddy and wide at flood stage. It sounded like booming Colorado rapids even on the mountaintop. A third of the Appalachian Trail lay behind at the James, along with more than half the trail's mileage in Virginia.

"Jeez, it's mobbed," I'd grumped, finally reaching Matts Creek and finding smoking fires, laundry lines, and five already camped.

"Oh, look!" came a woman's voice. "It's the Arizona family." Friendships mellowed from there.

We traded stories through dinner and answered assorted questions. They hung on each word, seeking, it seemed, some small measure of wisdom from hikers just in from Georgia. Not about to disappoint them, I offered notes from my log concerning three laws of the wilderness: *For every mountain you go down, there is another to go up; If you stay in the woods long enough, you'll get rained on;* and *There is no such thing as too much peanut butter.* Cheers and another round of beer followed.

We crossed U.S. Highway 501 early next morning. From the bridge over the rampaging James, we saw rushing waters reaching far beyond their usual bounds, inundating tree-grown flats normally green with brush and grass. Logs and debris lodged against trees. Water thundered over the spillway upriver and showed long patches of frothing white where it sped across unfamiliar ground.

Seventy miles of Appalachian Trail now led though the Pedlar District of the George Washington National Forest. Its opening challenge, Big Rocky Row, set the theme: five miles and twenty-six hundred vertical feet of "steep and difficult." We resupplied at Snowden's one-building downtown, then started up. We stopped often on the rugged trail to the top, resting where breaks in the trees offered views.

I looked back to dimly outlined radar domes on Apple Orchard Mountain where we'd been two nights before. There it was again: mountain majesty. What it meant was as big a mystery as ever. But I found myself looking ... standing and looking ... pleased to have climbed high enough to see what I was seeing, whatever it was.

We stood atop the fire tower on Bluff Mountain several hours later. A look around showed the final trees had leafed out, marking at last the full change of season. Mountain slopes and summits about us, once stark with the barren look of winter, now wore full measure of leaves in uncountable shades of green. We'd been walking since the first buds began to show, walking a trail that promised four hundred thousand feet of elevation gain and loss before it reached the end. I saw our progress written in the leaves. I was certain we'd still be around to see the season turn again.

The evening's program at Punchbowl Lean-to was already in progress as we arrived. Two southbound couples were camped there, but authoritarian tones in the one-sided conversation told us one held center stage. Mr. Klutz, as we called him, hardly paused at our arrival. He stated flatly, and without prompting, his opinions on everything. He expected no disagreement. He was the expert — on how many miles they should have walked that day, on how poorly the trail crew maintained the trail, on how uncommonly slow his wife walked.

"That stove's no good," he said, noting the one Jerri fired up to cook a quick dinner. "I had one once and got rid of it."

"We've used it for seventy-two days," she said, "cooking twice a day. It's holding up pretty well."

"The gas jets clog," he went on. "I soaked one in gasoline for a week and a half and it still wouldn't work."

"This one clogged once," I said. "I got some wire and carbon tet in town and cleared it out just fine."

"You'll see," he insisted, "it'll clog up. Then you might as well throw it away."

"How far have you walked?" I asked, changing the subject.

"We started in Shenandoah five days ago," he said. "We should have reached the James River today but the damn trail's all messed up. We'll get there tomorrow. If I can get *her* to go that far, we'll get to the Blue Ridge Parkway at Thunder Hill the next afternoon."

"That's twenty-seven miles from here," I said. "Some of it's pretty rough."

"We'll make it," he said, glancing smugly at his wife.

When I hung up our packs in a minute flat with my loop-and-carabiner number, it caught him unawares. But he was not to be outdone. He gathered gear and slammed it away quickly. Cursing the shortage of convenient hang-up nails, he finally hung their packs somehow with a stick. He glared at us defiantly, daring some challenge of his technique.

His wife, Mrs. Why-Me, sat downcast at the picnic table the whole time.

"Are you enjoying this?" Jerri asked her.

"No," she said at once. "I hate it."

"It has been rather hot, I guess," Jerri said. "But the woods are very pretty in May."

"I don't like it here at all," the lady replied. "Hiking is just torture and I hurt all over. I've been trying to get him to quit for days but he just pushes harder."

"How fast have you been walking?"

"About fifteen miles a day, but he wants to go twenty. I'll get used to it, he says. I just want to go home."

"How did you happen to come along?" I asked.

"I didn't know it would be this bad. I guess I should have. None of his men-friends will hike with him anymore."

The show resumed in the morning. While we still sat at breakfast, Mr. Klutz fumed and fussed, rolling up bags and jamming things away so they might be off early.

"You'll have tough going today," he told us. "Creeks are very high and you'll get wet at *all* the crossings."

"It hasn't rained in three days," I said. "The water should be down by now."

"Nope. All the rock bridges are under water. And it's just the opposite in Shenandoah. Water there is very scarce and is found *only* at the shelters which are *all* far off the trail."

He turned and set a brisk pace going south. Mrs. Why-Me struggled into her pack and hurried to catch up. We had yet to finish breakfast.

We crossed half a dozen creeks that day without the slightest dampening of boots. The other couple's advice didn't turn out much better, however. All downhill to Brown Mountain Creek Shelter, they'd said, and it proved to be anything but. We covered many miles uphill as another hot and sunny day wore on.

This led to another wilderness precept: *Never ask directions of anyone who's been on the trail less than thirty days.* Trail that seemed difficult going south one day wouldn't necessarily be easy going north the next.

Readjustment to steep ups and downs came as a shock after walking through half of Virginia on often-easy ridges. Elevation to be gained and lost in the Pedlar District's 70 miles was nearly that of the entire 250 miles of Jefferson Forest. We sputtered at suddenly steep grades, especially on days with four thousand feet of grinding uphill. One Maine-bound hiker kept things in perspective, however, saying this was "just an average day in North Carolina."

Arriving at Brown Mountain Creek Shelter, we felt as tired after eight miles as after thirteen on each of the three days before. Kyra rolled out bags in customary fashion, side by side in one end of the shelter with hers in the middle. We sat up till well after dark to talk and look out at night-time woods. Crickets chirped and June bugs buzzed that first day of June and we listened to a slight wind in the leaves. A moth fluttered busily around the lantern's small, warm glow.

I sat on the edge of the shelter platform, swinging my feet and looking into the dark. Perspective ... how many evenings had been so quiet, so pleasant, so detached from real world problems before we'd come to the AT? Jerri was right ... there were many things to see here, even in the rain, even in the dark.

I heard rustling in the brush.

"Hello," came a voice some distance away. "Hello, could you shine the light this way?"

I aimed a flashlight toward the voice, toward sounds of crunching leaves, breaking twigs, thrashing brush. Two figures emerged from the darkness and made their way toward us.

"Thanks," said one, catching his breath and slumping on the shelter floor. "Our flashlight died and we missed the shelter turn-off. We thought we were lost until we saw your lantern."

Ed and Shiela Long of Roanoke, Virginia, had made a Friday-night start for a weekend hike. Troubles quickly developed.

"We reached the trailhead late, then got disoriented in the

dark," Shiela said. "Besides that, Ed had dental surgery this morning and has been in pain ever since."

"Finding the shelter at all was a stroke of luck," Ed added.

Dogs Bowser and Babo immediately stirred out a skunk nearby and a rich aroma wafted through the shelter. That seemed to complete the day for our beleaguered companions. They wondered aloud what more could go wrong. Learning that the dogs had escaped serious dowsing relieved us all. Jerri offered remedies from her medical kit to relieve Ed's pain and the evening returned to comparative calm.

Ensuing days took us steeply uphill and down, through mosquitoes and nettles, through hours of hot, cloudless sun. Long Mountain lived up to its name, but Bald Knob turned out to be completely wooded. It led upward three miles past half a dozen false summits before letting on.

We paused on grassy, twin summits of Cole Mountain for lofty looks at mountains in all directions. The guidebook pointed out distant views of The Priest, The Cardinal, The Friar, Little Priest, and an acolyte and ring-bearer or two. We couldn't tell one from another in the haze. We also read of one called Three Ridges. Its description inspired a certain awe — a shadeless, three-thousand-foot climb in three miles with no water till much farther on.

Three Ridges was the focal point of the Pedlar District as far as we were concerned. Jerri thought we should climb it early and be well on our way before the day got too hot. That suited me. To get into position, we tramped fourteen difficult, uphill miles one day to sleep in the grass at Elk Pond Mountain, and another fourteen the next over The Priest and down to the dusty Tye River Valley to reach Harpers Creek Shelter. Kyra protested the long days and complained when we kept pushing on. There was good reason, I told her; from the mountain's base, we could get going early and make good use of our time.

But to "get going early" required a certain resolve. We could

146

sit around at nightfall and agree to spring forth at first light, but when morning rolled around, some of us forgot....

"Jerri ... wake up ... it's time to get up."

"... mmmmmm."

"Wake up ... we're going up Three Ridges before it gets hot."

"... wha ... what time is it?"

"Four-fifteen."

"You've got to be kidding."

"We said we'd get up early, remember?"

"It's still *dark* out!"

"The shelter is in a hollow. There's light through the trees, see?"

"What do we tell Kyra. It's her birthday, you know."

"That she can enjoy more of the day this way?"

"Oh, great...."

"Kyra ..." I said, moving to waken her.

"NO!"

"C'mon, Kyra ... wake up," I continued, shaking her gently, "It's only three miles. We'll take a nap on top."

"Leave me alone!"

We departed just before seven.

Considering the anxiety we'd invested in the project, the mountain disappeared swiftly underfoot. But it wasn't easy. Long switchbacks led steadily up the side through nettles that would sting and burn at the slightest touch. Temperature and humidity rose quickly to uncomfortable levels. We stopped in any patch of shade we could find, but there were few. We reached the top at ten o'clock. Had we made the climb at high noon, in temperatures well beyond ninety, we would have had it even worse.

We napped in the shade near a spring. Kyra asked a lot of questions.

"What are we going to do for my birthday?" she wanted to know.

"We won't make it to Waynesboro, that's for sure," I said. For days she'd been hoping we would.

"I wanted to have my party in town."

"We'll have one tonight," Jerri said.

"With presents?"

"Uh-huh," I said. "I have a bicycle here in the pack. You can ride the rest of the way to Maine."

"Sure, Dad."

"We'll have presents," Jerri assured her, "and a party in Waynesboro, too."

We descended again to the parkway three hours later, Kyra still pressing for details. A final climb to Devils Knob (restoring balance to the names in the vicinity, I thought) put us on an old logging road. We followed it three easy miles to water at Laurel Springs Gap. We camped in a secluded hollow barely fifty feet from cars passing on the parkway.

I baked a cake after dinner, cut a hole in its center, and inserted the candle borrowed from the lantern. I lit the candle and presented Kyra with a hand-lettered card.

"Whereas," she read by flickering light, "the Appalachian Ten-Year-Old has been a fine and pleasant companion for most of these 735 miles, she may redeem this certificate at trail's end for one ten-speed bicycle."

Taken completely by surprise, she giggled and squealed with delight. She'd wanted a bike long before the trip started, but hadn't expected it now. I cut the cake as candlelight danced in her eyes.

"You *did* have a ten-speed in your pack," she said with glee. "When I get home I won't have to *walk!*"

Jerri and I sang "Happy Birthday" with the wind and the leaves and the crickets. The fourth of June had come at last. The ten-year-old was eleven.

CHAPTER 13

Intruder at Sawmill Run

*You do not need to leave your room. Remain
sitting at your table and listen. Do not even listen, simply wait. Do not even wait, be quite still
and solitary. The world will freely offer itself to
you to be unmasked, it has no choice, it will roll in
ecstasy at your feet.*

— Franz Kafka

Four miles out of Waynesboro we waited for a ride. Cars went
by, one, then another, but none stopped. I'd followed the rules
for the short hitch to town, rules I'd developed during fifteen
years of travel by thumb. So far my strategy wasn't working.
Drivers stared straight ahead and passed as if we weren't even
there.

The highway ran straight with wide, uncluttered shoulders.
Motorists had plenty of time to see us and ample room to pull
off the road. I'd learned to pick a good spot (rule one), avoiding
curves, embankments, steep hills, and streets jammed with
parked cars in my efforts to offer drivers this convenience. Four
miles out of Waynesboro, no one seemed to notice my concern.

We'd washed up and changed clothes at a gas station to look clean and wholesomely non-threatening (rule two). Two cars approached, then passed. Maybe they didn't like my beard.

Perhaps if we walked, making some show of getting there on our own, we'd have more luck. Perhaps, but I thought it dumb to be walking backward down the road with my thumb hanging out. Rule three said "Don't walk." One could easily trade benign thirty-mile zones for high-speed traffic that way and no longer have a good spot. Staring blankly ahead, another driver passed without slowing. I'd had such trouble in Montana once, unaware I stood ten miles from the state prison. But in neighborly Virginia? How could anyone resist a ten-year-old? Excuse me ... eleven.

A sign showing the destination city name often helped (rule four) if the city lay within a few hundred miles. But at four miles away, I'd thought Waynesboro would be obvious. Whoosh, another car.

These people didn't appreciate refinements in my technique. I always made sure I knew where both we and the driver were going, for example, to avoid rides in the wrong direction. I carried gear for unexpected situations like darkness or rain. I would run toward a car as proper response if one did stop, but decline rides from those not in shape to drive.

As a final note of finesse, unmistakably setting us apart from novice hitchhikers, I positioned us *beyond* intersections and traffic signals so motorists could stop voluntarily. Intimidating drivers trapped at red lights I deemed poor taste. But my educated efforts seemed wasted. Cars continued on by, not even giving me a chance.

As desperation set in, I'd known hitchhikers to try more dramatic moves: asking for rides in restaurants or gas stations, linking arms to form a roadblock, stopping traffic with red construction flags, building fires in the road, or hiding a group in the bushes while one stood innocently thumbing. I'd tried them all myself, in fact (except building a fire, the ultimate in bad form), but ran a cleaner act now, especially on a family trip.

There was no need for special effects four miles from town anyway. We were close enough to walk, which we decided to do. But a hundred feet up the road, Jerri stopped.

"This looks like a better spot," she said. "Let's try it here."

Suppressing disdain, I shrugged and thumbed one more car. It stopped.

"Guess you're right," I muttered.

Mr. Harry Floyd took us to town. He waited while we retrieved Post Office packages, drove us on a motel shopping tour, then delivered us to our chosen room at the General Wayne Motor Lodge. Then he drove off — another stranger we'd never see again, leaving kindness for us to pass on. The room seemed too fancy for hikers. We took off our boots to go in.

We changed techniques again over the next two days. Jerri mail-ordered lightweight rectangular sleeping bags for delivery to Chester Gap at the far end of Shenandoah. Three of us could sleep in two bags if we zipped them together. That would save six pounds; sending down jackets to the Doerings until fall saved another five.

She also switched to granola for breakfast and to dinners that could be cooked at noon and eaten cold later on. We could rest during the heat of the day thereby, and walk in cooler evening hours before making camp. Lighter packs, less cooking, and longer hours sounded good to me. Already I could see the twenty-mile days.

We concluded Kyra's birthday party at McDonald's.

"I'll have one of everything," she said, still in an exuberant mood. I ordered somewhat less than that and carried the heaped tray to an outside table.

"We finished the Pedlar District," said Jerri. "I guess we should celebrate that, too."

"Definitely," I said. "You know, I've noticed that we walk

everything at about the same speed lately. We did the easy stuff in the Jefferson Forest at twelve miles a day, yet went through the Pedlar District at eleven and a half."

"Ah, the trip statistician," Jerri said in a patronizing tone.

"And Shenandoah's supposed to be *really* easy...."

"Don't get any big ideas."

"Where were we a month ago, Kyra?" I said, shifting to a game we sometimes played.

"Um ... Damascus?"

"Right. We'd just gotten there. How about two months ago, April 6?"

"... I can't remember."

"Brown Fork Gap," I read from the list I kept. "That's where we got rained out sleeping in the open. And three months ago?"

"Sixth grade."

"Sorry you didn't stay those two months of school?"

"Nope, I'll take the AT. Hey, look," she said suddenly, "it's Annie!" Short, pretty, with a red bandana tied around her close-cut brown hair, Annie walked toward us. We'd met her on the trail on our way into town.

"It must be party time," she said.

"Sure," said Jerri. "Join us."

Annie Halle had been with the New York Bunch, three men and two women hiking from Georgia to Maine. A broken foot sent one of the women home weeks before, and Annie had recently dropped behind to walk more slowly than the others.

"I've decided on a *purple* ten-speed," Kyra said.

"Considering how hard you'll have worked for it," Annie replied, "it ought to be *gold!*"

We bought and processed 170 miles worth of food during two days in town, enough to last to the next Waynesboro, just into Pennsylvania. Post Office connections had improved of late; we set supply drops for three intermediate points we could be sure of reaching during the week.

"We don't have enough crackers," I said as I packed boxes for mailing.

"I'll go to the store," Kyra said at once.

"Just for a change," Jerri said, "look for those little loaves of rye bread instead."

Kyra took off for the store. I had use for two loaves; she returned with six.

"I ask for bread; she brings me a bakery."

"But you gave me a ten," she said. "And you always buy *all* the store has of something you want!"

"No problem," I replied. "Hope everybody likes rye bread and peanut butter. Wow, and pumpernickel, too!"

Then we left town. We knew hitchhiking out would be pressing our luck. We weren't likely to catch someone going the exact zigzag route (stopping at the Post Office) who might deposit us precisely at the trail crossing on U.S. 250. Instead, we took a cab.

The trail now entered guidebook four. Elevation profiles on the backs of maps showed the ups and downs and the crossing didn't look bad at all. Perhaps Shenandoah would be easy like everyone had said. The walk began with eight miles of wonderfully graded trail through grassy fields and over open summits. We cruised into Jarmanns Gap, entrance to the park, still in early afternoon.

We tented at Sawmill Run Shelter a few miles farther on. It was Friday night in Shenandoah and the shelter was full. Through-hikers Mark Furman of New York and John Gantz of Florida tented nearby.

I woke toward midnight to the sounds of packs falling over. I reached for the flashlight, slipped out of my bag, and crawled to the front of the tent.

"What's wrong?" Jerri asked.

"Black bear," I replied. "It's fifteen feet away and into the packs."

"But the food is hung up."

"Uh-huh. It's checking the empty ones anyway."

I played light across the huge black face, the massive shoulders and back. It looked directly at me, then resumed pulling at something it had hooked with a claw on Kyra's pack.

"He sure is big," said Kyra, crawling forward so three of us bumped shoulders to look out.

"Especially from here looking up," I said.

We'd come prepared. When two bears tore up my pack in Yosemite, we'd scared them off by making noise, banging pots and pans and the like. Here we carried whistles. The bear looked our way again. Three flashlights shone in its eyes. Three whistles screamed in synchronous blasts. The bear looked on unmoved, then returned its attention to the pack.

Mark and John woke up. Shouting and shrill whistle blasts issued from three tents. The bear stood and stared, hardly taking notice.

"It didn't work, Dad," Kyra said. We yelled and blew whistles again. Nothing.

"I'm scared," she went on.

"It won't bother us," Jerri said. "But I'd sure like to get those packs."

Bored with us, the bear searched for better prospects. Mark and John had packed their food in a stuff sack and hung it from a cord stretched between two trees. Out of reach, they thought, but not quite — the bear found it easily by standing up.

It bit and clawed at the sack. The tightly packed cache bobbed away like a punching bag. The bear grabbed the sack and pulled. The nylon cord held. Holding the sack in both front paws, the bear sat down. Two three-inch trees bowed in to follow the descent. One snapped. Then the pickings were easy.

"Get out of here you hairy freeloader," yelled John.

Rrriiiip went the sack.

154

We'd all gotten out of tents by then and stood watching just beyond reach. The bear snuffled and stirred, spilling and biting into the sack's contents. No protest of ours seemed enough to make it go away.

I gathered the packs I'd left out and put them in the shelter. I returned to find the bear sniffing at the cord holding my pack in a tree. Bears would bite through sometimes, I'd heard, to bring packs crashing to earth. Or they'd climb the tree and break off the branch. It clawed and chewed, but lost interest. Back to the easy stuff.

"What do we do now?" asked John.

"We can walk to the road and hitch for more food," answered Mark.

"We only have three dollars. And our next supply is ninety miles north in Front Royal."

"You could buy a copy of *Stalking the Wild Asparagus*," I said.

"Our packs will be lighter without food," said John. "We can walk faster that way. Just think: thirty-mile days!"

"Right!" agreed Mark. "No more of the sub-ten variety."

Still the bear wouldn't go. Abandoning scattered food, it began doing tricks. It sat and looked at us for a while, leaning on front paws like a dog. Then it lifted a huge back leg and scratched behind its ear. Rolling on its back, it waved all four feet in the air. It paused after each routine and looked at us quizzically for reaction. We threw no offerings of appreciation. Our unwelcome guest finally got up and lumbered off, snapping twigs loudly as it went.

John reported that their food had been sampled but little was spoiled; they could go on without problem. He hung what remained in a much higher tree. We returned to our tents and slept — uneasily, and close, and with an ear tuned for noises in the night. I woke at once at three o'clock when the bear returned. I listened intently; it departed without incident.

I retrieved the packs at dawn and made breakfast and lunch outside the tent. We'd leave early on such a cool morning, so while Jerri and Kyra ate in the tent, I began to load packs. Then I noticed the bear had returned. It had its head poked into one end of John's tube tent just then; I hoped John wouldn't suddenly wake up. It wandered from there to the broken tree to sniff remains from the night before. Then it came to see me.

I was vulnerable. I hadn't a chance of packing things away in time.

"Jerri, the bear is back," I called toward the tent. "There's a lot of food loose out here." She joined me for the stand-off. We blew whistles and shouted. No effect. The bear advanced to within twenty feet. Kyra watched from inside the tent.

"Throw rocks," Jerri said. We reached trembling hands toward the ground. Twelve feet. Mark and John awoke at the ruckus and got out of their tents.

"Throw at the ground in front of it," she said. We threw. Rocks clattered off other rocks and bounced to hit the bear's front legs. We threw again. At ten feet away, the bear turned and fled.

We were ready to go in minutes. I held up packs for Jerri and Kyra to put on, then put on my own. Twenty feet up the trail Jerri stopped and turned.

"Welcome to Shenandoah, gang," she said.

_____

CHAPTER 14

Downwind, Boy; Downwind

The hiker can go without combing his hair or shaving and will be accepted as perfectly normal. He can get dirty and his friends will still speak to him jovially. His clothes may be in tatters, and people will think nothing of it. If there happens to be a little rock dust on his shirt or trousers, or if his clothes are a trifle torn, so much the better. Of such stuff are hiking heroes made. The hiker doesn't have to talk very much, say witty things, hold a glass in his hands, or laugh lightly at banalities. His is a world of opposites, and no one cares or worries about it.

- ANN AND MYRON SUTTON

SHENANDOAH PARK: two northbound lanes, slow traffic keep to the right. Blackrock Gap exit one mile. Emergency stopping only.

Or, if you prefer....

Shenandoah! Daughter of the stars. Elegant spring flora ... lush, rolling meadows ... glorious mountain panoramas.

Somewhere in between we looked for the reality of Shenandoah. We'd entered the popular area with a jumble of expectations — extravagant scenery, spectacular wildflowers, fast and easy walking, mobs of hikers, campers, and tourists. Almost none of it turned out to be true.

To begin with, the trail seemed more like a tunnel. It was wide and usually well-maintained, but solid ranks of trees with branches merging overhead formed walls and roof. Only on occasion did we find a window to the world outside. Distant views weren't required, but we expected the woodland path to offer more than the nearby highway, the Skyline Drive. Not so. Travelers in Shenandoah could see more from their cars.

Flowers? Mountain laurel were fragrant and beautiful at every turn, but azaleas had gone and rhododendrons were fading fast. The boot-top varieties Jerri preferred grew in abundance, however.

Easy trail? It was graded and not too steep, but still led uphill with casual disregard for plans reaching toward a quick seventeen-mile day. Ten miles that muggy June afternoon seemed like all we could do.

Crowds? We had the walk mostly to ourselves. In fact, so far in Boy Scout City, where predictions held we'd be overrun by urchin hordes in matching neckerchieves, we hadn't seen a one. Perhaps heavy traffic would come later.

We reached the side trail to Blackrock Gap Shelter in mid-afternoon. The day had been dreadfully hot and we agreed to retire early. We followed the path steeply down to the shelter and there found the reality of Shenandoah: two bank examiners and a through-hiker who hadn't had a bath in 350 miles.

The bank examiners were out for the weekend. They asked endless questions, viewed our answers skeptically, and ultimately held to the opinion they'd had to start with: no one in his right mind would hike two thousand miles. We busied ourselves outside and avoided them as much as possible.

Jerri called the other fellow Mr. Musty. He'd taken one bath so far, in Damascus, and there had given his clothes their only washing. He'd have a second bath in another hundred miles, he said, and perhaps would make it from Georgia to Maine on only three or four.

None of us were prom-night fresh after days of hiking in summer sun and we didn't expect others to be, either. But Mr. Musty carried the idea too far. A sickening smell drifted through the shelter every time he moved. There was no escape, save to sleep outside with the bears. And when he hung his food in that reeking shirt for the night, I was sure it would be compost by morning.

"What do we do if a bear comes?" asked one of the bank examiners as we settled into shelter bunks.

"Throw rocks," I advised. But with Mr. Musty around I didn't think we'd have to worry.

For breakfast he ate a can of sardines and a Three Musketeers bar. He dropped his trash into the fireplace, heaved on his bulging rucksack, and left before the rest of us had begun to pack. A hundred miles later in Harpers Ferry, West Virginia, he finally took the plunge for a second bath. The laundry eluded him, though, and his ghastly clothes remained unwashed all the way to Dalton, Massachusetts. Mr. Musty was more commonly remembered thereafter as Damascus-to-Dalton Bob.

We returned to the trail early next morning. Another clear day greeted us; cool morning air and crisp, sunlit colors made walking pleasant. The tunnel-like path broke open for mountain views on the rocky summit of Blackrock Mountain, then led down into trees again, crossing the Skyline Drive several times as it led back and forth over relatively easy terrain.

Eighty-two days ... we'd been walking the Appalachian Trail eighty-two days. Robert Manry, in a tiny boat named Tinkerbelle, sailed across the Atlantic in seventy-eight days. Columbus did it in seventy-one. We weren't even half-way.

Passing a litter barrel near the road, I stopped to dump our accumulated trash. Jerri and Kyra walked on and were out of sight around a bend by the time I hoisted on my pack to follow. The shoulder strap broke again. I installed the replacement I'd obtained, pitched the ripped one into the barrel, and went on my way in moments.

Interesting ... problems that brought alarm in early days of our walk no longer caused much concern.

I found Jerri identifying again. Some of her recent discoveries carried very strange names. Buttercups and columbines I'd heard of, and blossoming strawberries, blackberries, and blueberries. Even rosa multiflora and purple-flowering raspberry sounded fairly routine by now. But I wondered about vipers bugloss, whorled loosestrife, and showy skullcap. And fly poison and Indian cucumber root. Was she making these up to see if I was listening? I checked the book she carried; no, they were all in the index.

"Is it a problem if I don't remember all this?" I asked.

"You don't have to," Jerri said, "but the walk is more interesting if you know what you're looking at. If you'd both study the flower book a little you'd see."

"Thank you, Mother Tory Peterson," said Kyra.

Whatever the peculiarities of Jerri's underbrush tours, they were never so dull as the nature walk we passed through on Loft Mountain. Laid out for visitors to that popular camp area, signs pointed out the most ordinary trees and shrubs and advised gravely of local "phenomena."

We learned, for example, that we passed through a stand of non-native *shockus vulgaris* (common power poles). The Park Service hoped to replace the rapidly spreading species with one that grew only underground. Cute. We also found out that towhees said "drink your tea."

Now I got along fine with chickadees, jays, bobwhites, and whippoorwills whose calls were quite like their names. But I resented being told, for example, that ovenbirds called for "teacher, teacher, teacher," or that wrens from Carolina said "teakettle, teakettle." Robins might have cause to say "cheerily, cheerily," but why would a titmouse be looking for "peter, peter, peter"? I'd never even met a chestnut-sided warbler, much less one that would reply "please, please, please ta meetcha." And I was sure that no white-throated sparrow knew anyone named "PEAbody, PEAbody, PEAbody."

Learning a new useless rule of thumb was annoying. I never heard a towhee again; I could only hear "drink your tea."

We found the Boy Scouts at Pinefield Shelter. Tents dotted an open field as far as we could see and the noise of small boys continued without pause. They'd left the shelter empty though, so we moved in.

In the morning we were disturbed to note the entire group packed up and on the trail before we three veterans could make our "early start." We followed the milling throng and learned the secret: breakfast served from a truck a quarter-mile away. I looked for the scoutmaster to compliment him on that clever device. It got the boys up and moving early, left no food over-night to attract bears, and avoided breakfast campfires when everyone had been urged to conserve firewood. When our paths crossed, however, the conversation took a different turn.

"Any bears up your way?" the stocky scoutmaster asked.

"Not last night," I replied. "We had a skunk in the shelter for a while, but no bears."

"We must have kept them all away then," he said. "We had a big bonfire going all night and the kids kept a bear watch. They took turns staying up to feed the fire."

I reserved kind words for another occasion. I walked up the trail, picking my way through the mob, hoping soon to leave them far behind.

We reached U.S. Route 33 at Swift Run Gap early Monday afternoon. The southern third of Shenandoah Park ended there and beyond lay its more popular central section. While Jerri and Kyra waited, I thumbed a quick ride seven miles east to the town of Elkton to retrieve our supply box.

I found the Post Office easily and soon returned to the highway. A blinding sun blazed away and I could feel the burning heat of pavement through my Vibram soles. Looking up and down the roadway, I saw no cars. I walked a quarter-mile to the shoulder's only spot of shade, steadied my pack upright in front of me, and waited.

I wore a faded blue string shirt, ragged and wet with perspiration, and dusty boots, socks, and shorts. Sweat ran steadily down my face, dripped from my soaking headband, and left streaks on my arms and legs. My long, curly hair bunched in snarls in the humid heat. My shaggy beard bristled out of control. Getting a ride should be a cinch, I thought, standing in the high-speed zone. Sorry, I left my tie back at camp.

But they stopped. Two wildly gesturing plasterer-painter types in splattered white overalls and spotted bill caps stopped to offer a ride. I shoved aside ladders, crusty buckets and cans, and climbed over boxes and tools to a small space in the dusty-white back seat.

And they noticed right away. Even at sixty miles an hour with wind rushing in wide-open windows they noticed. Turning to offer a cold beer after a mile or so, the driver said:

"Fella, you need a bath."

Days continued to be hot. We sought to avoid the worst of it through afternoon rest periods, but heat came earlier and earlier till we thought the favored cool of morning would soon dissipate just before dawn. Evenings were cooler, though. Walking from five o'clock till dark helped restore the balance.

Scenery looked pleasant when we could see it through openings in the foliage or from atop rocky peaks. Tunnel walking brought new sights as well, reducing our focus to things we might have trampled on to see some far-off view.

Overgrown trail and nettles slowed us in several sections. Our token efforts to avoid becoming a smelly, musty trio were further complicated by itchy stings and bites. But we wouldn't wear long pants. Walking would be even hotter then. Jerri and Kyra even shed their shirts in favor of swimsuit tops. And every day we climbed mountain after mountain in the heat, verifying what hardly needed further proof: even in Shenandoah, uphill wasn't any fun.

An hour out of camp one morning we met three Boy Scouts heading south at a dead run.

"Anybody ahead of us?" one asked.

"Nope," I replied.

"Good," said another. "We want to find the shelter early before it fills up."

At eight in the morning? How crowded was it up ahead?

Another dozen hurried by shortly, and still later we found a group of fifteen sprawled over the trail in various stages of exhaustion. We talked with the scoutmaster.

"Doing the whole trail, eh?" he said wistfully. "I've often thought of that, just chucking it all and taking off." We'd heard such sentiments before.

"She's walked all that way, too?" he asked, referring to Kyra.

We told him yes and supplied the particulars. A mischievous smile lit his face and he turned to his recovering twelve- and thirteen-year-olds.

"All right, slowpokes," he said in a reproving tone, "look at how much this little *girl* is carrying — twenty pounds. That's more than any of you have and *she's* only eleven. And she's walked eight hundred miles from *Georgia* in eighty-four days. You guys better get with it!"

None of his winded charges appreciated these remarks. We set on our way as they groaned and struggled to their feet and soon I heard Kyra snickering.

"I think I ruined their day," said she.

"That's for sure," I replied.

"Pooped out after a mile or two and a *girl* zooms by. Ha!"

"I noticed one had a patch on his shirt. Something about '50 miles afoot-afloat.'"

"Whoo-pee."

"When you finish the AT you could get forty of them."

"Yeah," she said, "and make a whole shirt!"

Later, Kyra took off as though she'd fired auxiliary jets when a group of northbound boys tried to pass us. A shelter lay half a mile ahead and we'd planned to stop there for lunch. No boys were going to beat her there, it appeared.

She pulled out in front with a narrow lead. The boys passed Jerri and me in pursuit. The trail rounded a bend and Kyra sped from sight; the boys disappeared close behind. The gap had widened when we saw them again. We followed trail uphill, down, across a creek on a bridge of rocks. Still Kyra led. Boys had dispersed widely along the trail and many stragglers had lost interest. Only three had any chance of catching her.

The trail took a looping turn. One of the three sought to shortcut it and got tangled in the brush. Kyra left him behind. The shelter came into view. Kyra, lead widened to fifty yards, reached it easily and set her pack on the picnic table. We joined her there while the boys regrouped and went on.

The woods opened up in Shenandoah's central section as we crossed occasional fields of grass and ferns. The trail wound gently through the greenery, nicely blazed and manicured just like in all the pictures. I noticed things large and small, near and far, and stored each away for further thought. Yes, it was all very nice ... maybe that was enough.

Chipmunks chased each other through the grass or stopped to sit on rocks and watch us go by. Rabbits broke from cover to bound across or down the trail. One just sat and waited, deciding what to do, anxiety mounting as we approached. It sniffed the air, wiggled its ears, and breathed heavily as it looked up

164

and down the trail. Giving a tiny squeal, it finally hopped away. Another rabbit stopped to eat grass. It bit off a blade at the base, flipped its head so the grass stuck straight out of its mouth, and nibbled steadily until the morsel disappeared. Then it chose another blade.

We passed Big Meadows next morning, a popular tourist gathering point in Shenandoah's central section. The trail led widely around the area. As we crossed the far edge of the campground, people on morning walks stopped to chat. They asked questions we'd answered before, and listed the reasons they couldn't make such a trip — jobs, families, mortgages, and the like. One man, walking a small, yappy dog, said with a faraway look,

"Oh, it must be nice to have the time."

"Everyone has time for what he really wants to do," I replied.

At Skyland, another visitor spot, the trail led through the main grounds. We passed through later the same day, wondering if the gift shop sold candy bars. Tourists stood about, the fancy dress-up kind, and some seemed more than a little offended at our presence. One lady stared at us in near-shock, apparently unsure about whether to notify the police, the sanitation department, or the animal control shelter. We departed before she could decide; the gift shop didn't sell candy bars.

June 14: Jerri was dreaming. People were bringing her food — pies, cakes, and ice cream. She kept eating and they kept asking if she wanted more. She'd dreamed her way half through a piece of fried chicken when I nudged her awake.

"Breakfast," I said, handing her a cup of cold granola and powdered milk.

"Thanks a lot," she answered, rolling over to resume her dream.

Kyra expressed similar enthusiasm for her morning cereal. She opened one eye, wrinkled her nose, and with a sleepy "Yuck!" pulled her bag over her head. Cooperation was at its peak that morning. Everyone eventually got up but it took considerable persuasion.

We took it easy with only ten miles scheduled for the day. At a picture stop, with miles of scenic Shenandoah Valley as backdrop, Kyra posed planting her flag atop jagged rocks of The Pinnacle. At morning break we found a hand-worked stone water fountain labelled *Spring*. Later we turned to see rugged Stony Man Cliffs where we'd been the day before.

A side trip to Marys Rock led us off the trail and up a sharp ridge in mid-afternoon. Dramatic views suddenly opened all around us. I looked around with growing enthusiasm at mountains near in detail, far in shadowy haze, wondering if we should stay ... wait for sunset ... spend the night....

We stopped later for ice cream and to pose for tourists at breathtaking Panorama Coffee and Junk Shop at Thornton Gap ("You've walked *how* far?" ... "Oh, it must be nice...."), then continued our stroll. We crossed U.S. Route 211 to the northern third of the park where the tunnel resumed. Forest closed around us, guiding quietly, peacefully on another few miles.

"Would you still rather go to a warm motel?" Jerri asked Kyra as we sat at a rest stop.

"Not as much, I guess," she said.

"You're getting to like the woods?"

"Well, it is pretty, and quiet, and we've seen lots of nice things. Camping with other hikers at shelters is fun. It's sure different from what the tourists are doing."

"We're tourists. We're just walking instead of driving."

"I mean all those people we've been seeing at visitor centers," Kyra continued. "They spend their time in restaurants and stores and they buy all that junk and don't see anything."

"So?"

"It's so *different* from what we're doing. We're seeing neat things and they're not. We're living with what we can carry and they're buying junk. And they ask all those goofy questions."

"So what do you like to do in the woods now that you're not counting the miles to town?" Jerri asked.

"Have fun. You know — see things, make things, eat, crochet, whittle, play the recorder. Things that keep me interested and happy."

"How about walking?"

"That's okay, if it's not too steep and we don't go too far."

"Do you want to make it to Maine?" I asked.

"Yeah, I do."

"Not another one ..." Jerri said.

"I don't think about it much," Kyra hastened to explain, "but I guess I'd be upset if we didn't get to Katahdin. I've been writing all my friends about what we're doing. If we quit, I don't know what I'd tell them...."

We stopped for the night at Byrds Nest Four, the last of four stone shelters built as a gift from Senator Harry Byrd. Perched atop an open ridge, it offered distant valley views, five fireplaces and a picnic table in a grassy front yard, and an unforgiving concrete floor on which to spend the night. We shared the space with one other couple. Together we watched in fascination as deer ambled almost within reach to graze. Night brought a near-full moon to silhouette deer out front, and a raccoon that came to sit quietly on the picnic table and look around.

The skunk wasn't so polite. I was sleeping on my side and didn't know it was directly behind me sniffing at my ear. I rolled over — on top of it. I felt a momentary lump and heard my bedside canteen fall over as the skunk scurried away. Looking sleepily at moonlit white stripes, I prepared for doom.

"What's happening?" Jerri asked, waking at the commotion.

"Skunk. I rolled over on it. I'm waiting for a blast of Chanel No. 5."

"Hmmm," she said, looking over my shoulder, "more like Evening in Pearisburg, if you ask me."

The other couple didn't take it with such calm. Snacks they

kept handy for nighttime nibbling had attracted the visitor in the first place, but they didn't make the connection. They tried to shoo the skunk away as it rummaged through their gear. I thought they might take a hint when I hung our packs from the ceiling, but they didn't. The last I heard before dropping off to sleep was an anxious whisper, then another....

"Is it gone yet?"

"No, it's still here...."

The weather cooled for our last two days in Shenandoah and we covered the final twenty-five miles in routine fashion. We saw more deer, some grazing near the trail, others bounding across our path and into the woods, barely touching the ground. One stood near and still as we approached. As Jerri carefully prepared to take its picture, it carefully walked away.

Clouds finally opened for a full-fledged rain when we reached the park boundary the afternoon of June 16. We suited up for the first time in twenty days. Despite the dry spell, we'd found creeks and springs full and frequent throughout the park. The last piece of trail advice from Mr. Klutz thus proved to be as much baloney as the rest. Joseph's words on weather changes rang true again, however; full moon had come the night before.

Our nine-day walk through Shenandoah was pleasant in many ways, disappointing in others, but the most lasting impression came from the people. We'd met weekend and vacation hikers there, pickup-truck and motor-home campers. Walking to Maine was a foreign world to them. Most exchanges followed a predictable routine — How long will the hike take? How do you get food? How did Kyra get off school? Why did you come here all the way from Phoenix?

We'd answered those questions and more for nearly three months. By the end of Shenandoah, I was thoroughly tired of it. I wanted to get away, to leave the crowds and hike in more remote places. But summer had not even begun.

CHAPTER 15

_____

Visit to Headquarters

*The Appalachian Trail as originally conceived is
not merely a footpath* through *the wilderness but
a footpath* of *the wilderness.*

— BENTON MACKAYE

AT CLOSED, read the map; *use road.* I pondered what to do. Landowners in northern Virginia had "withdrawn permission" to use their land, and the trail and all its travelers had been booted out. Twenty-three miles of highway replaced what was once a wooded path, twenty-three miles of traffic, noise, and taunting *No Trespassing* signs. Whether vandalism or the general slobbishness so evident on easily reached sections of trail had been responsible, our information didn't say. The guidebook mentioned the closure only briefly, and held out hope for better news in the next edition.

Some hikers took an early running start where the pavement began and tried to walk the whole distance by nightfall. Footsore and weary, they'd drag to the end of the road at Snickers Gap, toss down a bedroll, and collapse for the night's rest they'd surely earned.

Others jumped the fence and followed the old trail, thumbing noses at signs and blackened-out blazes, hoping to find a safe place to camp before dark.

A few thumbed the cars and put the pavement behind more quickly. None of the options looked good to me.

We were camped at Mosby Shelter, three miles from the town of Linden where the road problem began. It would be hot along those twenty-three paved miles, and with no known place to camp or source of water, I knew we'd never be able to walk them. I kept such thoughts to myself. We'd spent the night with Charley; he had definite opinions on the subject.

Charley was Walking Every Inch of the Official Trail. He'd started in late April in Georgia, when we were already 250 miles along, and had caught up the day before in Chester Gap. According to Charley, only AT hikes that covered every inch of officially marked ground qualified as truly "end-to-end." There could be no shortcuts, no skipping ahead. He'd followed this rule since Georgia, he said, and even X'd spots where he left the trail for any reason so he could be sure to resume exactly there.

Charley demanded this authenticity not only of himself, it seemed, but of everyone. He spoke with contempt of "AT hitch-hikers" who thumbed rides around sections of trail, then bragged of it when they signed the next register miles ahead. Those who took occasional easier trails around peaks instead of over were cheating, too. Charley kept notes of such incidents, he told us, as did others. The information would find its way to headquarters.

Note-taker Charley made me uncomfortable. I hadn't asked his opinion; why did he think I cared? And why did he have to show up here? If we did skip the road ahead he would only catch up again. I wished he would pack his gear and his insinuations and leave. Damn! Now we were being watched!

Our morning walk to Linden went as slowly as ever. We plowed through jungle-like trail for two miles, battling branches and vines that blocked our way and tore at our packs and clothes. Turning at last onto Highway 638, Jerri showed no inclination to pick up the pace. It made me nervous. We had problems ahead. We had to get moving.

Then our speed diminished — the mulberries were ripe. Jerri and Kyra stopped at every bush, picking and eating without concern for the time. My patience wore thin. Why today? But I joined in; three could pick faster than two.

Jerri found a cherry tree next, with red, ripe cherries dangling just within reach. We picked a quart and tucked the container into the pack.

More mulberries. Already purple-faced and purple-fingered, we stopped again, and again. Would we ever get to town, or ever get anywhere today?

"Hiking schedules just fall apart during berry season," Jill Durrance said in one of the AT books I'd read. She'd sure had that right. We walked and stopped, walked and stopped, and finally reached Linden at noon.

It was Sunday and the store had just opened. I leaned packs against the building and Jerri dug out money to buy ingredients for cherry pie. I looked down the road leading out of town. No cars at all were driving north from Linden, Virginia.

"What do we do now?" I asked Jerri.

"We'll have to get a ride," she said. "There's no alternative."

"Right. Maybe I should call a cab."

She looked at me crossly and entered the store. Then I heard a voice just behind me.

"Hi," the young lady said. "Could you tell us something about the Appalachian Trail? You look like you've been hiking awhile."

Her name was Elaine. Elaine Wood, she said, with friend Nancy Barton. Nearby, they'd parked a Volkswagen bus.

They asked about food, trail markings, and shelters. I answered in polite detail. How long had we been walking, they wanted to know, and what was it like? I told some of what we'd seen in three months on foot — in the Stekoahs, the Smokies, the Pedlar District, in rain and snow and cold. We'd been forty-two days just in Virginia, I said, and likely wouldn't even see Mount Katahdin till October. Elaine and Nancy listened a bit wide-eyed. No problem answering *these* routine questions ... I moved on to a more urgent concern.

"Are you headed anywhere special today?" I asked.

"No, we're just driving around," said Elaine.

"I see. Well, we have this problem...."

They studied a road map as I described the trail just ahead. Twenty or thirty miles wouldn't be out of their way, they allowed, so sure, we could get a ride.

Jerri came out of the store as I loaded the packs aboard.

"Hop in," I said. "We're going to Snickers Gap."

"That was fast."

Right.

Our hosts took the nearest main roads and dropped us in Snickers Gap. Then they drove off, waving and smiling as though *they* were having the adventure. We were back on foot an hour after walking into Linden, two days forward in time. We had an easy walk to water, shelter, and perhaps beyond.

Had we reached town any earlier, of course, we might not have been so lucky. We might still have been wondering how to travel those twenty-three miles. I shrugged such thoughts off, wondering instead what Charley was going to say.

The trail followed the Virginia-West Virginia border from there, flopping back and forth between states on its final nineteen miles to the Potomac River. We climbed along Devils Racecourse, a long, stony streambed, then worked our way through stretches of loose and jumbled rock. Gathering clouds briefly brought rain. The afternoon cooled, rain and rocks ended, and the path became a grassy forest road. Smooth, wide, and easy: we picked up speed.

A summer tanager danced ahead, pale red among the green, shaking each branch it lit upon as it flew from tree to tree. We stepped over Indian pipes, tiny, ghostly white, growing in patches of decaying leaves. Views and picture stops slowed us at times, yet we walked at top speed. A quiet sense of well-being seemed to overcome us all. We'd gone beyond the day's problems, set a new goal, and suddenly felt all in tune. Walking in silence, watching scenes appear and drop behind, I sensed a certain harmony for almost the first time — among ourselves, and with the world we passed. Fourteen miles flashed by and we barely touched the ground.

We camped at a shelter in Keys Gap. Our long-gone-ahead friend Annie Halle appeared at dark, returning from dinner in a nearby town in time to join us for stove-top cherry pie.

The night cooled to almost cold as we retired to the shelter. Hard-lashing rain swept the camp and we snuggled close to keep out the chill. We slept in summer bags, two duck-down rectangles zipped together to make a warm, roomy envelope for three. I'd strapped them directly onto the packs from the carton received in Chester Gap. I hadn't measured, inspected, or even unrolled them. I'd simply mailed winter bags away.

We left the trail next morning to follow a two-mile path downhill to Harpers Ferry, West Virginia. The town occupied a point of land where the Shenandoah and Potomac rivers rushed together, and where the view from surrounding hills showed one of the more pleasing scenes on or near the Appalachian Trail.

The view from city streets was of museums and old buildings, graveyards and ancient oaks, and points of interest reflecting the town's catalytic role in the War Between the States. Harpers Ferry: a National Historical Park — a place of rebuilding, remembering, preserving.

It was also home to the Appalachian Trail Conference, the folks in charge of our two thousand miles of ups and downs. We'd come to pay a visit, but couldn't find them.

Guidebook directions ended at the edge of town, leaving us without trail, blazes, or any idea of where we were. We wandered city streets for half an hour, still wearing rain gear from a morning cloudburst, but found no evidence that the ATC was really there. I finally asked directions. We were at the wrong end of town.

"We can't go looking like this," Jerri said.

True, soggy string shirts and dripping rain gear would not make us welcome guests. We washed up in a public restroom and changed to clean, matching red shirts and zip-off shorts (the legs zipped off our jeans, converting them to shorts). Then we walked side-by-side down the sidewalks of Harpers Ferry to find the ATC.

The Appalachian Trail Conference was an organization of groups and individuals who supported and maintained the Appalachian Trail. It worked with government agencies and member hiking clubs from Georgia to Maine, establishing a protected route for the trail, determining proper limits of its use, and organizing maintenance of the footway itself. The ATC published guidebooks, maps, newsletters, and other trail-related information. It also promoted the Appalachian Trail idea: that of a pathway to wilderness adventure right here at home. More than half the country's population lived within a day's drive of the Appalachian Trail.

When we entered the spacious, many-roomed house that served as ATC headquarters, we heard typewriters clicking in an office at the end of the hall. Three women were at work there, answering requests for information that made a sizable heap on each desk. They knew we were coming. Typewriters stopped and eyes brightened with recognition as we walked in.

"I guess I don't have to tell you who we are," I said.

"Good heavens, no," said Jean Cashin, coming out from behind her desk. "And let's see those fancy zip-off pants. I've been hearing about them for weeks!"

174

Judy Van Gilder and Wendy Willcott added their greetings and work ceased for half an hour while we traded questions, stories, and trail news. Passing hikers kept them informed of our progress, they said, or perhaps our lack of it. Just an hour before, Annie had told them:

"Oh, they'll be here today. Just give them time."

The ATC welcome was so cordial and friendly that the list of guidebook errors and other complaints I'd collected, and often fumed about, paled to insignificance. They knew about the errors, Jean said. Corrections were already planned. She called to arrange bunk space for us at the youth hostel across the river and gave directions to the Post Office and grocery store.

We met Peter Dunning, editor of the monthly *Appalachian Trailway News*, when we returned from errands an hour later. He was a tall, slender man, younger than myself, who had walked the AT end-to-end two years before. He asked questions as we sat in his upstairs office. He was interested in how a hiking family was approaching problems of such a trip. We explained some of our techniques and recounted an experience or two. He chuckled and nodded approvingly, yet seemed to have something more on his mind.

"We sure had trouble finding this place," I said at one point. "A sign or a note in the guide would have helped."

"We do that on purpose," Peter replied. "By the time a hiker has walked this far he should be able to find us on his own."

"Maybe so," I answered, "but it took a lot of time."

He paused a moment, then turned to another subject.

"Considering that you're walking just ten miles a day," he said, "you folks are doing pretty well. You've probably seen more of what there is to see than anyone we've talked to lately."

"That's what we came to do," Jerri said. "Even ten miles is too fast sometimes."

"You're hoping to finish on Katahdin, I'm sure," he went on.

"But even if you keep on as you have been, I think you may have some trouble."

"Why is that?" I asked. "We've survived problems we had at first and are even with our plan — we've done nearly 900 miles in 90 days. At that pace, we'll be there in early October."

"Could be, but the trail up north is more difficult than you think. Parts of New Hampshire and Maine could slow you down and add many days. Winter comes early there. Some of the trail could be impassable by the time you arrive."

We'd read about Elmer Onstott, of course, who had walked all the way to Katahdin in 1968, only to be forced back, in October, by an early winter storm. He'd had to return the next year to finish.

"What do you suggest?" Jerri asked.

"I hiked the trail from the ends to the middle," Peter answered. "I walked from Springer Mountain to the halfway point, then from Katahdin south to the middle again."

"I've been thinking about something like that," said Jerri, suddenly interested.

I was thinking we didn't need this free advice.

But Jerri was off, and I didn't like the sound of it at all. I looked at Kyra, hoping to see some reaction. She slouched in her chair looking thoroughly bored.

"It worked out well," Peter was saying. "I avoided cold weather up north and also summer water shortages in Pennsylvania, New York, and New Jersey."

"We want to see fall in New England," I said, seeking to bury the idea. "That's one of the reasons we're walking north."

"I can understand that," he replied. "You don't have to turn around at halfway. Time it as you see fit."

"It would be a good compromise," Jerri said, running with the ball. "We could finish the trail as Mic wants to do, but without any pressure. We could see everything we wanted to see, and take almost as long as we liked."

"That's right," he assured her. "Give it some thought as you're walking along."

Kyra fidgeted in her chair. I leaned over to her.

"Let's go," she whispered.

"Wonderful idea," I told her quietly. I gathered my gear, noting aloud that it was seven o'clock.

Peter drove us back to the trail. It followed U.S. 340 at that point, leading back into Virginia and across the Potomac River into Maryland. After spending nearly a month and a half in Virginia, there we touched three states in less than an hour. We found the youth hostel, lights on and occupied, a quarter-mile past the bridge.

"Hi," said Annie, "you're running late, as usual, I see."

We'd expected to find Annie there; she'd also spent the day in Harpers Ferry. We didn't expect the other occupant: Charley. He'd caught up again with back-to-back twenty-plus-mile days.

"Picking up speed, I see," he said in a mildly accusing tone. "Hitchhike a bit of road, perhaps?" His manner implied an explanation was due.

"We couldn't do that stretch with no place to camp," I said, "so we skipped it."

"That leaves a break in your hike."

"So it does," I said, "but from what I've heard, I don't think we missed very much."

Annie and Kyra started chatting then, turning the conversation to more pleasant subjects. I updated my log by electric light for a change, then spread out the big double bag to retire. I lay in darkness, waiting for sleep, considering the turn of events....

Ends to the middle ... what a dumb idea. It's Georgia to Maine, remember? Springer to Katahdin. No variations on the theme, please. Turn around? Walk south? No, we wouldn't do that.

CHAPTER 16

Halfway

"Will you walk a little faster?"
said a whiting to a snail,
"There's a porpoise close behind us,
and he's treading on my tail."
          - LEWIS CARROLL

"Mom, what's a toepath?"

"It's the walkway mules once used to pull barges through the canal."

"But we've been on a *foot*path all along, now it's a *toe*path. I don't get it."

"This is a t-o-w-path, like in tow truck."

"Oh! (giggle) I see!"

We were walking beside the abandoned Chesapeake and Ohio Canal. A busy shipping lane in the 1860s, the waterway had been put out of business by railroads and floods and now looked like an Everglades swamp. Branches, logs, and summer growth clogged the channel. Patches of duckweed splotched the water's surface. Frogs and insects left widening ripples as they came and went.

The towpath was wonderfully flat. It led between files of picturesque trees grown up along the canal and offered hikers and cyclists a pleasing 184 miles. To our regret, the AT followed it for only two. About a hundred would have been more like it.

Weaverton Cliffs took over from there. The rocky, half-mile ascent was strenuous, said the guide, and from below it surely looked the part. We found it little trouble. We climbed at a leisurely pace, often checking behind for openings to expanding views. On top, I stood at cliff's edge to look over the Potomac River Valley. River and highway flowed across the land, flanked by trees and mountains at first green, then softening to hazy blue. I made out houses and meadows in the forested valley, linked by braided roads, looking dewy and damp under a Tuesday morning overcast sky.

From there the walk was easy. We followed simple ups and downs along the crest of South Mountain for six miles and reached Gathland State Park in early afternoon. We lunched at the pop machine.

Some later we passed a side trail where blue blazes led off through the trees.

"What's out there?" Kyra asked.

"Our Junior Woodchuck's Guide here says ..." I paused to consult the guidebook, "'... trail leads 300 ft. to a viewpoint on cliffs which should not be overlooked.'"

"Why not? Is it dangerous?"

"Doesn't say. Maybe it's not worth the trouble."

"Why would they blaze a trail if we shouldn't go see it?"

"Beats me. Maybe they had extra blue paint."

"Gee, first they send us on a *toe*path, now they say not to go see the view. This is dumb!" She looked at me slyly and snickered. Laughing in return, I gave her a shove and we went on our way.

So went day one of our three-day crossing of Maryland.

On day two, we visited the Washington Monument, a thirty-foot stone tower built in 1927 in a state park of the same name. An odd structure, it looked more like a large stone cream bottle with a door. We followed steps winding round inside to the top, glanced at the valley below, then wound back down to the trail.

Three miles later, we crossed Interstate 70 on an impressive concrete-and-steel footbridge built especially for the Appalachian Trail. I'd found a picture of the bridge in my reading, showing hikers crossing and waving to six lanes of Maryland motorists below. I'd wondered then if we had any chance of getting that far, any hope of reaching the bridge that took the AT in a great leap across the road. When we crossed, we waved to motorists, too.

Then things turned dull. That meant we could go faster, logic told me, faster and farther with fewer occasions to stop. And so, not stopping as often in the nondescript surroundings, we walked faster and farther. Level crest soon gave way to a series of mountains to climb and we grew tired. No matter; we were chalking up miles.

Jerri wanted to rest, so we rested. Often. Ten-minute breaks stretched to half an hour and we logged fewer miles. I grew anxious, wanting to move on.

"Time to get going," I said, as we sat in shade near the trail.

"Not yet," Jerri said. "We just got here."

"It's been twenty minutes."

"Who cares? What's the rush anyway?"

"I'd like to camp at Hemlock Hill tonight."

"How far is that?"

"Six miles."

"It's three o'clock," she protested, "and hot, and I'm tired."

"The trail description doesn't look bad," I said encouragingly. "We can make it."

"Why didn't we stop at the shelter two miles back?" Her tone said she wasn't pleased.

"Too early."

"Is there any place closer?"

"There's no water till Hemlock Hill."

"You didn't tell me that or I would have stopped at the shelter for the night!"

Which was, of course, why I hadn't mentioned it.

"If we do more today we can take it easy tomorrow," I explained, "and we'll be in position for Waynesboro on Friday."

"And if we don't?"

"We'll get to town on Saturday and lose another day to Post Office hours."

"I suppose," Jerri said angrily, "but I wish you'd tell me what's going on. You and your Gotta-Get-to-Maine. I thought you were getting over that. What good is getting there if you don't see anything on the way?"

"There's nothing to look at right now anyway. We may as well walk."

"There are things to see *everywhere*. Just look!"

We walked to Hemlock Hill. Jerri saw roses, honeysuckle, purple-flowering raspberry, and a thistle blooming in a burst of purple and green.

I saw miles: fifteen and a half that day, thirteen the day before. Winter up north could be avoided by stepping on the gas farther south.

We slept in the open, not bothering with the tent. It didn't rain. It was just as well.

Maryland gave us a parting gift next day of pleasant trail and long, hazy views. The scene up close continued to be more interesting to Jerri, however. She lay flat on the ground several times photographing mushrooms — one with an orange ruffled hat, one beaded and jeweled with moisture, another with a cap of red velvet. We crossed into Pennsylvania at the village of Pen Mar. Six states had dropped behind.

The state boundary was also the Mason-Dixon Line, surveyed and marked at that point, Milestone 91, in 1767 by a couple of so-named Englishmen. There we traded "down South" for "up North." Toast country. Summer began; it was June 21.

We camped just out of Waynesboro, Pennsylvania, at Mackie Run Shelter. The stream ran brown there, with bubbly suds, so we hauled water from farther back along the trail.

"Do you purify your water?" asked Steve of Steve and Jerry who were camping with us.

"Not usually," Jerri said. "But it looks like we might have to start."

"What do you use?"

"Something that's sort of like Clorox," I said. "It doesn't leave much taste."

"A friend of ours uses iodine," Jerri added. "She says it makes the water taste like Scotch. I tried it and realized why I never liked Scotch — tastes like iodine."

Jerry reached to dump spaghetti into a kettle of boiling water. He missed. The package slipped from his hand and heaped its contents on the ground.

"Pick-up sticks!" said Steve. "C'mon, Kyra."

The three squatted round the pile as the pot bubbled on.

"One for Kyra," Jerry said, as Kyra successfully extracted one stick. "Two ... three ... four! Okay, my turn."

Jerry picked two and dumped them into the pot, then Steve studied the tangled pile. Neither hurried. Steve got three, then Kyra followed with six.

"Wow, steady hands," Jerry said.

They continued turn by turn. Kyra deftly outpicked them each time as they cheered her on. Someone occasionally stirred the pot.

"Only a few to go," Kyra said, as Jerry completed a turn.

"I'll get those," said Steve. He bumped the pile and got none. Kyra handily cleaned up and dropped the last piece into the pot.

"The winnah!" Jerry yelled.

"Okaaaaaay," added Steve, and Kyra beamed.

182

The group of boys camped nearby wasn't having so much fun. They milled about with no apparent agenda until dark, then got caught with their tents down in a pounding rain. Soon they all huddled soaking wet under shelter eaves. We shifted aside to let a few in, but otherwise had little sympathy for the unprepared. We left them to shiver and watch the rain, and went to sleep.

We escaped Waynesboro in one day. We hitchhiked in in early morning, shopped and ran errands during the day, and packed food boxes in a motel room all evening. By check-out time we had enough food for 221 miles of Pennsylvania, in our packs and in the mail, and were ready to hit the trail.

We found a bakery as we left, the first we'd seen on the whole live-long trail. The very smell two steps inside its front door transported us into ecstasy. The taste of cream-filled, frosted doughnuts was something divine. We finished a whole sackful on the doorstep and went back for more.

A gas station attendant gave me an old automobile tire to fix our walking sticks which were slowly wearing away. I cut three rectangular strips from the tire's main tread, bent one across the bottom of each stick, and taped them firmly in place. Retreads: good for four months or a thousand miles, whichever came first.

And the cab driver who delivered us to where we'd left the trail said we were mighty lucky. The cab company picnic was in progress and he was the only driver on duty. We paid and thanked him for the ride and walked into state number seven.

Few people said anything good about the trail in Pennsylvania. Rocks from border to border was the word, with mosquitoes, dense jungles, sun-baked roads, and scenery of no redeeming value. We expected the worst, but the trail the next four days never approached the torture advertised.

Some parts were dull, of course, and others went uphill. We walked exposed roads in the heat at times and overgrown laurel and rhododendron thickets occasionally obscured the path. When wet with rain, they gave us goose bumps and shivers.

More often, though, it was easy. We walked frequent wood-land roads and followed well-maintained footway across low-lying mountain crests. Jerri added touch-me-nots, white penstemons, and moth mullein to her observations, and we passed through a half-mile forest of pines, walking needle-cushioned path. Some sights thought "magnificent" in the guidebook came closer to "well, not bad," but others were fine indeed.

We whiled away a whole steaming afternoon at Caledonia State Park, watching softball games and swimmers in the pool, moving only for raids on the refreshment stand. We loaded up on treats at an old general store at Pine Grove Furnace State Park, and watched swimmers in the lake. Berry stops came often. Summer had surely arrived.

People continued to offer variety. We met librarians — two women on their annual six-day outing. They were equipped to handle six days or six months, it appeared, yet they had a problem.

"We brought freeze-dried four-man meals," said one. "They're good, but they always make more than we can eat."

"I believe we can be of assistance," I said. Their leftovers that night were stirred into whatever we were having.

"You can have this, too," the other lady offered, "if you can think of anything to do with it."

Instant grape jam. Adding water per directions produced a gooey mass that looked and tasted like thick grape Kool-Aid. Its uses seemed limited.

"Put it in pudding," suggested Jerri.

The dishes of beautifully lavender dessert I produced failed to impress the librarians.

"I hope you like it," one said politely. We ate it for lunch that day. I wondered where I could get some more.

The people we didn't meet left notes. Annie had sprinted ahead once more but left us a message at Birch Run Shelter:

> To The Family:
> You went to Waynesboro on a good day. I got caught
> in the rain. I'm planning a 1,000-mile steak party
> soon. Hurry up and celebrate! Now I'm off to the
> firetower for a panoramic lunch.   - love, Annie

We'd come up in the world. To "The Family," from mere "parents of the ten-year-old."

Hikers often left notes in trail registers. We hardly passed a shelter without looking for the tablet, spiral notebook, or tin can full of loose pages in which hikers recorded dates of passage and comments, as well as occasional stories, poems, and messages to the world.

"Frodo lives!" asserted one.

"Fifth day of rain — why am I doing this?" wondered another.

We signed in, too, always with an accompanying GA →ME. Hikers behind easily identified us when they caught up.

We found a wealth of information at Birch Run Shelter besides Annie's note. Bill Rombin was only four days ahead; he'd probably taken a week or two off. Ned Barr had rested there three days recovering from a summer cold. Charley, thought to be light years ahead by then, only led us by a day. His pack had fallen apart, we learned, and he'd left the trail to buy a new one.

And someone had written: "How come we're only two days behind John Laming? Did he hitchhike backwards by mistake?"

Another note we found much later took the summer's prize. It told again of Annie, who hiked at times wearing only a fishnet shirt with no bra. Doug Wilson, a minister, he'd told us when we'd met in North Carolina, noted his reaction: "Met Annie today. She wore a string shirt with nothing underneath. My eyes misbehaved."

We hit the rocks our fifth Pennsylvania day. Beginning with a maze of random boulders on Rocky Ridge, we picked our way through crevice and crack, up chimney and ledge, and thought it all rather fun. Later on we thought it not so fun. A ridge heaped with jagged, odd-sized chunks led on more than a mile. Stepping stones thought to be solid would suddenly tip or roll; only quick use of walking sticks prevented many falls. Deciding where to take the next step became a full-time job.

Vibram boot soles softened sharp edges for our feet, but constant jamming in odd positions brought tension and twisting to ankles much happier with long, even strides. We moved along slowly, flailing for balance, watching for snakes, questioning motives of those who'd routed such a section of trail. Such a mere hint of what was to come. We felt relief when again on solid ground, not knowing that a mile of rocks would come to seem like nothing.

Gravel roads took over from there, leading out of the mountains and into Cumberland Valley farmland. Pavement began at an intersection under a huge sycamore tree. We walked toward the village of Churchtown, Pennsylvania, in hot, heavy air left humid by rain hours before. Mosquitoes carried off our lifeblood by the pint.

The good news said we'd done our ten miles. The bad: there were thirteen more to go. Water and shelter for hikers lay beyond the road through the populous Cumberland Valley, and a few miles up Blue Mountain. It was 4 PM.

No handy VW bus stood by to save us from our plight. The meager traffic didn't even look thumbable and the chances of getting past the pavement by nightfall seemed depressingly remote. We sat on the steps of the Churchtown Market to think it over. I finally went inside and bought a half-gallon of ice cream to assist our deliberations.

"Do you know of anyone heading across the valley soon?" I asked the woman behind the counter. "Thirteen miles is more than we can do yet today, unless we walk till midnight."

She rang up the ice cream.

"I get off at five and live out that way," she said. "If you want to wait, I'll drive you as far as I'm going."

We waited, and rode with Darla Harlacher as eight miles quickly dropped behind. We had time to finish the final five.

We reached Darlington Shelter at dusk. The dilapidated stone structure looked dreary and uninviting set off in a tangle of bushes, but we had little cause to be choosy. We were glad to be there at all. Through-hikers Jim Mendes and Alan "Two-Stick-Man" Sneeringer (who hiked with a walking stick in each hand as if skiing the trail) had already set up camp. We'd met them the night before and our arrival at Darlington left them a trifle surprised.

"We certainly didn't expect to see *you* here tonight," said Jim, sounding somewhat suspicious. "That was twenty-three miles."

"Yup," I replied, choosing not to elaborate. "Sure was a long day."

We saw the river the next afternoon. I'd imagined the view for days and mental pictures finally merged with the real thing. Blue-gray clouds became land on a faint horizon, gathered to darkening shapes on approach, turned detailed green nearby. A broad, sky-colored river flowed into the scene and out again along a grand curve. A town clustered at water's edge, its streets and rows of buildings bending to match the river's arc.

Here was a view I could appreciate. Here was a sight with meaning. The Susquehanna. Duncannon, Pennsylvania. Halfway.

We'd crossed Center Point Knob the day before. A plaque once marked its summit as midpoint of the Appalachian Trail. Vandals had taken that, so we'd found only a squared-off, milestonish boulder with four bolt holes. Routing changes had moved the trail's true center elsewhere anyway. Where, no one knew. No one cared. The center was at the river, where one left the land for half a mile and walked the bridge across the wide, dividing, Susquehanna. We had three miles to go.

Part way down the mountain, Jerri stopped with a sudden "Shhhh...." A copperhead lay in the trail, head arched high, tongue flicking the air. We watched without moving. We'd heard standard warnings and stories, tales of moccasins, copperheads, rattlesnakes, but having seen so few we'd paid scant heed. The snake just ahead commanded full attention.

It held almost perfectly still. Its rust-banded body described a graceful, wavy line on rocky ground and its tongue darted continually to sample the air. We stared, then Jerri moved to ready her camera. The snake dropped its head and slid into the brush, coiling and nearly vanishing among grass and dead leaves. We gave it wide berth as we passed.

"I've never seen one before," Jerri said, her eyes alight.

"Me, either," I said.

Kyra wasn't so charmed. Finding a copperhead where she was about to step shook her. She seldom looked at the trail as she walked, she said. Often her thoughts would drift till she barely noticed where she was. Realizing she could step on a poisonous snake before she saw it came as no comfort.

"I didn't see a thing for the next three days," she told me later. "I just watched the trail."

Walking down High Street in Duncannon that afternoon, we heard a shout.

"Hello, you must be The Family."

I looked around, saw no one we knew, no one who might have called.

"Hi, I'm up here," came the voice again. A lady waved from an upstairs window in a building across the street. We returned her wave and she leaned out between flapping curtains over two lanes of traffic to ask us about our trip. The conversation lasted nearly five minutes, shouted across the street as cars and pedestrians passed. Some stopped to listen. Like others, the lady upstairs had heard we were coming. Everyone else now knew it, too.

A routine supply stop readied our packs for the next fifty miles, but the search for a thousand-mile steak dinner proved to be another story. We'd hoped for a chance to clean up and find a restaurant for a fitting celebration. Our choices narrowed to a diner, a truck stop, and a dusty hotel coffee shop that looked dark and closed. Thoughts of wine and rare steak faded. We shrugged, and trod a reluctant path to the grocery store.

We considered the selection with dwindling enthusiasm. Weighing in a forecast of rain and the distance to camp across the river, we resigned ourselves to the inevitable — hot dogs. Jerri tossed in a cherry pie.

Then we crossed the Susquehanna, walking the symbolic half-mile on the Clarks Ferry Bridge. Noise and fumes from a steady flow of traffic accompanied my scattered thoughts.

Sir Vivian Fuchs had crossed Antarctica in ninety-nine days. Thor Heyerdahl sailed Kon-Tiki over the Pacific in a hundred and one. We'd walked a hundred days from Springer Mountain and finished half our two thousand miles.

Was that significant?

To us, perhaps; another thousand miles of adventures would begin next day. Had we seen and learned of the woods? Yes, we walked with confidence now. And we'd surely reached a new definition of what lay "within walking distance."

What else?

We'd stuck together those hundred days. We were still going forward. Some days we walked fast, some days slow. Some days it mattered, some it didn't. We only disagreed, at times, about which was which.

I looked over the bridge railing at water moving lazily below.

Maine ... halfway there. We'd do the other half now for sure. Yes, Katahdin Fever still burned ... quietly perhaps, but ready to erupt whenever forward progress was threatened. Something else was burning, too. I felt it on those mountaintops, and other times, too. Some feeling of peace, contentment ... something just out of reach. Where did that fit? Perhaps I'd learn more in the days ahead....

We didn't have to wait for adventures to begin. The trail crossed a highway at the end of the bridge, then railroad tracks, and a freight train stood directly in our path. I didn't want to be climbing through if it started to move, so took the long hike down to the engine to see if anyone was inside.

"Hello," I shouted at the open window. No response.

"Anybody there?" I shouted again, banging my fist on the side of the giant locomotive. Nothing.

"Hello, hello." BANG BANG BANG! The vibrating sheet metal stilled and a sleepy face appeared at the small opening.

"Will you be here long?" I asked.

"Don't know," the man replied. "Might be hours."

"I need to get across back there."

"Just walk around. We're waiting for another train so you'll be okay."

"The bank is too close on the other side. Can I climb through?"

"Sure, sure, whatever you want to do."

We found an empty auto transport car near the trail crossing. I boosted Kyra up, handed her the packs, then climbed into the frame of open steel girders myself.

"When does this rig get to Katahdin?" Jerri asked as I pulled her aboard.

"Don't know," I said. "Might be hours."

We buckled on our packs once down the other side and came face to face with the first of our next thousand miles — it was straight up.

"Already?" Kyra complained. Rain clouds assembled for the predicted storm as we began the climb. No one spoke of skipping ahead, turning around, walking south. No one mentioned beating winter up north by going there now, or the significance of splitting the hike in the middle. I climbed steadily northward, offering no reminders.

Susquehanna Shelter was built of logs and had a dug-out dirt floor. It looked as primitive as any shelter we'd seen. A stiff wind might topple it, and the roof seemed too flimsy to guard against rain. But we had it to ourselves.

We roasted hot dogs on sticks to the soft light of campfire coals. We heard wind in trees and nightsong of tiny creatures. Atmosphere. A candlelight dinner in town would have been no improvement. Then rain began. Thunder crashed, lightning danced in darkened sky, and rain fell as from buckets.

"So goes the simple life," I noted in the log.

I slept, and dreamed....

Rain flooded the shelter and we shivered in inches of water, our bags and clothes sopping wet. I rolled over in a vividly pictured splash ... and woke up. Rain still beat the shelter roof, but it had held. We were warm and dry. I went back to sleep, to dream again....

We were in Phoenix, just leaving for a wonderful summer's walk of the Appalachian Trail. The preparation was over and the exciting moment had finally arrived. We drove to Amicalola Lake, put on our packs, and walked up the trail with bounce in our feet and joy in our hearts.

After a short time, an hour, or maybe a day, Jerri stopped.

"This is just too hard," she said. "It's no fun at all. I'm going home!" And so we went home, and our adventure ended....

Then I woke up. Across the Susquehanna. Halfway along the Appalachian Trail.

CHAPTER 17

The Moth That Ate Pennsylvania

The rocks have a history; gray and weatherworn,
they are veterans of many battles; they have
most of them marched in the ranks of vast stone
brigades during the ice age; they have been torn
from the hills, recruited from the mountaintops,
and marshaled on the plains and in the valleys;
and now the elemental war is over, there they lie
waging a gentle but incessant warfare with time
and slowly, oh, so slowly, yielding to its attacks!
- JOHN BURROUGHS

"TO LEFT 300 YDS. IS FINE VIEW."

Three hundred yards, a third of a mile round-trip, wasn't much to invest in scenery, so we turned left. What Jerri expected to see on a foggy morning, she didn't say.

We saw fog: soft, swirling, out-of-focus fog. We'd climbed dead uphill an hour to get above it. Looking back on it, everything blurred and disappeared. Without fog we'd have seen down the leafy mountainside to where it flattened in a valley of jigsaw fields fitted together in shades of green and brown.

Commonplace, really. We'd seen it a hundred times. But "To left 300 yds. is *ordinary* view" would draw few hikers, so the guidebook rated it "fine."

Regardless of the quality of things to be seen, Appalachian Trail guidebook authors could be counted on to describe them with enthusiasm. Their directions led us to near views, far views, and wide views on the lower end of the scale, and to views forward and backward. Some views they classed good, fair, or fine. A few, unusually fine.

Difficult views were those harder to reach; those with narrow perspectives were called limited or restricted. Views seen clearly, however, ranged from occasional and unobstructed, to frequent, continuous, or continuing. Especially lofty points were rated panoramic, all-inclusive, or wide-sweeping, and even 360-degree.

We'd looked upon sights scenic and picturesque, and some graded impressive, expansive, or extensive. A few were deemed noteworthy, pleasing, or beautiful. Others were worthwhile or rewarding. One, the author told us, was particularly rewarding.

At times we'd followed trails to grandstand or commanding views; at other special times we'd seen things striking, imposing, or superb. Some scenes were ranked wonderful, remarkable, or splendid. One spot, however, overgrown in recent years, had been demoted to formerly splendid.

We'd ascended to extraordinary and exceptional views, while other climbs took us to scenes tremendous, excellent, and outstanding. We'd seen marvels inspiring, spectacular, and astonishing, and on certain rare pinnacles had viewed wonders magnificent, unequaled, and unsurpassed.

Descending into lower elevations, into regions of more farms and less wilderness, I'd expected the eloquence to diminish with the grandeur of scenes described. Valley views seen again and again ceased to be moving, after all. If anything, the authors had redoubled their efforts. "Magnificent panoramic views" thus looked remarkably *deja vu,* and "impressive, if not inspiring views" of a railroad yard and industrial site seemed overbilled.

A touch of realism seemed in order. An economy of adjectives so we wouldn't reach Maine so jaded we hardly bothered to look. I didn't expect it. The model of restraint appeared in the Virginia directions — "... short side trail to left leads to rocks which provide modest view" — but I didn't think the idea would catch on.

We walked a dozen miles of gravel road that day, June 29, following an arrow-straight forest cut atop Peters Mountain. Dissipating fog revealed scenes in the valley to our left, and to the right we glimpsed mountains in long rows, Third Mountain, Second Mountain, Blue Mountain, all level-crested and side by side like the giant caterpillars of Virginia. Jerri pointed out an indigo bunting, a brilliant blue bird darting from branch to branch, and we stopped for the climbing fumitory. The trail's only specimen of that delicate vine grew at Fumitory Rocks. In season, it produced pink flowers similar to bleeding heart. So far it had yielded only leaves.

Crossing Pennsylvania Highway 325, we entered St. Anthonys Wilderness, a forest preserve traversed by nearly sixteen miles of Appalachian Trail. It was Friday afternoon and the weekenders were out early.

"How far have you walked?" asked a man hiking with his wife.

One thousand seventy-six and a half miles, I said, counting mileage off the trail.

"Oh, from Georgia!" the lady exclaimed. "How do you get food?"

I told her.

"How long will you be out?" inquired the man.

October, I said, though I couldn't give the day.

"Will your little girl miss a year of school?"

No, I said. She would only miss a few months.

"What a wonderful thing to be doing," the lady prattled on. "I've often wanted to hike the whole trail, but we can't. We have a house, a mortgage, and Fred has such a good job with the telephone company in Harrisburg. We just couldn't leave."

"The Pennsylvania telephone company," I said. "I knew there had to be one."

"One what?"

"Pa Bell."

She didn't get it.

We climbed the flank of Stony Mountain to a spring and made camp.

"I'm not a *little* girl!" said Kyra.

"That's better than those two hiking grandmothers who thought you were a boy," Jerri said.

"Oh, *them!*" Kyra said with disgust. "Boys don't wear braids. Don't they know that? If they couldn't see any better than that, I wonder how they found the trail!"

We were sitting around a campfire baking a cake. A well-traveled cake at that: we'd mailed it to four postal stops before finally deciding to use it.

"We should make up some bizarre story," I said. "We could have leaflets printed next time we're in town and hand them out instead of answering questions."

"Good idea," said Kyra.

"Hmmm, I work for the telephone company ..."

"In Liberty, Pennsylvania," Kyra added.

"Arrgh ..." complained Jerri, fingers in her ears.

"... and I've taken a leave of absence."

"Leave of your senses, more likely," Jerri said.

"Kyra is a royal princess traveling with us ... and you're searching for a rare orchid to cure the common cold."

"And when I find it," Jerri said, "I won't tell where it is."

"Right."

"We started walking in South America," Jerri added.

"That's good!"

"When I was five," said Kyra.

"Uh huh, and we're headed for Point Barrow."

"We must have taken a wrong turn somewhere," said Jerri.

"Oh ... Newfoundland, then. Never was much on geography."

"How long will the hike take?" said Kyra, mimicking the typical questioner.

"Don't know, ma'am," I said. "Jus' gonna keep walkin'."

"And how do you get food?"

"From NASA. They mail us little capsules. Add a drop of water; get a whole turkey dinner."

"Or sukiyaki," said Jerri.

"Birthday cake," added Kyra.

"Coming up," I said, pulling a coconut-pecan special off the fire. Perfectly done. Delicious.

Rain sent us scrambling to put up the tent in darkness, but by morning the sky had cleared. We packed and moved on, following miles of old stage roads through St. Anthonys Wilderness. The area was uninhabited but evidence of coal mines could be found throughout, along with traces of villages that had thrived there the century before. The day became hot, yet we walked among tall, quiet trees that shaded our path. It felt again like real forest, more so than in many a day.

We camped after fifteen miles at a meeting of highways, pitching our tent among sun-dappled weeds in a grove of trees. Touch-me-nots and poison ivy grew in abundance. Traffic roared past on Pennsylvania Highway 72 just up the bank. Cars and motorcycles clanked across an old iron bridge over a creek a hundred feet away.

Sunset brought long shadows and deep, rich color to the creek and surrounding trees, and to the twin bridges of Interstate 81, the predominant feature on the horizon. We watched and took pictures. I rated the view as urban, Broadway, and beautiful downtown.

Kyra found magic in the twilight. She roamed the campsite catching fireflies, holding them in her hand, watching them light up. We slept soundly on the sandy ground, hearing nothing from the busy environs till morning.

We gained the crest of Blue Mountain a thousand feet up. The trail would be mostly flat the next thirty miles, I read, and we'd remain atop the same mountain for more than a hundred miles.

The morning seemed unusually hot. Sunlight hit the forest floor with full force; there was no shade. I could see into the valley through the trees as in spring before leaves had grown. Above me, naked branches stood still against a bright blue sky.

We walked an hour and nothing changed. Leafless, shadeless trees covered the ridge ahead and behind and those we could plainly see across the valley.

"Something smells dead," I said.

"I've noticed it, too," said Jerri, "especially since we climbed this mountain."

The stench increased as the sun beat down. I leaned against a tree and felt something squash.

"Gypsy moth," Jerri said, identifying the oozing caterpillar corpse in my hand. Then we saw them all around, dead and dying in the trees, on the ground, in the streams. Alive and eating what little they could find. Gypsy moths: turning the forest into a defoliated war zone.

We walked all day on the steaming, stinking ridgetop. It made little difference whether we walked in forest or on completely exposed roads; the sun hit us as though we crossed the desert at mid-day. We paused in any patch of shade we could find, but we found few. Miles passed quickly, adding up to nearly a hundred in the previous week — more than any week before or to come on the Appalachian Trail. The scene was sunbaked and putrid, and not at all worthwhile.

We stopped for our evening water supply at Pilger Ruh

Spring. A shelter once stood there but a nearby highway gave easy access and crowds had vandalized the structure. Tiring of that, its keepers tore it down. We made camp out of sight nearby. Then Charley showed up.

"*Now* where have you been?" I asked. "You were ahead of us not long ago."

"I went to Philadelphia for a couple days. Mind if I camp here?"

"No, there's room," I said. "And water not far back."

"I got some, enough for dinner anyway."

"What are you cooking?" Jerri asked.

"The one, the only: brown rice. I have it every day."

Afterwards he made tea.

"Want some?" he asked.

"Sure," Jerri said. "How long do you let it steep?"

"Please," Charley said with a grimace of pain, "don't use that word."

The scene did not improve next day. We walked roads that were gravel or dirt, that were long, straight, and flat, and the sun beat down. We stopped for water at every unpolluted spring and rested where we could. We waited in one spot of shade for Kyra who lagged out of sight again.

"A doe and fawn crossed the road right in front of me," she excitedly told us when she caught up. "They were *so* pretty!"

And the gypsy moths munched on. The patter of falling excreted leaf mulch could always be heard in the woods.

We walked into Port Clinton, Pennsylvania, on Tuesday, July 3. State Route 61 led through the center of town and we followed it to the cluster of stores that fronted directly thereon. Intermittent traffic, notably trucks, rumbled by, rattling store windows as we looked through them. The Post Office had closed but would reopen in fifteen minutes, said its sign, so we passed time in the grocery store. Even inside we found the sound of trucks disturbing.

"How can you stand living next to all that noise?" Jerri asked the lady behind the counter.

"What?" she said.

"Never mind."

Groceries and parcels safely packed away, we stopped at the Port Clinton Hotel to find a phone. We'd planned a rendezvous with our Rochester friends for the coming weekend. The estimate of our progress I'd given by letter needed updating.

I reached Fayne Doering and explained that they'd find us in Little Gap. The trail crossed a road there that led north from Danielsville, Pennsylvania. That was forty-two trail miles from where we stood, I told Fayne as she copied directions down. With more than three days to get there, we'd likely be waiting when they arrived.

We reassembled our parade on the hotel front porch just as rain began. We watched it. Huge droplets splashed and bubbled on the pavement; Jerri thought we ought to wait it out. I nudged Kyra, mentioning we hadn't been to a store for nearly twenty minutes. We dashed to the Port Clinton Peanut Shop for a sack of chocolate-covered peanuts. The shower ended as we finished them off so we began our march out of town. Rain politely waited until we'd climbed well up the mountain before resuming.

We descended a ridge and entered a rocky clearing around seven o'clock. We'd heard a new shelter had been built thereabouts and had counted on setting up camp right away. I couldn't find it. I looked farther along the trail: not there. Returning, I followed a sign that advised *500 ft →*. Not there, either. I walked again around the clearing.

Windsor Furnace once stood in that spot, maker of iron stoves and one of the most famous of the iron furnaces that flourished in Pennsylvania from 1740 until after the Civil War. Only bits of shiny slag remained. And rocks, like the pile laid out in the shape of an arrow. The arrow pointed to a blue-blazed trail which led to the shelter. Stupid: I'd stepped over and around the arrow several times. But it hardly mattered. Four people, two men and their sons, had already made camp. Though the large structure clearly offered room for eight, they hadn't left an inch to spare.

Oh, plenty of room, they told us — we could move in as soon as they rearranged their gear. They made no move to do so. They talked instead, asking questions about our trip and telling, it seemed, much of the stories of their lives. An hour went by. We stood around and waited. Jerri cooked dinner at the fireplace as they talked, still making no move. We finally got in near dark. The jabber continued unabated.

The two-hole outhouse at Windsor Furnace Shelter turned out to be the big attraction. It was a yellow-painted building set off in the woods. Its front door opened to an unusually spacious interior where seating came in two elevations: one normal, one eight inches off the floor. Windows provided ample light during the day; a box of old newspapers and magazines helped one pass the time. A bench stood outside. In case of crowds, one could wait one's turn as at a golf-course caddy shack.

Morning brought more chatter and irrelevant advice. We loaded our packs and fled to the woods, making our way over rocky trail and down shady sections of road.

Gypsy moths hadn't hit as hard beyond Port Clinton but the day felt hot and humid all the same. We took in views from The Pinnacle, from Dans Pulpit, from other points with no particular names. They were excellent and fine, but stopping to cool our feet in a stream was the most pleasing, rewarding, and splendid of all. Jerri topped off lunch by heaping strawberries and blueberries she'd picked on vanilla pudding, to make "red, white, and blueberry" pudding for the Fourth of July.

"How far is the next water, mister?" a boy of about fourteen asked me. A large group of youngsters was setting up tents in an incredibly rocky and weedy field.

200

"A mile or so north," I answered, thinking it odd they hadn't settled this before making camp. "That's where we're headed."

"What about behind you?"

"Two miles, but it might not be running. We didn't check."

"Guess we'll go north then," the boy said. "That's the way we came and it's really rough going."

"So we noticed." *River of Rocks* was how the map had put it.

"Rocky behind you, too, huh? Where'd you start anyway?"

"Georgia. The twenty-first of March."

"Oh."

The mile north proved routine like most trail segments that came with such warnings, and we set up camp at dusk. Three of the boys appeared later to get water. They joked and laughed on their way downhill to the spring. Heading back to camp juggling eighty pounds of water bags and canteens in their arms, they seemed less amused. The sky neared total darkness. Soon rain began, then came thunder, lightning, and a sudden wind that drove rain in solid sheets. I wondered if any of them had brought rain gear, or a flashlight.

Thoughts about preparedness and presence of mind were reinforced the following day. We met a hiker walking south, stepping carefully from rock to rock.

"I just got back to the trail," he explained part way into the conversation. "Two weeks ago I had appendicitis."

"Were you hiking at the time?" Jerri asked.

"Yes," he said, "along a ridge not far back. I felt a pain in my side that didn't go away when I rested. I sort of figured what might be wrong so I headed for town."

"How did you get out fast enough?" I asked.

"Lucky. I took the next side trail down the mountain to a road and hitched a ride. I got to a hospital soon after and had an operation the same day.

"I'm feeling pretty good now," he added. "I thought it was time to get back on the trail."

Rocks. Rocks we walked on; rocks we climbed on; rocks we stumbled and tripped on. Rocks *in* the trail. Rocks *were* the trail, in miles-long windrows we couldn't avoid. They'd been just an inconvenience at first. We'd passed one bad stretch before the Susquehanna and a only few more in the seventy miles after that. But after three solid days of walking on rocks we had our fill. Rocks were eroding, wearing away, geologists said, but not fast enough for us. We ached. We were tired. We were frustrated.

Moments of relief were few and largely intellectual. We followed the trail down a tree at one point, down a tree we hadn't climbed. It leaned at about sixty degrees and provided convenient descent from an abruptly ending ledge. Jerri found wood lilies, arresting flowers with brilliant orange, brown-spotted petals, growing in clumps along the trail. She stopped for pictures of nearly every one. Teetering along the crests of some of the bigger boulder piles got to be interesting at times as we looked through trees and over cliffs to valley scenes below. But our legs and ankles became increasingly sore as the days wore on. We wished the rocks would end, disappear, or that the path would go around them. To our disappointment, the trail would be rocky through the rest of Pennsylvania and into New Jersey as well.

We'd also seen and lived with enough gypsy moths to last a good long while. Small sections of forest beyond Port Clinton had not been badly damaged, but we'd left those behind and again walked shadeless trail in the heat. The stench of the dead surrounded us. Caterpillar corpses dangled from branches, littered the ground, floated in the water supply. They'd eaten everything, even scrub growth on the ground. In places we found them eating needles of hemlock and spruce as well. The view was of destruction. Whole mountains were stripped brown as far as we could see.

Through it all we picked blueberries. They were small and

sour at first, but Jerri and Kyra stopped to pick them just the same, filling empty half-pound margarine dishes we used as all-purpose containers. They stopped more often when they found bigger and sweeter berries, eating them in quantity out of hand and stirring them into our mid-day pudding. If I'd thought walking behind a photographer tested a man's patience, compulsive berry-pickers strained it even more.

I didn't complain. I wanted to walk, of course, to cover ground and not stop and dawdle all day, but we were doing well. We were actually ahead of where I'd thought we'd be. So I stopped and picked, too, growing restless, perhaps, only because I wasn't that fond of blueberries.

Five miles from our rendezvous point in Little Gap, we descended Blue Mountain to cross the Lehigh River and Pennsylvania Highway 248. We climbed Blue Mountain again from there, figuring to walk to the next water and make camp. Berries threatened our progress, as did views of the river and valley, but we stuck to it — and walked right past the spring. We ended up at the road through Little Gap at eight o'clock with no water aboard or nearby.

"I'll find some somewhere," I told Jerri, remembering how superior I'd felt to the boys carrying water in the rain. "Make camp under those trees while I'm gone."

I saw a car pulled off the road a short distance ahead. Collecting canteens and a five-quart water bag, I walked up the road to the car.

"Know of any water around here?" I asked the driver through the open window. "We seem to have missed the spring."

"Sure," he answered, "at my brother's farm. Get in and I'll take you there — it's better water anyway."

We drove a few miles, then walked through a farmyard to the spring house. Kneeling on the cool stone slab inside, I dipped eleven quarts of the coldest, best-tasting water we'd had in weeks.

"Thanks," I said, as he dropped me back at the trail. Jerri and Kyra had everything ready to go. We had dinner done and were asleep just after dark.

Paul and Fayne Doering arrived from Rochester early next day.

"Ready for a day off?" asked Fayne as we traded hugs and handshakes all around.

"You bet," Jerri said.

"I figured you'd want to retain the spirit of things," Paul said, in his usual straight-faced way, "so I reserved campground space for us all. There will be plenty of room for your tent."

"We also brought twenty boxes of your slides to look at," added Fayne.

"Wow," Kyra said. "Home movies."

We piled our belongings into their van and headed for town. Somewhere, miles from Little Gap and the Appalachian Trail, we ate a huge restaurant lunch, then checked into a campground for the day.

Standing in the office, I noticed posters warning of gypsy moths. A small television set turned on behind the counter showed news of gypsy moth damage. The commentator gave a minute's fast-paced description, showed an aerial film of the stricken area, then moved on to something else.

I was stunned. How could anyone grasp the problem's scope in that short a time. Mixed with segments of traffic accidents, worldwide tragedies, and other grim news, how could anyone understand in one minute that the forests were being eaten? We had walked in it *six days*. We'd smelled the death, lived the devastation, felt the burning heat of the sun through denuded trees. How could television viewed in comfort convey such a message?

We had left the city to live more closely with the natural world. I'd never expected to experience the difference quite that way.

CHAPTER 18

Trouble in DWG

Any man who goes to the big city deserves what happens to him.

- "HELLO, DOLLY"

JERRI STOPPED SO SUDDENLY I nearly ran her down. I glanced ahead at the cause: a three-foot snake coiled in the trail, its head and throat distended to twice normal size. From its mouth protruded the back end and legs of a toad. Stretching slowly to devour its meal, the snake forced the toad farther down as we watched. Soon only the feet remained visible.

Jerri moved to focus her camera. The snake crawled off, ungainly and overbalanced with its bulbous head held aloft. I tried to retrieve it for a picture but it eluded me. Kyra caught up just then.

"What's happening?" she asked.

"We watched a snake eat a toad," Jerri said. "You should have seen it."

"No, thanks," she replied. "I'll pass on snakes."

We continued on our way, Kyra resuming her position in the middle.

"What are you doing back there these days?" I asked. She'd been walking behind us nearly always of late.

"I'm decorating the inside of my house on the island. It has a room for ceramics where I'll make my own dishes, and a metal-working room so I can make silverware. And a wood shop for building furniture and a place to needlepoint rugs. I'm going to make everything myself!"

"Sounds like you're keeping busy," I said.

"Uh-huh, I'm decorating each room differently with things I make. I go to whichever one I want, depending on what I feel like doing."

"Are you going to build this house someday?"

"Maybe."

"With wave power, solar heating, a garden, and making everything yourself, you'll be almost self-sufficient. You'll live alone, I suppose."

"Oh, no," she said. "I'll have cats."

"Cats?" I said. *Nothing that eats* was the rule about pets at home, which had prompted her once to paint a horse on a rock for a pet. "How many cats?"

"Lots."

We walked on another half-mile, feeling the sun beat down on a blistering day.

"Have you thought about running away any more?" I asked.

"No, I decided it wasn't worth the trouble. But I still don't want to walk in the middle all the time."

"We ought to stick reasonably close together."

"I suppose," she said, "but I really like being by myself."

"To have your own adventure? 'Ten-year-old turns eleven on solo hike to Maine.' Something like that?"

"Uh-huh."

"You camp with us. Doesn't that mess things up?"

"Not really," she said. "We meet other through-hikers some-times and that's fun. The only time I feel funny is in town."

"Why? I thought town was the best part for you."

"I keep thinking other kids will see me and laugh because I'm with my parents."

"Parents are out for sixth-graders, huh? But these are pretty small towns. Kids here might have different attitudes."

"Maybe."

"What about groups of kids we meet on the trail?" I asked. "Or those jerks yesterday who told you to go home before you got lost?"

"I ignore the groups, but those other creeps made me mad. I know where I'm going. I got here from Georgia, didn't I?"

So she had, and if she wanted to lag behind and have her own experience, free of distracting conversation and parental advice, that was fine with me. She'd walked more than a thousand miles. She could find the way as well as we.

Kyra stayed with us after the snake encounter because she'd run out of water. So had we. The day was hot and we'd used the gallon I'd brought along to see us through eleven miles with no springs. Reaching a stream at day's end, a satisfying rush of water over mossy rocks, we drank and drank and filled canteens as if finding an oasis in the Sahara.

Noon the next day found us gasping at another stream, taking long drinks and soaking bandanas to tie around our heads. The day had been completely miserable. The path led constantly over jagged rocks and through dense underbrush. We met few other hikers as the sun scorched down from a sky that had been clear sixteen of the past seventeen days. We pushed on in silence, no relief in sight.

Hot ... hot, and no breeze ... air felt heavy, humid. We'd been perspiring for days. Our arms and legs glistened with it ... dust clung to it ... sweat made tracks in the dust. Sweat ran into my eyes, trickled down the lenses of my glasses and blurred the view. Wiping them with a wet bandana didn't help. Nothing to see anyway ... everything hazy and dull.

Mosquitoes ... biting, circling, buzzing loudly in our ears. Repellent wore off as we perspired, when we used any at all ... it made us smell even worse. Gnats followed us in swarms, hovering in front of our faces. Waving them away had no effect. They bit, too, but it was much too hot for more clothes to keep them away. We wore as little as possible ... settling one question anyway: a string shirt would give you a waffle suntan.

Rocks ... rocks at breakfast, lunch, and dinner, day after day. Ankles ached from twisting, turning, straining, jamming ... boots slipped as rocks tipped and rolled. Sharp edges scraped our ankles and legs, leaving bruises and wide, red scratches. Rocks covered only a third of Pennsylvania. A third of Pennsylvania was a long way.

Underbrush ... slapping us, clawing at us, snagging our clothes and packs. Leaves and grit clung to wet arms and legs ... fell down our necks ... worked under pack straps and back bands. How many days before the going got better? Before we found smooth trail and shady forest? Would New Jersey and New York be any better?

Rocky trail continued through late afternoon, leading over a ridge of heaped boulders that lasted four miles. Soreness in my legs and ankles and a feeling of endlessness wore on my nerves.

"I'll go crazy if we don't get out of these rocks pretty soon," I complained to no one in particular.

"We probably qualify already," Jerri replied.

"How did these rocks get here, anyway? Did glaciers push them up in heaps and rows like this?"

"The glaciers didn't come this far south."

"Well, something did. No farmer clearing fields made these piles!"

"No, probably not," Jerri said, making her way slowly along in front. "It's likely an old sea bed pushed up and cracked during formation of the Appalachians. Centuries of freezing and thawing have broken huge blocks into these smaller pieces."

"I'm not so sure," I said.

"Why not?"

"I think they were trucked in here by the ATC...."

"Sure."

"And former through-hikers haul in more every year to make the going tougher for everyone else...."

"Right."

"Then why does the trail have to go over *every damned one?*"

Next day we found berries. We stopped in every patch of shade and picked blueberries, huckleberries, and black raspberries until our fingers turned blotchy and we'd filled every container. We covered the day's seven steaming miles in irregular surges and finally reached the town of Delaware Water Gap at two in the afternoon. Half the trail's fourteen states ended there, just beyond the small town at the Delaware River.

We sat on a bench near a street corner thirty minutes later in an advanced state of confusion. We'd been to the Post Office and found things we'd mailed but had received no package from the Doerings. That meant no guidebook for the next two states. We could find our way without it but couldn't pick supply drops for two hundred miles of trail if we didn't know where it led.

We'd also been to the town's only store. We couldn't hope to find what we needed on its limited shelves. And rooms were priced beyond our budget. We sat on a bench and watched cars go by, looking for answers to it all.

I suggested moving everything to Stroudsberg, Pennsylvania, about five miles away. Jerri talked about picking food supply points from a gas station map. We considered hitchhiking to Stroudsberg and back for groceries. We discussed doing our whole town routine while camped out. We talked about getting food to last only to the next town, to see if things might be better there. We concluded nothing.

"One problem at a time," Jerri finally said. "Call Fayne and see if she mailed the guidebook."

I called Fayne Doering from the pay phone up the street. She thought she'd mailed the book as requested in our last letter, but would check.

"No, it's still here," she said, calling back moments later. "I'll mail it right now!" I walked back to the bench.

"The book is on its way," I told Jerri. "We'll get it tomorrow if we're lucky."

"That means we stay in town," she replied. "Did you check all motels listed in the phone book?"

"Yeah, too expensive. I didn't check the place recommended by the lady at the Post Office, though. She said they only rented rooms."

"Better call and find out."

I called Holly Manheim at the Bridge-View Inn. She had rooms, she said, also an efficiency apartment for ten dollars a night. Would that be okay?

Less than half what others were charging: I took it.

We packed our burdens back to a sprawling, two-story house we'd passed on our way into town. Sunlit shade trees surrounded it. Columns and railings on its wrap-around front porch gave it the look of a Catskill resort or a Southern plantation home. The paint had been a cracked and aging white for years but painters atop ladders and on the porch roof were turning it a fresh dark green.

Mrs. Manheim and several of her younger children showed us to our upstairs room.

"I'll be leaving for Stroudsberg in half an hour," she said, "if you need anything from the store."

We sat in the apartment again three hours later, surrounded by groceries heaped on the bed, the floor, the kitchen table, and jammed in the small refrigerator. We had 260 miles' worth of food and planned to have it under control in thirty-six hours.

We didn't make it. Morning a day and a half later found us not quite ready and being none too cordial about it.

"What is there left to do?" Jerri asked after an hour of avoiding the subject.

"Mail these boxes, write some letters, and clean the canteens," I replied. "We could be ready by noon if we wanted to."

"Don't we want to?" she asked, surprised.

"Not really. There's no camping allowed along the trail for the next twelve miles. It would be a pretty rushed afternoon."

"When has that stopped you?"

"It seemed like a good chance for time off," I said in defense. "I thought you'd appreciate a day of rest."

"Sure, I would. So why did you keep us up until midnight these past two nights getting things ready?"

"We couldn't decide whether to stay this extra day or go. I figured it best to be able to handle it either way."

"Now neither makes sense," she said. "There's too much to do to get away for an easy hike, not enough to make it worth staying in town. I thought you were in a rush to get to Maine. Now you want to take an extra day off. I don't understand."

"We'll make it to Maine. Half a day won't make a difference."

"Goodness, let me write that down."

"What I meant was, we're doing okay."

"Fine, but look at the nice blue sky out there again today, just like yesterday. It sure seems stupid to sit in town during good weather."

"You mean hot weather," I said, my exasperation showing. "But we can still go on if you prefer."

"We should have turned around here instead of continuing north. The Delaware River is a logical breaking point just like the Susquehanna, maybe more so. I wish we'd skipped to Katahdin to walk south."

"It's too late with all this food packaged up," I said. "Besides, you seemed quite confident solving all our problems yesterday the way you did. Why didn't you say something then?"

"I didn't think of it in time. But you could still readdres

those boxes to points in Maine and call Fayne for another guidebook. The one she just mailed got here in a day."

"I don't want to walk south."

"Why not?" Jerri asked.

"It's more logical to walk straight through."

"I can't see how it makes any difference. You'd be sure of finishing by doing northern mountains now and we wouldn't have to care about miles per day. We wouldn't worry about crossing the Kennebec River in Maine, either. We'd be on the north side where the man with the boat is."

"We're doing fine," I went on. "At our present rate, we'll reach Katahdin in early October just like we've always planned."

"You've missed the point, as usual," she said in a loud voice. "I'm *tired* of 'our present rate.' I don't *want* to go as fast through New England as we did through Pennsylvania. The country is too pretty up there to *run* through!"

"Well, it's too early in the season," I replied. "It's only July 12. Black flies will be ferocious in Maine for another month."

"*Make lunch, not war!*" called Kyra, still in bed. "How about French toast? We have berries for syrup!"

We ate French toast, and stayed the day.

And a completely undistinguished day it was, filled with such inspirational events as scrubbing moss out of canteens (sugar from lemonade had fostered growth of black algae inside them), and hauling boxes of supplies to the Post Office to be mailed. We tried to take naps while house painters laughed, sang, told stories, and clumped about heavily on the roof outside our windows.

We departed the following morning. Blue sky had given way to black clouds. Thunder crashed directly overhead. Lightning split the morning air; painters dashed for shelter under the eaves. Holly Manheim and her youngsters gathered on the front porch to watch. And we walked down the streets of Delaware Water Gap heading north in the pouring rain.

CHAPTER 19

Cold Shower in the Girls' John

*Wheresoever little children are gathered together
in the wilderness they will be playing in the fire,
throwing rocks in the water, or chopping down
trees.*

- JOURNAL ENTRY

THUNDER BOOMED AND CRASHED ABOVE US like freight trains colliding in the sky. Wind whipped tall oaks and hemlocks and rain beat savagely down. Lightning flashed so near we could hear it, see it, smell it in the morning air.

Rain had ended once we'd crossed the Delaware River into New Jersey, then had begun and ended again as we'd climbed to the crest of Kittatinny Ridge. As we passed Sunfish Pond it came once more, stirring the moody waters, lashing the forest into a frenzy. Then clouds broke and parted. Sunlight lit trees in broad patches. With a final blast of thunder, an afterthought almost, the morning storm departed. The woods fell to stillness once again.

After 115 days on the trail, we knew just about when to expect rain. Full and new moon brought weather changes, we'd learned and observed — rain had dampened us on six of seven such occasions. This was more than coincidence. We later found a National Weather Service study documenting it: ten percent more rain and periods of heaviest rain fell on days following new or full moon.

We'd suspected less scientific causes at first. Putting up the tent at night once appeared to be a factor (rain for sure if we didn't), as did the length of time since our boots had been weatherproofed (no rain after a new application). Drying, folding, and packing the rain gear away always seemed to bring rain, too. But after sleeping several nights in the open without rain, walking through recent storms with freshly weatherproofed boots, and being showered on while actually wearing our rain gear, we'd come to discount these theories.

One relationship endured, however. I wondered why we hadn't noticed sooner. We'd been to twenty-one towns so far and rain had occurred in eighteen. Whether postal stop, crash stop, or just passing through, nearly every town visit brought rain. That was strong medicine. In Delaware Water Gap, with full moon two days away, the weather should have held. Town-rain medicine had proven stronger.

Branley Owen reported only eight rainy days on his 1970 AT hike, and after his 132-day walk along the Pacific Crest Trail, Eric Ryback told me he'd had no rain at all. Our luck was different. We could hire out to break droughts. Even with hot, clear weather through Pennsylvania, we'd still seen rain on 51 of 115 days. All we had to do to get more, it appeared, was go to town.

The trail led through swamps fed by coffee-colored streams and over rock-strewn ridge the rest of that day and into the next. We stopped for views of the valley from lookouts atop sheer cliffs, and listened as we walked to sounds drifting up from below — dogs barking, roosters crowing, people shouting across farmyards. Twelve miles passed each blue-sky day and we met no one. Gypsy moth damage appeared lighter in New Jersey. With surviving caterpillars emerging as moths, we hoped for continuing improvement.

At length we reached Rattlesnake Mountain. Proceeding through dense brush, Kyra moved to follow Jerri, stepping down over a narrow ledge of rock. I heard a sudden, unmistakable buzz. Kyra jumped back in alarm. A black timber rattler slid away as we cautiously looked down. All but the tip of its six-rattle tail disappeared behind a rock.

I crossed the ledge ahead of Kyra, discovering as I stepped that the snake wasn't out of reach at all, but rattling loudly again directly under my boot. I veered to one side and shooed it from the path with my walking stick. We continued without further disturbance, at least from the snake.

"Why can't snakes stay off the trail?" Kyra said. "There are plenty of other places for them to go. I *hate* them."

"This is Rattlesnake Mountain," I replied. "We're *supposed* to see one here."

"Can't we just see a picture of one?"

"We saw apple trees on Apple Orchard Mountain didn't we?"

"I guess so," Kyra said.

"And we had sassafras tea in Sassafras Gap."

"Yes."

"Well ... some things just have to be, that's all."

"There weren't any cherries at Cherry Tree Shelter."

"No," I replied, "but we went for a walk on Walker Mountain."

"I didn't see any angels on Angels Rest."

"It was raining."

"Are they excused on rainy days? What about Humpback Rocks? I didn't see any whales there, did you?"

"Perhaps not, but we were miserably hot on Bake Oven Knob and Dismal Creek Road was mighty dismal as I recall."

"Hmmm," Kyra mused. "Do you think there are bears on Bear Mountain and pigeons at Big Pigeon River?"

"Sure, and Groundhog Creek has groundhogs that see their shadows!"

"I wonder if there's a good place to rest in Davenport Gap."

"That would be nice," I said. "Especially after you'd just walked a mile from Camel Hump Knob."

"Enough, you two," Jerri laughed from the head of the line. But by then we'd left all trace of the rattlesnake behind.

Blue sky and sunshine were gone by morning. Rain began at 6:15 AM; the moon turned full at 7:56. We weren't concerned about rain, fog, swampy trail, or socked-in views, however. We had one destination in mind, a scant four miles from camp on U.S. Route 206: Worthington's Bakery. We'd read about it and heard of it from other hikers and were closing in fast. I only hoped they'd be open that drizzly Sunday morning. They were.

Breakfast began with a whole nut-covered coffee cake, enjoyed in the comfort of a side yard under a broad-branching tree. A trip back for jelly doughnuts followed, then brownies, cupcakes, and a large can of fruit juice. Still we couldn't leave.

Churchgoers on their way home crowded round the counter and supplies ran disturbingly low.

"I'll wait," I said on my final visit. "Another half-dozen doughnuts, please."

They were brought to me straight from the fryer, soft and warm and clouding the clear plastic bag. We savored each bite, finishing them off as we walked slowly down the trail.

We climbed through a forest of dripping hickory and scrub oak, making our way five miles to the top of Sunrise Mountain. A picnickers' pavilion stood at the summit. Clotheslines full of waterlogged socks, shirts, and rain gear hung throughout and abandoned tents stood off to one side. No sunrise was seen there, campers reported — only rain that had left them drenched.

From there we followed ridges, rocks, and roads. We picked dewberries, red raspberries, and high-bush blueberries. Jerri found basswood, creeping bellflower, spotted wintergreen, and slammed to a halt for smooth false foxglove.

"It's in the snapdragon family, Kyra," Jerri said. "Remember how snapdragons work?"

"Sure," she replied. "You squeeze them on the side and they open their jaws. Snap!"

We also started counting red efts. We'd seen but a few since early Virginia, but damp leaves and puddled trail brought them out again in force. All afternoon we rambled along the ridgetop, stopping ... four, five ... to see them pad in a rush across moist forest floor ... eleven ... to watch them turn and stare at us from rocky perches ... sixteen, seventeen ... to note them scrambling through leaves to escape our prying eyes.

We came to a shelter as we counted ... twenty-three ... but a troop of Boy Scouts had moved in and more were on the way. We walked on; there would be another shelter in two miles.

We hadn't found it in three miles, nor in four. It wasn't shelter we cared about, but water — we had only a quart.

"What do you think?" Jerri asked, stopping at a wide place in the trail shortly before dark. "Should we go on or make camp while it's still light?"

"Let's keep looking," said Kyra.

"We've missed the shelter," I said. "We'd do better to stop."

"I think so, too," agreed Jerri, and we quickly made camp.

The quart of water vanished quickly into dinner but breakfast next morning came easy. We stirred sugar into a quart of accumulated berries and ate a treat second only to the bakery stop the day before. A mile and a half later we found a drive-in camper park, with fireplaces, picnic tables, visitor center, and water from a pump.

"I guess you were right, Kyra," Jerri said. "We should have kept looking."

"We might have seen more red efts," Kyra said with a grin. "We only counted twenty-nine."

Our northeasterly course led to the uppermost corner of New Jersey and to High Point State Park, home of 1,803-foot High Point, the highest mountain elevation in the state. The "peak" made little impression on the skyline but we had no trouble identifying it — a 220-foot stone obelisk had been erected on its summit. We saw it for miles as we approached, saw it up close as we passed through the park, and saw it pointing skyward behind.

We stopped to talk with a young couple resting on the roadside some distance on. I mentioned that we were walking the whole trail.

"We planned to walk to Maine, too," the woman said, "but now I don't think we'll even get to New England. We're in terrible shape and walking on these rocks is just awful."

Odd, they looked healthy and trim to me, and I'd thought the rocks were easing up.

"Where did you start?" Jerri asked.

"Delaware Water Gap," the fellow replied.

"That's forty-five miles or so," I said in an encouraging way.

"Yes," said the woman, "but we've been hiking *three weeks!*"

Maybe she was right; a new plan would be appropriate.

They kept pace with us that day as we crossed into New York at the town of Unionville. They joined us for pie at the Side Road Pantry pie shop, passed us as we snacked on the outskirts of town, and joined us again as we walked miles of hard-top road through Walkill Valley farmland to a place called Liberty Corners. We chose a campsite there, in a ridge-top pasture behind a row of houses. Our supposedly slow-moving friends elected to go on, preferring, they said, a bit more seclusion.

"They walked as far today as in any other five days," I said to Jerri after they'd gone. "Maybe they'll pick up the pace."

"I don't think so," she replied.

"Why not?"

"Surely you noticed."

"Um ... noticed what?"

"Their problem isn't that they aren't in shape," she went on. "They are obviously just married."

"Oh," I said. "That explains why they passed up this great spot."

"Amazing. But I don't like it, either. Do we have to camp here?"

"The trail looks pretty brushy ahead," I said, puzzled. "What don't you like? It's quiet here, with big trees and a great view of the valley. We haven't seen anything nicer."

"The place makes me nervous. Being this close to those houses down there bothers me."

"I'll pitch the tent where no one can see it," I offered. "We'll disturb our friends if we go on."

"I suppose," she said reluctantly, "but I still don't like it."

A barking dog outside the tent woke us at one in the morning. We heard no other sounds and saw nothing amiss, so ignored the noise until it went away. Night passed without incident otherwise.

Morning brought sun and clear sky and another view of High Point Monument across a fluffy, fog-filled valley. We continued across the ridge, passing the couple's tent and leaving the lovely camp at Liberty Corners behind. We were lucky. A story we heard later made clear why Jerri had reason to be nervous.

Carl Windle had hiked through the area a month before. As he'd passed the houses along State Line Road at Liberty Corners, two dogs ran to attack him from a nearby yard. Readying his Mace and facing the dogs, he'd then seen a man pick up a baseball bat and come toward him from the same yard. Carl expected him to call off the dogs or chase them away. Not so. The man had come for Carl.

"What's that in your hand?" the man demanded.

"Dog Mace," Carl said.

"Drop it! Drop it!" came the threatening reply.

Carl dropped the can and the man picked it up and batted it far into a field. He waved the bat, shouting,

"You no good bum! Don't you ever come by here again and pull that stuff. We have ways to deal with people like you around here!"

Carl, tired and sick from polluted water, turned and walked away, continuing along the trail.

"And you better not go over that mountain," the man shouted, running after him.

Carl walked on, figuring he hadn't hiked twelve hundred miles to be stopped by a nut with a bat.

"I told you not to go up that mountain!" the man yelled once more.

Too weary to run, Carl dropped his pack and picked up a large rock, resting it on his knee. He pictured the newspaper headlines — "Heart Fund - Policeman Hiker Kills Man on Appalachian Trail" — as he faced his still-shouting assailant.

"Shut up," Carl said. The man muttered and glared, then he turned and walked back to his house. "Saw one hawk, two deer, one squirrel, one crackpot!" Carl noted in his journal for the day.

We'd just camped within sight of the house at Liberty Corners. Had no one seen us? Had no one been home? What of the dog that barked at our tent in the night? We would never know.

The trail led back into New Jersey beyond the ridge and commenced meandering along roads and through fields, up and down brushy ridges, across buggy, mountaintop swamps. We passed water often but found it stagnant, dark brown, or running out of pastures. No wilderness feeling accompanied our progress. The press of urban and agricultural development left the trail anything but remote. We felt we were just walking through it to get somewhere else.

In late afternoon, having run out of water for at least the

third time, we stopped near a house on Willow Brook Road. I collected empty canteens and chanced to pull out and read again a post card we'd received in Unionville.

"Great," I said to Jerri. "We were supposed to call Doug Wilson at Homestead Camp yesterday when we got this card. I missed that line when I first read it."

"We'll be there in a couple of days," she said. "Better try and call him now, I guess."

I knocked at the first house. The middle-aged lady who answered said I could get water out back from a faucet but I couldn't use the phone. No one could use it. She'd been stuck with long-distance bills of too many hikers.

The guidebook mentioned the Willow Brook Inn a mile away. After filling up on water and sending Jerri and Kyra to make camp, I walked the mile. I found the inn but no one seemed to be around.

I entered the deserted dining room. Dim light made its way through curtained windows, sending irregular shadows of tables and stacked chairs across the floor and up the walls. I listened for some sign of life. Sounds came from the kitchen. Through an archway, I saw a telephone on the kitchen wall. I strode through the doorway to inquire about making my call.

A frail, older lady looked suddenly in my direction. Her startled eyes widened in fright and she shrank away, raising a hand to her gaping mouth. I made no move. After four months on the trail, and more days than I cared to remember of summer's suffocating heat, my appearance was anything but reassuring.

"May I use the phone?" I asked politely, seeking to calm her.

She said nothing, but nodded and waved me toward the phone.

"It will be long distance," I said. "I'll pay you."

She continued to point and nod, saying nothing.

I dialed the number Doug sent me. Waiting for an answer, I glanced through an open door into another room. A short, stocky man sat at a desk ten feet away, staring at me with unblinking eyes. I looked away; someone had answered.

No, the man on the phone said, Doug wasn't around. Yes, he'd tell him we'd be there in three days. Would Doug know who we were? Who were we anyway? I explained. Doug would remember us, I assured him. I hung up after obtaining charges from the operator.

"Thirty-five cents for the call," I told the man at the desk.

"Just leave it on the phone," he answered in a wary voice, watching my every move.

I left a quarter and a dime and departed past shadowy tables and chairs. I heard no resumption of sounds from the kitchen.

I found Kyra's note back at the trail — "Dad: camp is not far. The swamp is very tricky, hop from island to island. Follow trees up hill." — and made my way to camp. Kyra sat on a rock at the hilltop watching for me. And thirty miles away at Homestead Camp, my message had already been forgotten and would never reach Doug Wilson.

Mile upon mile of dusty roads, dismal swamps, and shadeless, carbon-copy ridges resumed next morning. The trail had entered New York once again, leaving another state finally behind. Rocks had diminished and changed in character from jagged chunks to smooth, glacially polished boulders. But in summer's heat, the excitement we'd once felt was gone. In another season — spring, perhaps, or fall — the trail through Pennsylvania, New Jersey, and New York might be vibrant, colorful, and alive as the guidebook continued to portray it. But with heat and bugs and boring terrain, with house and highway never far away, our enthusiasm for each new day was gone. Walking the trail had just become something to do.

So many accounts of hiking the Appalachian Trail were misleading in this regard. Written after years had passed, after occasions of misery and boredom vanished in a rosy glow, they'd assured us that every step was a pleasure. Every moment was fascinating, unique, and special. Every day brought nearly endless unfolding of wondrous experience.

Walking through dull terrain that seemed much like that of the day before and days before that, beset by conditions described, I couldn't help but think the authors had been over-generous. I wondered, sometimes, if they'd even been paying attention.

Hiking the Appalachian Trail was not non-stop ecstasy. It offered highs, but also lows. It brought joy, but also drudgery. One could take the bad with the good, one could grow from suffering as well as rapture, one could be as positive and high-minded as one liked, but some days were hardly worth the effort. Some days were just filler, spaces between more interesting times.

Finally, a milestone. Standing atop Arden Mountain in southeastern New York next afternoon, we looked down at two strips of pavement stretching across the Ramapo Valley as far left and right as we could see. The New York State Thruway: a visual boundary that marked progress like nothing we'd seen in recent days. We hurried down to cross it, descending 660 feet in less than half a mile on a cliff face known as Agony Grind.

We found Harriman Park beyond the pavement, with grassy woods and pleasant trail once again. The change seemed sudden, but had actually come upon us over many miles. Barren stretches had slowly given way to forests of oak, beech, and maple, and we'd been stopping more often to see the sights. I didn't fully notice the effects until we crossed the road.

We made camp late in the day at the end of a gravel road near Island Pond. We would have preferred to go on; a dozen other campers and fishermen nearby were blaring music on portable radios and frying sausage and potatoes upwind. It was the last source of spring water for several miles, however, so we stayed — and couldn't find the spring.

A few evenings before, Jerri had been about to fill canteens from a creek near our camp when she'd abruptly decided to check farther upstream. There she'd found a group of boys wading and bathing in the water supply. Another recent time, directions to water had been "a ten-minute walk to the right." I'd walked down a road exactly ten minutes and found spring water gushing from a pipe. On the way ten minutes back, I'd listened to wind swaying the trees, the regular clump of my boots on pavement, and the far-off sounds of Jerri playing her recorder. The quest for water often added dimension to our days. But with the crowd at Island Pond, we purified water from the lake. At least there was plenty of it.

Then came raccoons; a bold mother and young one walked right into camp and nearly lifted the pot lid to sniff what was cooking. I chased them away. After midnight I woke to find them parked in the vestibule of the tent, staring at us through the front netting.

"I gave at the office," I told them, and they padded silently off.

Next morning we negotiated the "lemon-squeezer" — a narrow passage around, beneath, and between huge boulders, up cracks and chimneys so tight we had to remove our packs to get through.

From there we followed the Long-Arden Interchange — a merging and separating of trails, lacking only a cloverleaf, in which the Appalachian Trail led forward marked by white blazes; the Arden-Surebridge Trail joined, then split north in red-dot blazes; the Long Path (blazed green) followed for three miles then departed north to the Catskills and Adirondacks; and the Ramapo-Dunderberg Trail merged in the eastbound lane bringing red-blotch blazes. The confusion yielded some very slopped-up trees for several miles, but we arrived without mishap at Lake Tiorati Circle.

We threaded our way through crowds of Friday-afternoon picnickers and sun-bathers, refugees from big-city offices, and

224

set up to hitchhike south on the Seven Lakes Parkway. Homestead Camp lay in that direction. There we could take the rest of the day off.

After half an hour of blank, look-straight-ahead stares from passing drivers, I abandoned the hitch and called the camp for a ride. Whoever answered didn't know who we were or why we were bothering them, but eventually agreed to send a car. Which left me a bit puzzled — to pick up three hikers and three fully loaded packs, they sent two people in a Volkswagen sedan.

Homestead Camp looked to be a quiet place set among tall trees along a lakeshore. It had a scattering of permanent, weather-worn buildings and rows of look-alike wall tents that lined paths through the camp. I saw people wandering idly about and heard occasional cheers and shouts. No one took the slightest notice of our arrival.

We asked around and found Doug Wilson and Jeff Menzer, whom we'd also met on the trail in North Carolina. The two had hiked together to Harpers Ferry, then left the trail to come to Homestead. They planned to start at Katahdin after the camp closed in late August, Jeff said, and finish the AT hiking south. Doug gave us the use of his wall tent, showed us the swimming hole, then left to attend a meeting.

"Where's the shower?" I asked one lad after my dip in the lake.

"That building over there," he replied, "the Girls' john."

"Isn't there a Men's?"

"Sure, but we all use the Girls'. It's closer."

I used it, too. No one seemed alarmed at my entrance. No one thought the presence of a complete stranger at all odd. One young lady on her way out even sought to be helpful:

"The water heater broke this morning," she said. "I think all the hot water is gone."

Under the circumstances, I entered the shower fully dressed. I draped my clothes over the shower wall and discovered at once the young lady was right. I emerged dressed again a very short time later, feeling about the same as when I'd jumped in the lake.

After dinner we hauled our gear to the "Wreck Hall" to talk to the kids about our hike. This was why we'd been invited, and quite a few youngsters showed up. Many seemed interested enough to ask questions. Then a driving rainstorm broke up the session and the group dispersed in a run. We headed for our quarters as well.

Doug drove us next morning to where we'd gotten off the trail. Camp counseling hadn't turned out to be the great experience he'd expected, he allowed, but it would be over soon and he'd be back on the trail. We soon heaved on our packs, said our farewells, and continued on our way.

I walked down the trail chuckling at something I'd seen just before we left. I'd walked through a vacant room, one with walls high and low and ceiling as well completely given over to graffiti. I'd stopped to read, finding this scribbled item:

> *Beauty is truth*
> *Truth is beauty*
> *Rooty-toot-toot*
> *Rooty-toot-tooty.*

CHAPTER 20

Rainer

Allons! the road is before us!
It is safe — I have tried it — my own feet
have tried it well — be not detain'd!
Let the paper remain on the desk unwritten,
and the book on the shelf unopen'd!
Let the tools remain in the workshop!
let the money remain unearn'd!
Let the school stand! mind not the cry of
the teacher!
Let the preacher preach in his pulpit!
let the lawyer plead in the court,
and the judge expound the law.

— WALT WHITMAN

THE STATELY, GLASS-LIKE HUDSON RIVER flowed imperceptibly beneath us, mirroring clouds and lush, green hills. Patches of wispy fog hung in the winding valley, outlining interleaved mountains that sloped to the river's shore. A single-span suspension bridge soared from bank to bank in a graceful economy of lines.

It was the most spectacular view we'd seen in weeks and we weren't even on the trail.

We were walking a road above the Hudson's west shore, returning to the trail after a night in the town of Fort Montgomery. Jerri stopped to raid a wineberry patch. She noticed the view and we paused to take it in. We might never have seen it had the trail not been closed the night before.

Before 5 PM, the Appalachian Trail led through the Bear Mountain Trailside Museum. After five, an alternate route led around. We'd arrived too late to go through and stayed the night so as not to miss it. It was worth the wait.

Not for the nature trail that led past identified specimens of trees, shrubs, and flowering plants. Not for the modest zoo with its caged ferret, raccoons, and sleepy bears. I could have missed the AT's lowest point (115 feet above sea level, near the bear den) without problem, and clusters of Sunday-morning tourists. ("Dey's goin' hikin'," said one lady pointing us out to her youngster. "See da big shooze?") But the statue of Walt Whitman was worth waiting to see.

Hat in hand, coat open to the wind, the life-sized figure strode across a massive boulder, walking the open road of which Whitman had written. Sunlight played through fluttering leaves over its rough-hewn features, lighting the craggy face and rambling beard, the outswung arm and leg. The man on the rock seemed to move, seemed bound in the direction of that steady gaze as though to pass us quickly by. I stood struck by the power of this confident figure, almost hearing familiar words cut into the rock at its feet:

> Afoot and light-hearted I take to the open road,
> Healthy, free, the world before me,
> The long brown path before me leading wherever I choose.

The ring of those words seemed to recharge our spirits in the summer heat, and seemed to bring renewal for the 750 miles of Appalachian Trail to go.

Paying our dimes at the toll booth, we walked across the Hudson on the Bear Mountain Bridge. The river spread half a mile wide below us, its passage rippled by barges and speedboats, its course dividing the land in a great swath of blue. Pedestrian toll on the bridge had been a nickel until 1971. Eastbound tolls had been doubled then and charges for westbound traffic had been eliminated. Perhaps this was an argument for walking the trail the other way.

We'd been "discussing" the issue again. We could escape hot weather by skipping north to walk south, Jerri had said; the Hudson would be a significant dividing point.

Not during black-fly season in Maine, I'd answered. We were already being eaten by bugs, she'd countered; how could it be worse? And again she'd expressed concern about crossing the Kennebec. We'd reached no conclusion.

Across the river atop Anthonys Nose, we met hikers just back from vacation in Maine. Bugs, they reported; bugs that sent you into screaming frenzy. I thought the information timely. But it wasn't the real reason I didn't want to walk south. Black flies were just buying me time.

I didn't know the real reason. I wanted to walk straight through, GA →ME, as I'd written in registers for 124 days. It was the logical, orderly thing to do. Wasn't that enough? Okay, maybe there was more to it but I couldn't grasp what it might be. I wanted time to figure it out. I'd be patient, I'd stop for whatever reason, just leave me time to figure this out. If we could just keep going as we were, avoiding any more "significant" major rivers for a while, maybe I'd have a chance.

Life, meanwhile, went on. The trail led up steep ridges, along roads, and past miles of low stone walls built of rocks cleared from fields. We ran out of water one afternoon. I stopped along a road and filled up at a garage sale. My pack strap broke again. I installed a spare with hardly a second thought. Mosquitoes, gnats, and no-see-ums attacked in swarms. We waved them away with bandanas during the day and avoided them at night by retreating to our tent. When we could stand them no longer, I hitchhiked to a nearby town to replenish our bug lotion supply.

"Dad blew his mind on repellent," Kyra wrote in her log. "What will we do with five different kinds?"

At Raymond Torrey Shelter, Kyra dove inside the tent as soon as I'd put it up.

"Ha, ha, can't get me you dumb bugs!" she taunted, zipping the netting tight.

We no longer used the open shelters because of the bugs. If we found one at all, we pitched our tent near it, sometimes in it. That evening Kyra rolled out the bags and stayed inside, nodding off to sleep before dinner.

Another hiker arrived and pitched his tent near ours. I recognized the tall, thin young man from times we'd seen him the past few days. He introduced himself as Rainer Ober.

"Have you been on the trail long?" Jerri asked. "We've seen a lot of you lately."

"I started in Delaware Water Gap," he replied; "a couple weeks ago — July 10, I guess."

"That's when we were there," I said. "We'd just pulled in."

"You've been taking your time, I gather," said Jerri.

"Yeah," Rainer went on. "I'm not in any rush. I get up late and mosey along until I feel like quitting. I usually sit out rainstorms in my tent."

"Sounds wonderful," said Jerri.

"Well, not always. I don't have a guidebook and I'm never sure of where I am. I've gotten lost a couple times."

"Off the trail, you mean," she kidded. "AT hikers never get lost."

230

"I remember seeing your tent," I said. "We walked past it in the rain at Lake Tiorati Circle. You had a radio going."

"Yeah, I was listening for the weather. Rained like crazy later. I woke up in the middle of the night to find a river running right through the tent!"

"You'll have plenty of rain if you're near us," Jerri added.

"I was wondering ... " he said hesitantly. "Would you mind if I walked with you a while? I've been alone for two weeks and could use a little company."

"How far are you going?" Jerri asked.

"Wherever I get in another week."

"We walk rather slow," I said. "Anywhere from zero to sixteen miles a day. You might find us pretty boring."

"That's fine," he said. "At least you know where you're going." Thus our band of three became four next morning, heading north through the final miles of New York.

We met two hikers coming our way as we took on water barely a mile out of camp. Richard Judy and Doug Hellie, they said as introduction — southbound from Mount Katahdin. Doug was headed for the Pennsylvania line. Richard led the summer's pack of Maine-to-Georgia hikers.

"I guess we can all go home now," I said. "Together, we've hiked the whole trail."

We talked a while, sharing news about the trail, but everyone seemed ill-at-ease. We each had information of use to the other; no one wanted to start the exchange. They told a story or two. So did we. I shuffled my feet, wondering what to say next.

"How were the White Mountains," I finally asked, "and the Mahoosucs?" Those were the trouble spots — 125 consecutive miles of rugged mountains in New Hampshire and Maine.

"Don't be worried," Richard said. "You'll get through them just fine. It's a beautiful part of the trip."

"Will the scenery improve soon?" Jerri asked. "We can't exactly recommend what we've just been over."

"There's nice country just ahead of you," he said. "You're almost out of the bad stuff."

"What about the rocks?" Doug asked.

"New York and New Jersey are rocky in places," I replied, "and the eastern third of Pennsylvania. But it's not as awful as everyone says."

"And the Stekoahs?" asked Richard.

"You shouldn't have any trouble. Half that section has been rerouted over graded trails and the rest isn't all that bad."

We traded more notes, each assuring the other that everything would be fine, there was nothing to be concerned about, and went our respective ways.

How quickly we forget. How quickly the pain of yesterday's struggle pales before today's. The hundred miles of rocky trail had been terrible and we'd found the Stekoahs especially hard. Why was *I* painting such a rosy picture all of a sudden? Well, these fellows were seasoned, fast-moving hikers. They wouldn't have the problems we'd had. Nor would they want to admit it if they did — especially knowing a through-hiking ten-year-old girl had been there before them.

One of the hikers we'd asked about was Carl Windle. His entries had grown old in registers and we could only learn more from someone who'd met him farther north. The news from Doug and Richard fit the pattern, the continuing saga of Carl's hard-luck hike.

Crossing the Bear Mountain Bridge, Carl had walked back past the toll booth to give someone post cards to mail and had been charged toll twice. He'd followed twenty-five miles of detours at flooded Clarendon Gorge in Vermont, just to get past one raging stream. Diarrhea plagued him for eight days in New York and New Jersey. In the White Mountains he'd run out of food. Where one might hope to find exhilaration and freedom in the wilds, more often Carl had felt fever, low spirits, and exhaustion. We wondered what drove him on.

The final chapter of Carl's story was being played that very moment. He climbed Mount Katahdin that morning of July 24, climbed to the end of his 101-day hike of the Appalachian Trail.

"It was no easy trip by any means," he wrote. "I suffered hardships, but rather than quit, I continued on. I found out what I was made of."

Rainer walked at the rear as we climbed Shenandoah Mountain and descended to cross the Taconic State Parkway. We followed crisp, white blazes through forests of maple and oak, and at one point passed through a maple sap gathering operation. I found it not at all like pictures I'd seen.

Collecting sap for syrup meant hardy New Englanders to me, a horse-drawn wooden sleigh and a fresh blanket of snow. I pictured sap dribbling from trees into buckets hung on pegs. I saw a tall, slender man — red bill cap with the earflaps down, red-and-black-checked lumberjack shirt — gathering buckets and replacing them. Icy puffs of breath from horse and man hung on still, cold air. Bright sun brought sparkle to the bluest of sky, the whitest of snow. I'd seen it on a Christmas card, no doubt. The process worked slightly different in New York.

Small-diameter tubes ran from each tree and coupled into other tubes that lay along the ground. Sap flowed continuously through them like water through a hose. Small tubes joined larger ones, directing the accumulating output of the forest to a large vat at the end of the line. The boiling and bottling works took over from there.

Another image shattered. Automation had struck again. Tubes in trees would never make it on Christmas cards, I decided. The place looked more like a blood bank.

We covered miles quickly that day, walking territory that varied from wooded ridges and mountaintops with views ("surprisingly fine"), to swamps and orchards of old apple trees. We followed roads past weedy ponds and exclusive summer cottages — *Private-No Trespassing; No Turning in Driveway; This*

Land is My Land! Jerri stopped to identify things — purple loosestrife, Asiatic day flower — and Rainer maintained polite interest. Kyra was catching cold and complained of an earache, yet cheerfully kept up the brisk pace in the company of our new-found friend.

Obtaining water at a mobile home on the outskirts of Holmes, New York, we ended a sixteen-mile day pitching tents in an open field. Weeds grew waist-high and dense. Tent floors puffed up like pillows but mashed down to disappointing lumps. We cooked over a campfire and talked with Rainer until dark.

I heard a faint and faraway sound as I lay awake in the darkness. It grew to a distant rumble that became steadily closer and louder. A train was coming. We'd camped a hundred feet from the tracks.

Rumble became roar as the engine drew near and soon we were awash in sound. The ground shook. The noise engulfed us. I thought for a moment the hurtling train would rampage right through our tent. A whistle shrieked as the engine thundered past, then chattering wheels set up a rhythmic beat. My focus narrowed to that repetitive sound; I could hear and think nothing else.

The noise slowly faded as the last car passed (another whistle blast, faint, far-off), then the train had gone. We were left in the dark and the quiet in a weed patch in Holmes, New York.

Kyra woke up crying. Her ear ached and she couldn't get back to sleep.

"What's wrong?" Rainer asked, getting up.

"Her ear still hurts," Jerri said. "The train woke her and probably made it worse."

"Maybe some oil would help," he said with concern.

"It might."

"I never heard of that," I said.

"It eases the pressure sometimes," Jerri said. "Will you get it from the pack?"

I got the pack from the tree.

"It's cold," Kyra shuddered as Jerri dripped cooking oil into her ear. "And it gurgles!" But she fell asleep soon after and by morning the pain was gone.

Adding Rainer to our party gave everyone's spirits a boost. But he was a quiet sort, and though he'd followed us patiently for a day, stopping when we stopped, joining conversation when there was any, we'd learned almost nothing about him. He lived in Queens, New York, he'd said, but that was about all. Jerri began to inquire.

"What's it like in Queens?" she said.

"City," he replied. "I have an apartment there."

"Do you like it?"

"It's okay."

"What brings you to the AT?"

"I like to get away from the city sometimes. Getting out to the mountains and lakes and woods is good once in a while."

"What do you do?"

"I repair oil-burners and furnaces. Sometimes I'm pretty busy. Other times there's nothing much going on."

"Like now, I suppose."

"Yeah. But there'll be work when I get back."

"Your name sounds a bit German," I said.

"It is," he went on, "but Ober isn't my real name. It's much longer. I got tired of spelling and pronouncing it for everyone and shortened it to the first four letters."

"No one pronounces our name right, either," Jerri said.

"How far do you think we'll get in a week?" he asked.

"Connecticut tomorrow," I replied. "Maybe to Massachusetts in a week."

"Could I stay with you that long?"

"Of course," Jerri said with a smile.

Kyra seemed pleased as well.

We reached Pawling, New York, at noon. We'd planned to

tent in Edward R. Murrow Municipal Park there and take advantage of hot showers. Arriving at mid-day ruled that out. We spent the afternoon on a shaded park bench waiting for the heat of the day to pass. We retrieved a food box, bought repair and supply items, and made frequent trips for food. Rainer sprawled on the grass to rest as the sun crept across the sky. Kyra bought a puzzle book and doodled for hours. We left again at half-past three when the day seemed to have cooled. The bank thermometer still said 101 degrees. I wondered what it had been before.

Everything went fine for six miles. We walked routine roads, climbed routine ridges, and had everything planned for dusk arrival at Webatuck Shelter in another three miles. Then the trail took an unexpected turn. Fresh blazes led ahead and bushes sported small streamers. Relocation: the trail had been moved off the road. It would still go to the shelter, most likely, but by what devious route was anybody's guess. We followed the winding, backtracking trail for miles with no idea of where we might be.

We reached a dirt road near dark. A concrete outbuilding offered space to sleep four, but needing water, we kept on. We crossed a brook. I suggested we fill up and return to the building. Jerri wanted to check on ahead.

She returned in twenty minutes. She'd found another road, followed it to a house, and negotiated tent space in the owner's yard. It had all the fresh well water we could drink. We hit the trail, arriving at the home of Ben and Phyllis Fischer at nine o'clock. We put up tents in the dark on a manicured lawn, ate a quick dinner, and hung our packs in an apple tree. There would be rain before morning; we battened everything down.

In the morning, in the driving rain, Mrs. Fischer invited us in for breakfast. While we ate and answered questions about our walk, she pointed out items around the house she and her husband had made over the years.

236

The kitchen floor and walls were of hand-made and hand-set tiles of their own design. They had hand-woven the living-room rug. To the drapes they'd added a row of heavy-stitched birds that appeared to stand and strut all through the house. She showed us wall hangings, ceramics, enamels, and pottery. We saw something new and different everywhere we turned.

Jerri could have stayed for a week. Kyra found enough ideas to add several rooms to her house. They admired and discussed each item in such enthusiastic detail that Mrs. Fischer went on to show them more. Cooking and natural foods became the topic. I left them poking through a whole shelf of cookbooks when, noticing the rain had ended, I went outside to pack things to go.

We crossed into New England at noon. A flat, table-sized rock near the summit of Schaghticoke Mountain showed *N.Y.* painted on one side of a white line, *CONN.* on the other.

"That's nine states," I said to Rainer, "and two-thirds of the Appalachian Trail!"

We noted continuing changes in the terrain the next few days. The mountains rose no higher than fourteen hundred feet, yet the climbing came harder and more often. Descents seemed harder still. We scrambled over jutting boulders and precipitous slabs of rock whose slick surfaces presented few good holds. Ledges, they were called. Something new.

We picked our way carefully down the Grand Staircase off Mount Algo, and the steep and spectacular St. Johns Ledges off Calebs Peak, both in one day. Other unnamed and unadvertised descents in between proved even more difficult. This was prelude. The trail would regain four- and five-thousand-foot levels before long and the work of glaciers would figure more prominently in our days.

Forest almost constantly surrounded us. We passed through stands of enormous hemlocks and dark groves of majestic pines. We followed roads through plantations where tall trees stood on either hand in orderly, close-packed rows. The guidebook pointed out birch, white pine, and rolling expanses of mature hardwoods and conifers. It all meant miles of welcome shade, miles of softly sunlit canopy.

I stopped to look, trying to absorb the scenes around me, looking for whatever it was I was supposed to be seeing. Trees and mountains. Was that it? Did it add up to something more? Hello? I'd expected to have more of an answer by now....

The trail led along the Housatonic River Road for several picturesque miles, and through ravines — Dark Entry Ravine, Deans Ravine. Streams passed in a rush over slippery boulders in those sheltered places, cascaded in random leaps down rocky slopes, trickled lazily over stepped stone slabs. The sun shone nearly always, dappling a forest floor that lay deep in pine duff, bursting through overhead branches in visible, slanting rays.

We camped exclusively by tent. Shelters had been grim, unusable caves since early in New Jersey and were oddly spaced. We passed up to four in a day but were rarely close to one at night. Beneath immense, magnificent trees at Cathedral Pines, we sought to spend a night sleeping under pinpoint stars on soft, comfortable ground. Stars gave way to rain clouds at three in the morning. We dove into hastily erected tents.

Our quiet friend became part of the family as days passed. He seemed content to follow at our pace and stop for each day's collection of views, plants, and creatures. He never showed impatience or a desire to break loose and walk ahead. He kidded with Kyra much of the time, always gently and in fun, and helped with camp and cooking chores. Had we looked for a hiking companion, we couldn't have made a better choice.

When Jerri made a subtle effort to polish his camping manners he was initially taken aback. His stone fire rings began to disappear in the mornings, however, and he would leave a spotless camp in exemplary fashion. One evening, Jerri cooked something none of us had ever tried.

238

"What's that?" Rainer cautiously asked.

"Day lily buds," Jerri said. "I picked them this afternoon. Want to try some?"

"Hmmm ... I don't know."

"Here, have a couple. They're better than green beans."

Rainer ate one, then another, then asked for more.

"Tomorrow, let's pick more lilies!" he said, finishing them off.

Rainer built a fire another night and he and I sat around it eating marshmallows as quickly as Kyra could roast them. Jerri had wandered off some time before. Returning at dark, she told how she'd been sitting quietly on a rock some distance away, listing for sounds of the deep woods — fluttering leaves, nightsong of insects, perhaps the delicate leaf-crunch of a scampering squirrel.

A hawk suddenly swept into view, descending with a rush of air through outstretched wings toward a landing on a nearby branch. Spotting Jerri just as it touched down, it instantly resumed flight in one continuous motion.

"Touch and go," Jerri said, "as if it had planned it all along."

Kyra continued to greet mornings grumpily on occasion and at such times I normally left her alone. The guidebook didn't say we *had* to be cheerful, after all, and her spirits would recharge before long. But Rainer took the matter seriously one morning and banished her grumps in half a minute flat.

"Have some of this," he said, offering to share his breakfast.

She took a tentative bite, then dug in with enthusiasm.

"What an improvement!" she said pointedly. "*We* ought to have good things like this."

And while Jerri and I slogged through our usual hay, Kyra and Rainer ate Mountain House scrambled eggs.

Descending Barrack Mountain later, Jerri braked to record another find.

"*Amanita verna*," she said of a white mushroom bursting from the ground. "I've been looking for one of these."

"Is it poisonous?" Rainer asked.

"It's also called 'Destroying Angel,'" I said.

"I see."

Then our friend's hike ended. He was due at work in a couple of days, so at our stop in Salisbury, Connecticut, he inquired about transportation home. He would have to walk six miles to Millerton, New York, and camp another night to catch the morning bus.

Though we'd met Rainer only a week before and still knew little about him, we seemed to linger when it came time to say goodbye.

"I guess we didn't make it to Massachusetts," I said, "but we came within seven miles."

"It was a pretty long walk for me," he replied. He'd covered 210 miles in three weeks of moseying along.

I loaded supplies while Jerri wrote post cards, Kyra worked puzzles while Rainer organized his pack, and we passed nearly three hours in idle conversation on the Post Office lawn. In his pack, Rainer found a packaged breakfast he would no longer need. He insisted we take it.

"Mountain House scrambled eggs," he said with a wink. "It might help Kyra get going some morning."

With just time to reach a campsite before dark, we all finally heaved on packs and went our separate ways. Rainer walked west to Millerton on U.S. 44. We headed north toward Massachusetts on the Appalachian Trail.

CHAPTER 21

An Appointment Kept

But I have promises to keep,
And miles to go before I sleep.
- ROBERT FROST

"ITS MORNING," I said, peering into the tent. "Anybody awake?"

No reply.

Why couldn't people get up? We agree to start early to avoid the heat, then nothing happens. I'd been up an hour, packing what I could. I'd run out of things to do.

"Breakfast time, everybody. C'mon, I want to take down the tent."

Jerri struggled to wake up but repeatedly lost to weariness that had been building for many days. Kyra never even tried.

"Hey, time to get going. You're supposed to be used to this by now." It was July 31, our 133rd day.

"What time is it?" Jerri asked.

"Seven o'clock."

"Leave us alone a while. It's early yet."

"Another clear day out here. It'll be hot before long."

"Go away."

I milled around camp amid growing frustration. We were doing so well: 50 miles in four days, 120 in the last ten. We'd make Katahdin with no problem on that schedule. But we had to keep going, I'd made every accommodation — taking afternoons off on hot days, walking behind at Jerri's pace, stopping for every flower, mushroom, and berry. Why couldn't I have this one favor in return? Why couldn't we leave early without hassle?

"Eight o'clock, Jerri."

"Okay, okay."

Rainer was gone, that was it. Everyone was so polite while he was with us. Now we were back to normal.

"Find the coffee," Jerri said, groping her way out of the tent. "I'm going to need it today."

I grabbed the bottom of Kyra's sleeping bag and dragged her from the tent.

"No, I don't wanna get up!" she protested. "*No hablas Ingles.* You have reached a *dees*connected number!"

"Time for breakfast."

"Not for me — I'm sick of that junk. I want Frosted Mini-Wheats."

"She needs coffee, too," I said to Jerri.

"Quit bothering her and take down the tent. Kyra, eat your hay."

"Yuck."

I took down the tent. Kyra scowled at her granola.

"Out of the bag, young lady. Got to pack it away."

"Grrrrrrr."

"Gee, nice to have everyone so cheerful this morning."

"You're no bargain yourself," Jerri said. "Can't you let us sleep in *one* morning?"

"I thought I had. We've been getting up at six."

"Seven o'clock is *not* sleeping in."

"I want Frosted Mini-Wheats," Kyra said. "This is awful!"

"And I want to get moving before noon!"

"We'll get to Maine," Jerri said. "Take it easy, will you?"

I jammed the bag into its stuff sack and strapped it on the pack. Make it to Maine — by spring, maybe. Didn't anyone understand setting goals and sticking to them?

Jerri finished breakfast and heated water for coffee.

"Is the sewing kit handy?" she asked.

"Why?"

"I want to fix the zipper Kyra ripped out yesterday."

"Do you have to do it now?" I asked, digging into a pack pocket for the 35mm film can of sewing supplies.

"It won't take long. What's with this press, press, press, Gotta-Get-to-Maine? Can't you leave off that?"

"We agreed to get going early, remember? It bothers me to waste time."

"Give us a break now and then. And drinking coffee is not wasting time!"

I finished packing while she mended. We finally left camp after nine o'clock, walking slowly, struggling up the easy slopes of 1,738-foot Lions Head as if it were the tallest mountain in the world.

We put a few miles behind on a stretch of level plateau and good humor gradually returned. Atop Bear Mountain in early afternoon, Kyra and I climbed the face of a forty-foot stone tower. I couldn't get down. This is great, I said to myself. I go through three rock-climbing schools and I can't get down.

I surveyed my situation, convinced myself that I really could move one foot, then one hand, and worked my way to the ground. Kyra made it up and down easily. She charitably refrained from comment.

We descended steeply over ledges into Sages Ravine. The trail followed a brook for a time, meandering among trees that crowded the rocky hollow, flowing past soft, green ferns that stood motionless in still air. We rested at a waterfall. Jerri sat down for another cup of coffee. Kyra and I climbed along the twisting watercourse, noting sun-sparkled colors on smooth, wet rocks and at the bottom of quiet pools.

We entered Massachusetts across the brook and met two women hiking south from Katahdin. We stood talking at the boundary, they with four states complete, we with the same four to go.

More changes: mountains rose above two thousand feet and the forest atop them dwindled to scrub pine. Peaks bunched closer together. The next day brought seven mountains in nine miles with deep gaps between each, just like old times. Bear Mountain faded behind in fog as we crossed Race Mountain (2,365 feet), then both became receding blue mounds as we ascended 2,602-foot Mount Everett. Then came Mount Undine, Mount Bushnell, and Mount Intermediate #1. ("Cross intermediate peaks at 7.9 m. and 8.5 m." the guidebook said.)

There we met the first northbound through-hiker we'd seen since Pennsylvania. He'd started June 5, had experienced near-drought conditions most of the way, and had seen only one hour of rain since Tennessee.

"Get out your rain gear," Jerri said. "You've just met the Lowthers and it rains every time we go to town. We just came from Salisbury — it's definitely due!"

Clouds gathered by the time we traversed the remaining two peaks and descended to a campsite along Jug End Road. Rain began as a sprinkle during dinner and drove us to the tent as it swelled to a pounding torrent. Sheets of water drummed taut walls around us and the roof stretched over our heads. The sound of the nearby stream grew to a roar. It was the fifth storm in three weeks, I noted, paging back through the log. Did we take a wrong turn? Was this North Carolina?

Five AM: time for an early start. Six-mile days and nine-mile days (our previous two) wouldn't cut it; we had to get away early. Six miles of road walking ahead ... a good stretch to

244

finish before the day got too hot. I moved to get up and rain began again, as hard as the night before. I went back to sleep.

Eight o'clock: still raining. At nine I emerged to find the tent awash in a sea of mud. We packed our dirty, soggy belongings and started down Jug End Road at 10:30. Dogs barked at us on Bow Wow Road. We passed wet, abandoned lime kilns on Lime Kiln Road. Kellog Road would be next. Perhaps we'd find breakfast there. It rained. Our boots leaked. My pack strap broke.

"I have this idea," Jerri said.

"What."

"Let's go to town."

We met a fisherman calling it quits and loading gear into a pickup truck. He offered a ride. We took it.

"Been hiking long?" he asked.

"Since March."

"Appalachian Trail, eh? Seen any snakes?"

"One rattler a couple weeks ago," I answered.

"Did you get it?"

"No, we let it be."

"How come?"

"They don't bother us in our home," I said. "We don't bother them in theirs."

Another snake-basher. Why did people feel compelled to kill them? Other hikers' accounts were full of such incidents (Snake! *BASH.* Heh, heh, heh.) in which rattlesnakes, copperheads, or snakes of any kind were manfully dispatched, along with woodchucks, porcupines, and everything but fellow hikers. One hiker said he turned turtles over to give them something to do!

The fisherman took us three miles off the trail to Great Barrington, Massachusetts. We checked into a motel, piled wet clothes on a heap, and added what we were wearing as we each showered. Jerri and Kyra hauled it all to a laundry. With nothing to wear but a motel towel, I stayed in the room.

Sorting through mail we were still carrying, I found a letter from Chuck Downing, a friend in Phoenix. Chuck had given me a Long-Walk Emergency Kit (his business card and a dime) before our departure and we'd received several letters from him since. He'd been thinking of us on a camping trip of his own....

"We challenged nature in the raw by parking the trailer in a campground approximately forty yards from the water faucet, thirty yards from the outhouse, a mile from the general store, and ten yards from three hundred people in a huge recreational vehicle. We sat about the campfire in the evenings coughing from smoke and scratching deerfly bites. Someone asked, 'How do the Lowthers live in the wilderness months on end?' No one knew.

"After three days we had seven hundred pounds of filthy, soggy clothing, miscellaneous cuts, bruises, and blisters, not to mention an organization problem as each of us tried to out-maneuver the others to stay upwind."

Wondering how we'd gone this long without a homicide, he went on to comment on what he considered the most remarkable aspect of our walk — "three people living together for months under conditions allowing few social gimmicks.

"If you are still talking to each other, you have achieved something wonderful and rare and experienced by few."

Interesting. We were still talking to each other, if not always in friendly tones. The problem still remained: Jerri wanted to live each day as it came; I wanted to hike to Maine. We'd each gone to great lengths to suit the other's wishes without giving up too much. Thus a new set of "gimmicks" had arisen: the early start scenario, the skip north and walk south dilemma, pressing on in irresolution.

I wandered the room, trying to think this through. I'd come to the woods for adventure. I'd found it, all right, in mountains to climb, wilderness to see, problems to solve. I'd been apprehensive at first, set on edge by unfamiliar sounds and surroundings. That had gone. I felt at ease now. I'd learned when to get water, where to make camp, how to find the way, how to get along with what we had. And I'd grown strong. I could keep going day after day. Important things. Critical things.

But Jerri had done these things, too, and none of it counted for much with her. They were means, not ends. We'd walked 1,350 miles in 135 days. She could have spent the same time doing five hundred miles, or fifty, or five. Just being there seemed enough for her. Why? I'd walked the same path, viewed the same views. I'd seen the same birds, the same flowers, and heard hundreds of names I could never remember. I kept wanting to go on, to arrive at some place that hour, that day, that week. Jerri seemed content where she was. What was the difference? What did she see that I didn't?

The object was adventure ... to see things, to be on our own for a time. But that was at first. Once I'd realized we could really walk to Maine, other objectives came along. Like achievement, whatever that was worth, and completing what we'd set out to do. Achievement meant little to Jerri. Her goal, as far as I could tell, was to *be* where she happened to be, and to move on when she'd finished. If that was the secret I was looking for, I was missing something. Maybe if I thought more about it, but I had something else to think about now....

Walking south. To complete the trail in a convenient way, to try and meet everyone's wishes, she kept pushing the idea of walking south. Whatever progress I'd made had been derailed. Whatever understanding had begun to awaken was brushed aside by threat of having my trip dismantled. I wasn't ready to give it up. We had come this far, done this well. I had to finish....

I heard a knock at the door.

"Guess what," Jerri said, letting herself in.

"I give up," I said; "the rain quit and the sun came out."

"Right."

"We found a bakery!" said Kyra.

"Tell me about this bakery...."

Tyringham, Massachusetts: we followed the trail along roads and through mucky swamp, over mountains with views of nothing, into a blueberry heath with no blueberries. We walked cushioned, springy path in a dense spruce plantation. Tiny leaks of afternoon light glowed red on tree trunks and bare lower branches, and on a forest floor layered deep in fallen needles. We came to more roads then, looking for a campsite as afternoon waned. Countryside gave way to estates and farms, to cottages and roadside homes, and to Tyringham, Massachusetts. Downtown. The next water and wooded area lay five miles ahead.

"Any rooms or places to camp nearby?" I asked the postmistress, who was also keeper of the general store.

"None that I know of," she said.

"I'd hoped to find something so we wouldn't have to walk after dark to get out of town."

"People have camped across the way a time or two."

I glanced out the window at a stone-faced building across the street. A library. Public property, most likely.

"Thank you," I said.

We pitched our tent under an immense weeping willow just off the library lawn. Cars passed regularly on the town's main road fifty feet away. Occasional pedestrians stopped, glanced our way, and walked on. After dark, a street light shone in our front door. Then rain came, dripping in great, thumping drops from branches overhead. We passed the night undisturbed.

"The dog takes the cat, the dog takes the cat, hi ho the derry oh ..."

Kyra was singing The Farmer in the Dell. I wouldn't have thought it unusual, but it was six-thirty in the morning.

"Are you okay, Kyra?" I asked.

"The cat takes the mouse, the cat takes the mouse ..."

"Amazing."

"Let's go before the library opens," Jerri advised.

'The mouse takes the cheese ..."

"By all means," I replied; "an Early Start!"

We were on our way at 6:45.

'The cheese takes the crackers, the cheese takes the crackers, hi ho the derry oh...."

The trail continued to offer little of interest as it led uphill and down, through brambles and swamps, to the shore of Finerty Pond. We decided to break for lunch there, at a small clearing we could see just ahead. But the clearing was already in use. We emerged from bordering brush and stumbled upon a naked, middle-aged couple who had obviously not expected to be disturbed.

The man lit out on all fours for the bushes. He lay there on the ground, eyes closed and white bottom up, as if doom were about to descend. The woman sat up in confusion, grabbing for clothes and clutching them about her in wads. She glanced desperately around, looking for a place to hide. No one spoke. What does one say? We walked on without a sound, postponing lunch for at least a quarter-mile.

Such encounters were reported by other hikers. Walking after dark in eastern Pennsylvania, Dorothy Laker had unknowingly entered a local lovers' lane:

"It was too late to avoid being seen, so I focused my flashlight on the ground and kept walking. I began flushing lovers from the underbrush like grouse. Young men began hauling young ladies to their feet all around me in the woods. I heard several muttered questions of 'What was that?' as I pressed on, leaving the lovers behind."

We climbed through October Mountain State Forest that afternoon to the top of Bald Top Mountain. Groves of pine, birch, and spruce brought improvement to the scenery, as did views from the summit and from points along the mountain ridge. We walked among bushes thick with ripe chokecherries and reached paved Pittsfield Road at the crest of another rise. A two-story frame home stood nearby. We'd planned to pay a visit there since our very first days of reading about the trail.

I walked up the path through the long front yard. An elderly, white-haired lady sitting on the front porch noticed my approach and stood to greet me.

"I'm *so* glad you could come," she said.

"I'm glad we didn't miss you, Mrs. Hutchinson," I replied. "Had you heard we were on our way?"

"Yes, weeks ago. I thought perhaps you'd passed by."

Mrs. Genevieve Hutchinson had lived beside the Appalachian Trail since before the pathway had become so known. She'd welcomed passing hikers over the years, offering water and occasional tent space in her yard. Each visitor signed her guest book. Her volumes of signatures dated back thirty-five years.

She invited us to join her on the porch. She asked about our hike, about Kyra and each of us in turn, and soon brought the year's register. We paged through familiar names, then each signed it. She drew stars next to each of our entries.

"That means you're hiking the whole trail this year," she said. "If you send me a card when you reach Mount Katahdin, I'll color the stars to show you've finished."

As I gathered our gear to leave, she showed us a birthday card she'd received from the White House. She would be ninety years old in six days.

We felt privileged to meet that grand lady of the Appalachian Trail, and to spend those few minutes visiting on her porch. It was the final summer for hikers to do so. Genevieve Louise Hutchinson's last days came the following February. The news made her parting words especially memorable:

"Share your experiences with others," she said.

I assured her that I would.

CHAPTER 22

Stormy Birthday at Bromley

Thursday's child has far to go.
- ANONYMOUS

THE SIGN HAD BEEN TAKEN DOWN.

NO
SWI
MMIN
G

it had read, the framed, hand-lettered sign we'd seen nailed to a tree when we'd last visited Berry Pond. We'd asked directions then, as we had times before to find the side street leading from Pittsfield, Massachusetts, to the mountaintop pond in Pittsfield State Forest. Berry Pond was well-known for its fields of wild azaleas that bloomed in early June. We'd always arrived in September on our way to somewhere else. Brilliant fall leaves, often shrouded in moody morning fog, made the detour especially worthwhile.

We found the setting pleasant August 6 and 7 as well. Days

continued hot and clear but they passed quickly. We had time to do our work, time to see the woods, time to watch tiny creatures dart about the pond. At evening, the sinking sun set the woods aglow. Bullfrogs and crickets sang in starry darkness as wind swayed the trees. Morning fog, the sun a burning disc clearly outlined, made everything seem as it had been years before. Except for the leaves that hadn't yet turned, and the sign that had been taken down.

We'd rented a van and gathered food needed to walk to Hanover, New Hampshire. That would take fourteen days, including supply stops at Bennington and Wallingford in Vermont. I'd had my boots resoled. Fourteen hundred miles of walking had worn them flat.

I'd also called the Doerings to have down jackets and winter sleeping bags sent to Glencliff, New Hampshire. We would climb into the White Mountains there, just beyond Hanover. With our Rochester friends about to leave on vacation, Jerri thought it wise to get winter gear in the mail. Evenings had already begun to cool. We'd need more than a lightweight summer bag at five thousand feet.

And while shopping, I'd bought Frosted Mini-Wheats. Anything to smooth out mornings was a good investment.

We left Berry Pond August 8, driving once again through fog down the steep mountain road. We dropped Kyra and the packs where we'd left the trail in Dalton, Massachusetts, then returned the truck to U-Haul. The dealer had been less than enthusiastic about the transaction in the first place but was cordial and helpful upon our return. Anxiously so, in fact. His conversation hardly varied from a single word.

"I brought your truck back," I said, turning in keys and contract at the counter.

"Beautiful."

"I gassed it up and checked the oil."

"Beautiful!"

"I backed into a tree and broke one bumper support."

"Beautiful!!"

Perhaps mentioning that I worked at the company's home office made him ill-at-ease.

The way led steeply up along a rutted road to the top of Jones Nose and across twin summits of Saddle Ball Mountain. We negotiated a ridge-top bog among spruce and balsam trees, walking on a corduroy footway of logs. Jerri added bead lily and turtlehead to her flower observations. At the end of seven uphill miles, we stood atop 3,491-foot Mount Greylock. "Extraordinary views" were extra ordinary, lost in the haze of a sticky-hot summer day. Even the mountain's stone memorial tower offered little of interest. It had been dismantled for reconstruction and lay in pieces on the ground.

We crossed two more peaks in the Greylock State Reservation and made our way down Mount Williams. Near the bottom, a day's worth of altitude lost behind in just over an hour, we came to a fork in the trail. White blazes led two different ways. The right-hand route looked newer so we took it and camped near a creek a short distance on.

"Which way?" Kyra asked next morning. "New trail or old?"

"The new way," I said. "It'll meet the other trail somewhere."

Fresh-cut path wound through mixed forest for a mile and a half, then dead-ended in a grove of spruce. Footway, blazes, cleared walkway and all ended as though the trail crew had thought better of the whole idea and gone home.

"We're out of trail," Jerri said. "Now what — go back?"

"Not yet, there's water running ahead."

Pushing on, I reached a concrete retaining wall. I climbed it and looked out on a large, misty lake, its surrounding trees and distant mountains mere suggestions of color in morning haze. A red-roofed cylindrical tower stood near the water's edge.

"There's some kind of tower there ..." I paged ahead in the guide.

"Yeah, this is Mount Williams Reservoir. The trail is on the other side."

We followed the bank around, found the trail, and went on. Five miles. Uphill. To the Massachusetts state line.

Three states remained: Vermont, 134 miles; New Hampshire, 154 miles; Maine, 277 miles. That meant fifty-seven days to reach "The Big K." It worked out again to October 6, the same answer I'd gotten in Suches our third day and every other time since. We would make it. The trail ahead couldn't be that much different on the average from what we'd already done. We could keep walking north and make it.

The afternoon wore on, insufferably hot as it had been for days. Each uphill grind drained energy and enthusiasm as if someone had pulled the plug. We stopped to rest on the way up each peak, on top, on the way down. At a shelter we lingered over the usual assortment of register entries (Annie was a day ahead; Ken Bailey passed through a month before) but learned nothing vital. The chance to rest a few moments more kept us turning the pages, reading even of those we didn't know.

Finally, after three miles looking for drinkable water on relocated trail (the creeks looked uninvitingly yellow and brown in most cases), we made camp in a hollow near a tiny stream. A telling change in the weather gathered above us.

"Either it's blistering hot or it's raining," I wrote in the log as wind picked up and thunder and lightning closed in. "Some choice."

The Appalachian Trail in Vermont shared its pathway for ninety-five miles with the Long Trail, another well-known and well-traveled route. From the Vermont-Massachusetts border, the two led north through the Green Mountain National Forest, near such towns as Bennington, Manchester, and Wallingford, Vermont, to Sherburne Pass on U.S. Route 4. The Long Trail continued north from that point another 165 miles to the Canadian border. The AT turned east, heading for New Hampshire and Maine. We'd already met several Long Trail hikers. They thought it a rugged, beautiful trip, whether preparation for a longer walk on the Appalachian Trail or a significant adventure in itself.

Our second day of it brought less significance than we'd hoped, however. Rain continued off and on all night. It was off at 5:15 AM when the first two hikers passed in the dark (Early Start!), still off at 6:30 when another came by, and promising to clear when we got going at eight. But it didn't. An intermittent drizzle returned, increased, and achieved certified downpour ranking long before we got into our rain gear. Wet again.

We had to go to Bennington anyway. After nine miles of slogging, dripping, and grumbling, and facing a seven-mile no-camping zone beyond Vermont Highway 9, we elected to hitchhike to Bennington and stay. Our ride left us at the Post Office in the middle of town.

Rooms read the sign on the weather-worn house near the sidewalk pay phone. The man in the phone booth looked like he'd be a while so I went to check it out.

I climbed creaking steps to the porch and knocked, rattling the window in the wooden door. I glanced inside through a slightly parted curtain. Parchment-yellow light glowed through a drawn shade in a distant room. A shadowy table and part of a cushioned chair were visible through a doorway. A dimly outlined banister told of steps leading upstairs. No one answered. I knocked again.

Movement. A slender shape seemed to flow down darkened stairs. A hand drew the curtain briefly back. Regarding me from the shadows, I saw the long, thin face of a fragile old woman. Straight, stringy hair hung limply to her shoulders and beyond. The door opened slightly. Expressionless, she stared at me, saying nothing.

"Um, I noticed your sign here," I said. "Do you have rooms available?"

Had she answered, "The professor is expecting you, this way ..." I would not have been surprised. But she said nothing. She only stared and slowly shook her head from side to side.

"Thanks," I said, relieved. I hurried back to the phone booth.

I called the motels: all full. The hotel: too expensive. Working through a list of tourist homes, I found them booked solid as well.

"One listing left," I told Jerri. The Molly Stark Inn had one room and would hold it until six o'clock.

"Eleven dollars, and we have to be there in half an hour."

"Where is it?" Jerri asked.

"Beats me. I don't even know how to get back to the trail."

"Call a cab."

I called a cab. We arrived just as the proprietor was removing *No* from the *No Vacancy* sign.

Beyond Bennington the trail led along gravel roads toward Glastenbury Mountain, 3,748 feet. We climbed through hardwood forest that merged with spruce as we ascended. We hiked in dry clothes once again, but not for long. Within sight of shelter, rain cut loose and drenched us even as we dashed for the protecting eaves.

A group of eleven boys wearing a rainbow assortment of plastic ponchos followed close behind. Some joined us inside; others stood about in the rain. One said they were headed for Kid Gore Shelter.

"So are we," I said. The shelter, four miles on, held eight.

"We'll have to have it," said another. "We didn't bring tents."

"I thought Boy Scouts always came prepared," I said, my contempt a little obvious.

"We're not Boy Scouts."

"Oh," I said; "that explains it." No one replied.

Hours of rain and sloppy trail later we found them occupying the shelter, wet gear everywhere, no space remaining. We went on to smaller Caughnawaga Shelter where three campers graciously made room. It was the first shelter we'd used in three hundred miles.

The condition of the trail gradually convinced me that rain had turned the whole state of Vermont to mud. The path led continually through puddles along ridgetops and through knee-deep oozing wallows below. A chorus of splashes and slurping, sucking sounds accompanied us wherever we went. With rain every two or three days, and wet underbrush and dripping forest in between, it seemed like it might be years before we or anything else dried out.

Beavers got into the act as well. Their damming of creeks formed ponds which frequently engulfed the trail. Looping relocations led us around older ones; we avoided more recent invasions on squooshy routes of our own.

"The worst mudhole in the state is between here and Bourn Pond," one of the caretakers at Stratton Pond told us. "Once you're through that, the rest isn't so bad."

We had no trouble finding it. The trail sank into a bog of yellowish slime within a mile or so and threatened to gobble us up, packs and all. A log footway led safely around the soup, however, and except for improvisation in areas where logs had sunk into the murky depths, our crossing was uneventful. Other less-publicized stretches, described blithely as "continue ahead," made for extremely slow going as we jumped from rock to slick, muddy rock, and teetered on logs and sticks to make our way through the muck. Deep, water-filled footprints showed where others had slogged on through, even where a stream flowed right in the trail. We slipped and fell on occasion, splashing and slopping ourselves and each other.

A wooden trail sign we found one afternoon summed it all up. *The Long Trail*, it said, to which someone had added, "The longest river in Vermont."

We spent our 146th night in South Bourn Pond Shelter.

"Aha, the famous Family," the caretaker declared when we arrived. "I wondered when you'd get here."

"A soggy family, I'm afraid," Jerri replied.

Night brought a raccoon prowling the premises and an army of mice that scampered over everything. Familiar sounds ... sounds that were part of our lives after 146 days. In 1955, at age sixty-seven, Grandma Gatewood had walked the entire AT in that length of time. Two years later she'd done it again in 142 days. Our trip had definitely grown long ... and nights had definitely grown cool for a summer bag. I huddled closer to Kyra for warmth.

Then it rained. After a tour of Bourn Pond, a pond with character for a change (weeds, lily pads, beaver lodges, forested islands), after a restful walk through birch forest and the first good views in days, another drizzle began.

"Not again," Jerri groaned. "We're turning into prunes!"

"It has been rather damp lately," I observed.

"Damp?" she said. "I wouldn't go *that* far. Not unless you think seven major storms in a month is *damp!*"

"Seven, huh. Does that count this one?"

"No, it's not major yet."

"When does major happen?"

"In an hour or when my boots leak."

"When my pigtails drip," added Kyra.

"Last night was full moon," Jerri went on. "We might as well count it now."

"Our boots leak all the time in this mud-wallow," I said. "You'll need a new definition."

"I know major when I see it, and I'm tired of it I want you to know!"

"You must be if you're keeping track. That's my job."

"You don't keep track of the right things."

Crossing Vermont Highway 11, we found deserted Bromley Cabin in mid-afternoon and ducked inside.

"Are we going on or staying here?" Kyra asked.

"I don't know," said Jerri. "Ask the tour guide."

"It doesn't look good," I said. "The next shelter is three or four hours away. We'd get there after dark, in the rain."

"We're staying," they both said at once. Rain gear, boots, and wet clothes soon hung everywhere.

Three southbound hikers arrived.

"What's it like ahead?" I asked.

"Wet," one said.

"Crowded," said another. "The next shelter will be full if you're thinking of going on."

Rain drummed the cabin roof. No, I told them, we weren't going on. We would bake a cake instead. The next day, August 15, was my birthday.

Rain: I went to sleep to rain; I woke to rain. Glum and disappointed, I stared out the cabin window next morning at rain. It was major, all right, number eight in a month, falling harder than ever. We hadn't even counted smaller showers in between. I was tired of rain. I took down the packs to get ready for another day.

Raining on my birthday yet. The universe was not being kind. Rain gear was still wet from the day before and spotted with mildew like the packs and tent. It hardly seemed to matter whether we wore it or not. Our clothes clung lately with a dampness that wouldn't go away.

The three hikers with us stared solemnly out windows. Jerri and Kyra slept. I got out breakfast things.

Three-fourths of the way. We'd walked almost three-fourths of the muddy trail that passed outside the door. Only 520 miles remained to Mount Katahdin, to the end of our long walk. That was significant. We should celebrate the milestone, along with my birthday. But it rained. At least we were inside, in a four-walled cabin with a stove and a roof that didn't leak. Six of us jammed bunks for four.

Getting time to go. I set breakfast within Jerri's and Kyra's reach and woke them. Rain drummed the roof, the windows, the trees just outside. Major. It hadn't let up all night. The trail *would* be a river soon. I stuffed things in the pack, preparing to depart.

"Time to get up and ready, Jerri," I said. "Looks like we can make Lost Pond today."

"I'm not going."

"What?..."

"You heard me," she said. *"I'm not going."*

CHAPTER 23

The Pattern Changes

*What could I say to you that would be of value,
except that perhaps you seek too much, that as
a result of your seeking you cannot find.*
                                              - HERMANN HESSE

"NOT GOING," I said. "In the rain? Today? Ever?"

"I'm not leaving this warm bag and dry cabin just to get wet," Jerri answered.

"It's grim out there, all right. Maybe it'll let up."

"I don't care what it does."

I walked to the window, wondering what to say.

"We ought to do a few miles today," I ventured. "Lost Pond is thirteen, but Griffith Lake is only nine."

"Nope."

"What do we do? Rot in this cabin all day?"

"Maybe, but I'm not going on in the rain."

Kyra looked expectantly between the two of us. The three other hikers gave us nervous glances and busied themselves with breakfast.

"I'm sick of rain, too," I continued, "but how else will we get

261

anywhere? We didn't quit every time it rained or snowed in North Carolina."

"I realize that," she said firmly, "but I've had enough."

I walked again to the window. Rain had not slackened.

"We could use the time to skip ahead," she said after a while.

"I don't want to do that."

"Yes, I know, and we've missed a number of good chances as a result."

"There's no need to. We're doing fine. Ten-mile days will get us there in plenty of time."

"We aren't doing fine. We're walking in day after day of rain." She got out of her bag and sat at the table for breakfast.

"Where are the maps?" she finally asked.

I tossed her maps of New Hampshire and Vermont.

"Skip ahead where, Katahdin?" I said. "We don't have the Maine information."

"No, to the White Mountains. You're worried about getting snowed in up north. Let's do the tough stuff there now, going north, and take it easy."

The others, packing their packs, looked to be groping for something to say.

"That's a hundred thirty-some miles from here," I said, checking the book. "There's no reason to skip that much trail. Unbroken road walking was one thing. Rain: no."

"We won't *skip* it. We'll come back after Katahdin and walk it in the fall. Trees should be gorgeous here by then."

A hint of relief showed on Kyra's face and she began to pack.

"What makes you think weather will improve farther north?"

"It can't be any worse. Besides, we'll gain time to wait out storms instead of having to push on."

"Going north, huh," I said. "How?"

"There's a town just down the road," one of the other hikers pitched in. "You could hitch a ride from there, or get a bus."

"Yeah," said another, "we're going there, too, to go home."

262

"How long have you been out?" Jerri asked.

"This is our third day and it's rained the whole time. We're going back to New York."

"What about the stuff in the mail?" I asked.

"The Leapfrog Box is in Hanover," Jerri said. "We can go there today and get whatever food we'll need. The winter gear is in Glencliff. We can start the Whites there tomorrow. That leaves a box in Wallingford — we'll call the Post Office and have that one forwarded somewhere."

"You have all the answers," I grumped. "It sounds like you planned this all along."

"No!" she bristled. "I'm trying to save this adventure and put some fun back into it. It may be our last chance!"

I looked around at a roomful of eyes meeting mine.

"Okay," I said. "Let's go to town."

The town just down the road was Manchester Center. We hitched a ride there in short order, bought bus tickets to White River Junction, Vermont ("Just across the river from Hanover," the agent said), and spent the hours till departure taking in the town's sights — the bakery, for example, and the grocery store. I called the Wallingford Post Office to have our box sent on. The postmaster had another idea.

"The bus goes right past our door," he said. "Ask the driver to stop. I'll have your mail ready and you can run in and get it."

The bus driver told me otherwise. That wasn't a scheduled stop and he was already twenty minutes behind. I said nothing further and we took seats near the front of the bus.

We pulled out of town at 2:45 PM heading north on U.S. Route 7. I watched out rain-streaked windows as Manchester Center slipped quickly by. I wondered whether I'd ever see the place again, whether we would really come back and finish. And if so, what would be the thrill of ending our two-thousand-mile walk not on Katahdin, not on The Big K, not even in Maine, but in some dumpy cabin in the woods. Bromley Cabin. The

Big B. I nearly laughed right out loud. Now we'd be headed for The Big B. Jeez.

The bus slowed as it passed the Wallingford Post Office and stopped at the next intersection. The traffic light was red. I saw the driver reach to open the door.

"Okay," he said to me, "the Post Office is back a few doors on the right. Better make it quick."

I was gone. I said hello in the Post Office, received a stack of packages and mail, and dashed out the door. The light was green and the bus was moving. I caught it across the intersection and jumped through the open door.

"Thank you, sir!" I said to the driver.

"Oh, good," Jerri said. "This saves a lot of trouble."

"We're getting these town stops down," I observed. "Thirty seconds, maybe less. Not bad."

White River Junction: across the river from Hanover, New Hampshire, all right, but about six miles downstream. A woman we met on the bus offered us a lift. Soon Jerri and Kyra and I, packs on our backs and "What now?" looks on our faces, stood on a crowded sidewalk in front of Hopkins Center at Dartmouth College in Hanover. There was a place for AT hikers to stay somewhere on campus. I only had to figure out where.

I found the Dartmouth Outing Club office and got directions to The Tabard, a fraternity house a few blocks away. I checked the hikers' register as I left and noted we'd have company. Charley had signed in. Vigilant note-taker Charley, joining us just like the last time we'd skipped ahead. I could hear the conversation already:

"Oh, we'll do this section after Katahdin."

"Right, Mic. Sure."

Summer residents of The Tabard had turned a large front room over to hikers. It contained the old, overstuffed chairs and couches one expected of such places, plus a few aging tables and lamps. Guests obviously slept on the floor. Back-

264

packs leaned against walls around the room but no one was there. We cleaned up, left our packs, and headed out to dinner.

"Would two large pizzas be enough for three people?" I asked the tall waitress who stopped at our table.

"Well, *I* think so," she said, wide-eyed.

We ordered two large pizzas and beer. Some time later, the waitress collected two empty pans without comment.

Back at The Tabard, Jerri explained it all to Charley.

"Hitchhiking again, I see," he said.

"We took a bus to catch up and find out how everyone was doing," she told him. "Without through-hikers roaring by toward Katahdin every day, we got lonely."

"Sure," Charley said, rolling his eyes.

"Oh, we'll come back and do every inch of this section, don't worry about that."

"Right," he said, but he was laughing along with the joke by then, apparently unconcerned whether we walked, rode, or flew the Appalachian Trail.

"Has anyone here come south?" I asked.

One of the half-dozen hikers in the room had. Tracing the route on a map, he described each section of White Mountain trail. Within half an hour we'd planned our next hundred miles.

Everyone bedded down around midnight. I stayed up a while, writing the day's events in my log, explaining the value of jumping ahead. Philosophical stuff. Positive, good-attitude stuff. I didn't believe a word of it.

I phoned the Appalachian Mountain Club next morning and made reservations for White Mountain huts we'd selected. We settled food needs, stripped packs to their lightest weights so far, and by early afternoon were again on our way. There were no buses to Glencliff, New Hampshire. We would have to hitch-hike a quick forty-five miles.

The first ride took us twenty miles. A jeep passed a while later, turned in the road, and came back.

"Where to?" asked the driver, Willis Applebee, getting out to help load things aboard.

"Glencliff, on Vermont 25."

"I'm headed for Haverhill — I'll take you there."

With a broad, friendly smile, the red-shirted construction worker began stowing our packs inside. To make room he pulled a cooler onto the jeep's tailgate.

"Have one," he said, opening it to reveal iced pop and beer. "You look like you've come a long way."

The drive took us north along the Connecticut River. Mr. Applebee spoke in crisp sentences typical of New England folk. He'd lived in the northern woods many years, he said, and his confident manner suggested he knew all about them. He laughed at some of our adventures. He answered questions Jerri posed about things we'd seen. We had followed a frog one night, she said — at least she'd thought it was a frog. It had quacked like a duck. We'd searched along a road with flashlights until we'd found it in a grassy puddle.

"A frog, all right," he said. "Frogs croak; toads trill."

At Haverhill ("Av'rill," he pronounced it) he kept on driving.

"Glencliff is just up the road," he said. "It'll be suppertime soon and you'll want to be on your way."

"Won't you be late getting home?" Jerri asked.

"Oh, no worry there. After all these years, my wife knows I'll be home when I'm ready."

The Glencliff Post Office was closed. I looked around for a place to camp nearby.

"Hello," came a voice behind us. Postmaster Charles Bilyea, thirty-five years on the job in that location, had seen us from the adjacent house where he lived.

"Hold on and I'll open up," he called from a window.

"Any packages for Lowther?" I asked, as he let me into the Post Office.

"Yes, I have one. Let's see ... 'Quiet! Sleeping bags,' it says."

266

"That must be it."

"You'll need a fire permit, too," he said, and he wrote us one.

I pulled winter bags, down jackets, and down longjohns from the box, and stuffed and strapped them to our packs. I mailed the summer bags away.

Ready to go once again, I thanked our rescuers and heaved on my pack. I nearly sank to my knees. Pound after pound I hadn't carried since Virginia threatened to drive me into the ground. Mr. Applebee chuckled at my pained expression.

"Good luck in the White Mountains," he said. And as Mr. Bilyea returned to the meal we'd interrupted, Willis Applebee drove off to suppertime in Av'rill.

We walked the mile and a half to Great Bear Cabin in daylight that remained. The cabin was locked, but the roofed front porch made one of the best shelters we'd found in several states. Looking up through tall surrounding trees, we watched for shooting stars from the Perseid meteor shower in a patch of night sky, then went to sleep in downy comfort on the wood plank porch. And it did not rain. It hadn't rained all day.

Mount Moosilauke rose to 4,180 feet. We'd been warming up to such elevations through Vermont but our leap ahead had cut that process short. We started our 150th day prepared for the worst. It turned out to be no problem at all.

We followed an old wood road for two and a half miles through forest at the mountain's base. Another road took over from there. Trees grew ever shorter as we ascended, diminishing to sparse clumps of scrubby, wind-flattened pine and finally disappearing altogether. Beyond tree line we crossed barren, rocky ground. We reached the boulder-strewn summit at noon.

We took in hazy views, ate our panoramic lunch, and declared it all worthwhile. No sweat, I thought. Nothing to it. What was so tough about the White Mountains? Then it came time to climb down.

The going became steep, muddy, and slow almost at once.

We'd allowed plenty of time for the three-mile descent, but we soon knew we had little to spare. We slipped in the mud, slid on the scree, and teetered across slides of small stones. Steps down sent us surging forward. At times we had to grab or crash into trees to prevent a downward plunge. As the way grew steeper, I thought we would soon be looking and climbing straight down.

A group of seven boys caught up with as we worked our way along. They knew we were headed for Beaver Brook Shelter. So were they.

"Your trail goes that way," said one, directing us down a spurious side trail.

"No, thanks," Jerri said. "The one we're on has been working just fine."

We moved ahead as they stopped to rest, then they caught up again. An unstated race developed. Kyra, not to be outdistanced by mere boys, pushed into the lead.

The way became impossibly steep. It dropped over rock ledges, down eroded washes, past plunging cascades. It slithered through mud and slid down banks of loose dirt. Log ladders had been built into nearly vertical sections. With three or four steps missing from some, they did little more than point the way. We held onto rocks and grabbed branches and vines to ease our way down.

The boys followed as fast as they dared. They jumped from rock to rock and fell as rocks tipped and rolled. Some clung to tree roots to negotiate steep drop-offs. Others slid on the seat of their pants. They ran, panted, tripped, stumbled, and got in each other's way.

Kyra raced recklessly ahead. She jumped steep slopes and hurtled down long dirt slides. She deftly dodged rocks and trees and never stopped, hesitated, or looked back. Shelter lay just ahead. Kyra plunged forward at a dead run. Seven grim-faced, out-of-breath boys swarmed steadily behind. We lost sight of

Kyra. We lost sight of the boys. Only rocks and huge trees remained, and a trail that plummeted down.

Breaking into a clearing at last, we looked ahead into the open front of the shelter. There sat Kyra, smiling as she chatted with another hiker. Her pursuers milled around outside. Jerri and I filed in; the Moosilauke Seven put up their tents.

More people arrived, all walking in from Highway 112 through Kinsman Notch two-tenths of a mile away. Single hikers came, campers by threes and fours, an entire church group. They spread sleeping bags on the ground and pitched tents, tarps, and sheets of Visqueen for shelter in ever-widening circles around us. It looked like Opera in the Park and we were on stage. A babble of excited voices communed with nature by the hour, engulfing us in a tide of "Groovy," and "Oh, wow!" It was Shenandoah all over again in the White Mountains on Friday night.

The church group, twenty of them, started singing. "Jesus Loves Me." Spare me, please. "We Shall Gather at the River." Give me a break. They sang till I thought I'd go back up the mountain. And evening passed into night, and for a second day it did not rain.

When rain did come, turning the trail to familiar oozing slop, we felt almost thrust back to the day we'd fled Vermont. Almost ... except that hiking in New Hampshire seemed different. Storms came and went quickly and with little warning. Rain lasted an hour, perhaps, or half a day, instead of becoming part of one's lifestyle. Mountains were higher, steeper, more rugged. Climbing them felt again like strenuous ascents of earlier days on the trail. On summits, when we stood at viewpoints or sat on edges of sheer cliffs, we looked out over slashing ravines and miles of unbroken forest. Row upon row of mountains stretched before us, each appearing still higher, still steeper, still more rugged.

In gaps we found brooks that widened into clear green pools

and bubbled down frothy cascades. We passed isolated ponds, marshy and dotted with water lilies. We looked up at soaring cliffs of glacially polished stone. Hiking up steep trail, we had but to turn around at times to see the vastness of what we were leaving behind: blue sky and blue-green carpets of forest; mountains that looked jagged even in the distance. We knew more of the same lay just ahead.

And all the climbing, all the straining to reach those pinnacles to see where we were going and where we had been — it all seemed worth it. Worth seeing, worth struggling for. It was different, somehow, than I'd felt before. So different, such a change even from Vermont, that I could tell we'd left something out. The continuity had been broken. The pieces did not fit. Had we skipped a hundred miles of Pennsylvania, we might have never noticed. But there, in the north, I could tell.

Maybe this was it. The trail had been flat and dull so long, at least compared to this. Maybe spectacular scenes were what it took ... because I didn't want to hurry there. I wanted to stay, to see, to understand. Pieces to a puzzle ... important ones....

We reached Lonesome Lake in late afternoon August 19. Our plan showed us reaching Liberty Camp yet that day but it lay five miles ahead and up another mountain. We wouldn't have a chance, I figured. Though scenic, stupendous, inspiring, and all that, the going in those parts was slow. We headed down the path to Lonesome Lake Hut, one of several mountain inns run by the Appalachian Mountain Club, to ask about staying.

"Liberty Camp?" said the young lady in charge. "I think you should give it a try. The first three miles are flat to U.S. 3, and the next two aren't all that bad."

Should I mention, I wondered, that we might be somewhat tired after riding roller-coaster peaks all day? Maybe not. The frail looking youngster probably packed in hundred-pound loads before breakfast.

"We've already had a pretty hard day," Jerri said.

"Well, it looks like good weather tomorrow for the peaks beyond Liberty if you can get there. You have three hours till dark, you know."

We took her advice and went on, reaching the road in slightly more than an hour.

"You have some rough hiking ahead of you," a gentleman day-hiker volunteered as we met him a while later.

"We've done four miles since four o'clock," Jerri said. "We should have enough time."

The man looked at his watch in surprise and stared after us as we climbed out of sight. It was 5:45.

Farther along we found two teenage boys slumped beside the trail, gasping for breath.

"I didn't know I was in such bad shape," I heard one say. We passed by and never broke stride.

A full hour of light remained as we finished the day's eleventh mile and walked into Liberty Camp. There was no shelter there anymore, the caretaker said, but we'd find room on tent platforms a short way on. Wooden platforms, accommodating two tents each, had been built among the trees over rocky, sloping ground to reduce campers' impact. Most were already full. Noting a lone green tent on one, I hopped aboard.

"Don't bother with your tent," the occupant, Paul Cassidy, told us. "I'm sleeping out tonight. You can use mine." We did.

We climbed Little Haystack Mountain next morning, rising above trees again and following a narrow ridge toward Mount Lincoln. Lichen-crusted rocks protruded at random on slopes falling steeply away to either side. Patchy mats of green covered open ground. Scrub pine a few inches high grew in hollows and the lee of large rocks. Clumps of moss spread out in irregular mounds. We found mountain avens, yellow buttercup-like flowers several inches high, along with alpine cranberry and diapensia, white blossoms that rose on stems from tangles of tiny leaves.

The trail followed the center of the ridge — a sandy, rocky path through scattered green. One could see it crossing peaks in the distance, appearing only wide enough in places for hikers to pass single file.

The weather changed as we walked. A world of sunlit peaks and enchanting vistas one minute turned to solid white the next. As if manufactured on the spot, a cloud appeared and cold winds drove it toward us. Mount Lincoln vanished. The path led forward into nothing. We could see barely ten feet except where sags in the trail took us below the swirling cloud.

We climbed 5,108-foot Mount Lincoln, saw nothing, then walked another mile of treeless, misty trail to Mount Lafayette. Fog alternately parted and gathered. Views materialized and dissolved as if on distant projection screens. We couldn't have been more thrilled. To be swallowed by weather shifting with dramatic suddenness, to have changing moods of those grand peaks demonstrated as if on command, seemed like a bargain and a half.

Traffic on the trail seemed heavy for a Monday. Day-hikers and vacationers continually passed us and appeared as colorful dots on the trail ahead and behind. With spectacular White Mountain scenery on every hand, and with nine Appalachian Mountain Club huts providing lodging and meals at intervals of five to nine miles (though one was thirteen), the region's popularity was understandable. A hiker could stroll from one hut to the next and carry little more than a rain suit, warm clothes, and lunch.

Hardier travelers could camp in shelters or in tenting areas scattered along most of the way. Many through-hikers did so, especially those who thought huts too expensive, or too commercial. But with a reasonable supply of that single most versatile backpacking item, folding money, one could see all the same sights on an uncomplicated schedule with a lot less work.

As a compromise position, and to part with our cash at a

272

more moderate pace, we'd planned stops at only three of the huts. Unlike sightseeing day-pack dawdlers around us, we were not exactly taking our time.

Atop Mount Garfield in late afternoon, we could see our first stop, Galehead Hut, three miles away atop a ridge. The path off the mountain's east slope dropped almost straight down. We had three hours. Slowly, painstakingly, we climbed down plunging rock ledges and up and over ensuing hills. We had to hit the last mile at full throttle to arrive in time for dinner.

Galehead Hut was a sturdy wood building located on the west slope of South Twin Mountain. It had a central, open room used as dining hall and congregation area, and dormitory rooms to the left (men's) and right (women's). Each had rows of bunks stacked up to three high, giving space for thirty-eight guests.

The hut crew consisted of half a dozen young men eighteen to early-twenty years old. They'd been chosen from the annual flood of applicants for the jobs and almost all were back for their second or third year. As "hut boys" — and there were "hut girls" in many of the huts that year — they packed in supplies almost daily in sixty- to one-hundred-pound loads. They maintained facilities and trails and assisted anyone hurt or in need. They also cooked. The lavish, family-style dinner of roast pork and ham served that evening was the equal of any fine hotel.

We talked with the hut master after dinner. Ten-mile days had become a tall order of late, I allowed; perhaps he could help us rearrange our plans. He suggested several changes to give us more time, including five hut stops instead of three and a tent-night at a sixth.

It seemed like a good idea. Spending an extra day or two in those incredible mountains, especially when we'd gained nearly two weeks, was the only logical thing to do.

CHAPTER 24

The Three Most Perfect Days
of Summer

All I could see from where I stood
Was three long mountains and a wood.
- EDNA ST. VINCENT MILLAY

WITH OUR PLANS REDONE, the going got easier. Long ridges and
flat creek-side trails smoothed arduous ups and downs, and we
passed easily along old logging roads. We stopped at every
lookout for the view. I didn't complain; we had plenty of time.

We also had plenty to see. Peaks such as South Twin,
Mount Guyot, and Zealand Mountain gave windows to breathtaking sights, views of an imposing land that rose and fell
around us. We stopped for off-summit scenes as well: cliff
faces, lakes, and streams; flowers, rocks, and huge trees.

The guidebook was very reserved about it all. It dropped a
"fine" or a "splendid" now and then but left most of the spectacle
undescribed. The writers apparently thought we didn't need as
much convincing than in less interesting terrain.

Kyra became quite a hit among the many hikers we met. A

youngster — a girl! — with full pack was curiosity enough, but one that had walked from Georgia proved more than many could resist. We would sometimes find her surrounded by young and old alike, fielding questions with relative ease and telling of things that to her had become second nature.

"How long have you been walking?" asked a man one day, his two young daughters in tow.

"Since March," Kyra answered.

"Where do you get food?" a lady wanted to know. "I've heard some hikers bury it along the trail."

"We don't do that. We go to town every couple hundred miles and pack supply boxes and mail them ahead."

"My, how clever."

"Don't you meet bears and things?" asked a girl, whose pack was a plastic wastebasket strapped to her back.

"Sure. And skunks and raccoons and porcupines. They come through our camp while we're sleeping sometimes."

"Aren't you afraid?"

"They don't bother us much," Kyra answered, nonchalant.

"What about snakes?" asked a lad hiking in sneakers, T-shirt, and shorts.

"I don't like snakes...."

"Does it ever rain?" a young girl asked.

"Does it ever!"

"What do you do then?"

"We just keep going."

"Isn't your pack *heavy?*" asked another girl.

"It's twenty pounds, twenty-five sometimes."

"Mine's less than that and it *hurts!*"

"The straps are loose," Kyra said. "Tighten them like this...."

We also noticed her wide-eyed looks at the hut boys. One, packing supplies up the mountain, carried boxes and crates of food lashed high on a wooden pack frame that towered above his head. I asked what the load weighed. Ninety-six pounds, he replied. Tall, muscular, wearing shorts and no shirt, sun-tanned shoulders held rigid in the pack straps, he moved steadily forward under that load — and passed us by.

Clear weather our first day out of Galehead Hut turned to a bizarre sunset over Ethan Pond. Blotchy, Van Gogh clouds in thick blues and grays wrapped the sun and painted the reflect-ing pond. Cream-colored light leaked around edges of the shift-ing mass and punched through in visible rays.

The next evening brought rain. We cared less about the inconvenience than what it meant for the following day. The trail rose again above tree line less than a mile from where we tented at Mizpah Springs Hut and would stay there for thirteen miles. That stretch crossed the Presidential Range and was what most hikers came to see.

Storms reached their full fury there, rising quickly and with savage violence. Hurricane-force winds and freezing conditions were not unusual, even in summer. A scattering of wooden crosses along the route served as reminder of those who hadn't made it. We'd planned most of three days for those thirteen miles; rain the night before did not bode well.

But morning dawned clear. A Forest Service sign warned of "the worst weather in America," but it all seemed irrelevant in the sunshine. We had food, we had rain gear, and we had enough goose down on board to outfit a flock of Canadian honkers. We were ready, come what may.

Emerging from dwindling trees atop 4,312-foot Mount Clin-ton, it looked like we'd found the top of the world. Rows of mountains, even those in the distance, lay crisply outlined under brilliant blue sky. Feathery clouds hung below us, moving on a wind that still blew strong and cold. The path led on, crossing hulking mountains that rose to five and six thou-sand feet just ahead.

The Appalachian Trail through the Presidentials offered alternatives. A path led around each peak as well as over, for

276

use in escaping bad weather or for times when clouds obscured views from above. Signs marked many other trails as well. The AMC map of the region showed miles of routes wandering afield to nearly every local summit and ravine.

We stuck to the main route, heading over (not around) Mount Eisenhower, Mount Franklin, and Mount Monroe. We checked in at Lakes-of-the-Clouds Hut just after lunch.

"What now?" Kyra asked. Her answer lay dead ahead.

"We're going up there," Jerri said, pointing.

The hut was built at the five-thousand-foot level where the Appalachian Trail began its climb of Mount Washington. The mountain was tallest of the presidential peaks (6,288 feet), rising nearly two thousand feet above tree line. It had originally marked the AT's northern end until a route was mapped across Maine. The severe climate in Mount Washington's upper reaches approximated that of northern Canada. Clouds obscured the summit two days out of three. Clear days were rare, one of the hut boys said. In fact, he couldn't remember an afternoon as nice all summer. Stuffing down jackets and rain gear into an emptied pack, we started for the top.

The trail wound past two rock-bound lakes from which Lakes-of-the-Clouds Hut had taken its name, and past cairns topped with orange-painted rocks to mark the way. A file of hikers in multi-colored outfits stretched ahead of us and behind. We walked easily with one light pack, but we could feel the temperature drop as we climbed higher. On top on that sunny, once-in-a-summer day, the wind chill factor equaled fourteen degrees.

The Mount Washington Cog Railway train, puffing and chugging up three and a half miles of twenty-five percent grade track, disgorged another load of visitors. Men in T-shirts, women in shorts and high heels, stood about or gathered tentatively at lookout points, then gravitated toward the Summit House lunch-room to escape the cold.

In the museum and weather station, we looked over historic Mount Washington artifacts and read of the area's extreme weather. Five hundred fifty-six inches of snow fell there in the winter of 1968. The summit had never been warmer, at least on record, than seventy-one degrees. A 231-mile-an-hour wind, the highest ever measured on Earth, was recorded there in 1934. Gusts more than two hundred miles an hour were not uncommon. Buildings had to be anchored to the ground with heavy cables to keep them from blowing away. And in 125 years of record-keeping, eighty people had died in storms on Mount Washington alone. Some of the weathered wooden crosses stood within minutes of safety.

Clear weather held the next two days. A steady wind made down jackets necessary much of the way but we made no complaint. We were warm, and we could see. Sunlit peaks near and far stood out clearly on every side. The route that could easily have been clouded, stormy, or impassable led distinctly ahead. It was luck beyond expectation.

If anything, terrain in the northern Presidentials became more desolate. Vegetation grew in connecting patches on the slopes but thinned to disappearance toward the summits. The trail passed through gritty, sterile ground or crossed an occasional field of wind-combed brown grass. The predominant feature was rock — rocky fields, jutting rock cliffs, rocks in twisting, jumbled slides that reached down from the peaks. Rocks of odd, angular shape and varied size, wind-pocked, frost-cracked, lichen-blotched, massed in giant mounds to make mountains all their own. We climbed them, threaded through them, and stood atop the highest ones to look around.

And the miles passed quickly. "Always rising, but never steeply," read a plaque bolted to a rock in Edmands Col. Expertly graded trail crossing Mount Clay, Mount Jefferson, and 5,798-foot Mount Adams proved the statement true. Blue sky held as our measured pace took us up and down and the sun lit every step of the way. We walked in silent single file, filled with feelings to match that massive place, feelings heightened knowing it could all turn solid white in minutes, marooning us on a piece of trail that led ten feet forward, ten feet back.

We looked behind us from Mount Madison, past cloudy Mount Washington to peaks in the Franconia Range, and to North and South Kinsman where we'd climbed five days before.

And ahead ... ahead I saw peaks in Maine ... *some of those far peaks were in Maine.*

At Pinkham Notch Camp, set in trees at the two-thousand-foot level on New Hampshire Highway 16, we paid social calls. Four months before we'd met Jonathan Coe in Hot Springs. A couple weeks later we'd talked with Tom Barringer heading south to finish an end-to-end hike he'd begun two years before. Both worked at Pinkham, and both said we'd had fantastic luck; they hadn't seen three such clear days all summer. To have spent them all in the Presidential Range above tree line seemed incredible timing.

"We have an arrangement with the weather," Jerri said. "When it really matters, the weather cooperates. When it doesn't matter, watch out!"

Tom was encouraging about our prospects of finishing the trail.

"You have it made now," he said. "Another three or four hundred miles will be the perfect finish to what you've already done. I hit the end May 29. It's a dynamite feeling!"

"We've been expecting you for weeks," Jonathan told us at dinner in the hut cafeteria. "I've been asking passing through-hikers where you were. They've all said the same thing — 'Oh, they're back there somewhere, but they're coming.'"

Jerri asked where we'd find Adele Joyes who had been with him in North Carolina.

"She's caretaker at Speck Pond in the Mahoosucs, about fifty miles from here," he said. "I'll let her know you're on your way."

Tom stopped by our table at breakfast.

"Headed for Carter today?" he asked.

"Yeah," I said. "What's the trail like?"

"Oh-ho, lotsa fun," he said with a hearty laugh. "Lots of good times on Wildcat Mountain."

Wildcat Mountain could be found among the top three on anyone's list of most difficult spots along the Appalachian Trail. But we'd climbed many mountains by then, perhaps three hundred, and we'd gained and lost 310,000 feet of elevation in the process. I didn't figure one more pile of rock to register as any big surprise.

So it had five separate peaks and rose three thousand feet in less than four miles. We'd done that two or three times some days.

So the weather had lost its benevolence and sent us wind, clouds, and the beginnings of rain. We hadn't walked in rain for eight days. We'd seen steep climbs with all the trimmings before — how could this be anything new?

Thus we started up. The path ascended steeply to be sure, but it all looked quite ordinary to me.

The wind picked up, the air turned cold, the fog thickened and dissipated in its fashion, and all things one expects to happen when climbing came to pass. The rain retreated after a brief shower. Yes, the strain of the steep ascent became more and more noticeable. And the incidence of clutching in rock cracks for hand holds, and of grabbing at trees to pull our way up did seem unusually high. Yet I figured we were doing pretty well. I counted three summits in an hour, oddly named E, D, and C on our large-scale Appalachian Mountain Club map. We'd knock off peak B in no time, then be headed up Wildcat Mountain itself.

I looked again at the map. Funny ... we should have passed a ski lift summit station between peaks E and D. Maybe I hadn't noticed. I climbed on; it couldn't be the wrong trail — there was only one with white blazes. The fog briefly cleared at a lookout point a few moments later. I saw huge peaks towering above. I suddenly realized we were still climbing the first peak, E, and we had a long way to go.

The mountain lived up to its reputation in the hours that followed. We struggled to each windy summit and plunged to gaps in between. The day dragged. We grew tired, sore, and irritable, far more than in many a recent mile. Peak D came quickly after we'd at last reached E, but the route to C added another hour down and up.

Atop another summit and thinking it B, I counted the peaks to go: two. The one we were on didn't even rate mention. Those ahead looked days away. Wind beat at us and rest stops had to be short. And we kept climbing, always climbing.

I saw back to Mount Washington at a point along the way. Clouds blanketed the area, yet a look to those mountains renewed momentarily the good feelings they'd given. Walking had been sunny, scenic, almost easy there. On Wildcat the view looked terrible. Looming, monster peaks demanded we go on yet gave no hint of what for. I remembered something I'd had occasion to note before: *Views of mountains climbed yesterday are more inspiring than views of those to be climbed today.*

Onward: we didn't worry about sudden storms or finding the way on that thickly wooded route, but I was certain we weren't getting anywhere. Carter Notch Hut lay but five and a half miles from Pinkham and I'd thought we would arrive early. I began to doubt we'd make it at all.

At last, peak B. Once more down and up. At least once anyway.

My mind drifted as we plodded along. What kind of endurance test was this? How could one mountain be so hard? Had Swim Bald in the Stekoahs been easier? Had we done the Stekoahs on this same trip? Who would name a mountain Wildcat and let it go at that? Peaks B, C, D, and E? Strictly amateur. Mount Jefferson had a meadow called Monticello Lawn. Mount Adams had one peak named Sam and another John Quincy. Ahead were South Carter, Middle Carter, North Carter and the like. Surely with such theme peaks in the area one could do better than B, C, D, and E!

Polecat Dome came to mind. And Big Fraidycat Knob. The view from C hadn't been bad; how about Mount Magnificat? And by the time one gasped to the top of B, Catatonic Peak might seem just. Much better, I decided. More appropriate names for those concatenated Wildcat Mountains.

Atop the main summit at last, we sat for a well-earned moment of views and afternoon lunch. It did not cheer me. I could see the trail dropping seventeen miles straight down to the hut (though the guidebook thought it closer to 0.8) and the Carter-Moriah Range in the distance looked the equal of what we'd just climbed. With the Mahoosucs beyond that, we wouldn't be taking it easy anytime soon.

After dinner at Carter Notch Hut, Andy, one of the crew, invited the few youngsters present to the kitchen to bake chocolate chip cookies.

"I don't have a recipe." he said. "We'll just have to guess at what goes in them. Any ideas?"

"Flour?" ventured one little girl.

"Got to have flour, all right," Andy said, hauling out a bag of it. "Anything else?"

"Chocolate chips."

"Good *idea!*" he said. "Here they are."

"Sugar?" asked one little boy.

"Right, sugar. Two kinds, I think. Any eggs?"

"Not too many," a small voice said.

"How many is too many?"

"Oh, not more than a dozen."

"We'll get lots of cookies with a dozen eggs," Andy laughed.

"Good, that's what we want," they all agreed. "Lots."

282

"Put some raisins in," said the boy.

"No raisins," I heard Kyra say.

"Oh, nooooo," said Andy. "Not in chocolate chip cookies...."

The results were served hot to the guests. One boy who hadn't participated thought they might be poison and refused. The rest of us thought them delicious.

We climbed in the Carter Range next day on trail that proved alternately difficult, routine, exasperating, beautiful, flat, and hand-over-hand. Fog swirled about us at some points; the way had blown clear at others. We crossed a summit about every mile and a quarter. I noticed again that the day dragged on.

On Middle Carter, grappling our way up a very steep slope, we met a whole family of spruce grouse on the trail. Mother grouse dallied about, casually unconcerned, while seven or eight nearly full-grown chicks moseyed this way and that. Only papa seemed aware of our presence. He threw out his chest, fanned his tail, and strutted about fiercely as if to take us all on. We watched from less than ten feet away and nothing much changed. Mama loitered, the chicks milled, papa put up his dukes. We almost had to shoo them aside to pass.

North Carter, sixth peak in the series, yielded to our efforts as the sun sank behind a ridge. A mile and a half remained to shelter. We started down, easily at first, then probing for footholds and hanging on with our hands. The trail dropped over rock ledges and grew steeper and rougher with every step down. Level trail took over at the bottom and led around Imp Mountain to a four-sided shelter on the mountain's north side. The sky was fast turning dark as we arrived.

Nine hikers let us in and shuffled closer together to make room. They were talking about food. Some had hiked many miles, others had come but a day from town, yet the subject of fast, back-home food pressed uniformly on everyone's mind. The view from the shelter's front door brought it all on. Looking northwest down the ridge in the dark, one could see lights in the distant city of Gorham. Most prominent among them shone McDonald's golden arches. Ecstasies of Big Macs and Quarterpounders invaded every topic. Visions of French fries and thick chocolate shakes took them all by storm. I thought the whole bunch might pack up and head down the mountain right then.

Clouds rolled in and heavy rain began.

"You deserve a break today ..." I heard some one sing.

Winds that would exceed a hundred miles an hour slammed rain and tree branches against creaking shelter walls. We shut and barred the door.

"You deserve a break today ..." the chorus went on.

Campers whose Visqueen tarp disintegrated in the wind came to pound at the door and plead for entry. We let them in.

"You deserve a break today...."

CHAPTER 25

Mahoosuc Notch:
Love It or Leave It

It was a very strenuous trail, very time-consuming, very dangerous, and very hard on gear and the seat of the pants. I recommend it only for the masochistic and those doing penance. I had a horrible time, absolutely awful. At one point I lay down on the rocks and cried.

- Dorothy Laker

I STOOD IN THE DARKENED PHONE BOOTH in Gorham and considered the news. Heavy trucks rumbled by, making it difficult to hear, but I knew I'd made no mistake: our Rochester friends couldn't meet us at Katahdin as planned.

"We're very disappointed," Paul said. "We've looked forward to this vacation for months, but my new job just ruled it out."

"That changes things, all right ..." I said, my voice drifting off, "but maybe it's just as well. We'll have some trail left to do then anyway."

"Oh? How is that?"

"We skipped a piece of Vermont a while ago. Having you drive twelve hundred miles round trip to drop us there was getting to be a lot to ask."

"We would have happily done so," he said, "but as it is, we can't go anywhere. We're still expecting you here when you finish, though."

I told him we'd work out a new plan and let him know. But Mount Katahdin wasn't exactly a stop on the subway; we would have to come up with something good.

I told Jerri the story. Her solution didn't take long.

"We could finish the Mahoosucs," she said; "that's about twenty-four miles. Then we could hitch to Katahdin and complete the AT walking south."

I didn't react.

"With Katahdin behind, we wouldn't have to be concerned about winter."

I nodded.

"It would be easier to get *into* Baxter Park now than *out* in October."

I agreed.

"Crossing the Kennebec will be easier going south," she went on, "and we'll be back here at the end of Maine. Getting to Glencliff to finish Vermont will be less hassle. It makes sense, don't you think?"

Calmly, I said yes.

I had no arguments to counter Jerri's logic. I'd let the fragmentation begin at Bromley; turning around now hardly seemed to matter. It certainly wasn't worth another argument, particularly when Jerri had all the cards. We'd met several "ends to the middle" hikers recently, including one whose chosen mid-point was Worthington's Bakery. None appeared overcome by any great loss.

We would do it. We would walk south. It was okay.

Accordingly, we bought food to last the next thirty-one days, or for all the AT north of Gorham. We loaded supplies in the pack to last to Grafton Notch in Maine, the jump-off point, and sent a box to Millinocket for the trip south from Katahdin. Boxes mailed to Monson, Caratunk, Stratton, and Rangeley in Maine would handle the remaining distance. The only problem was Katahdin to Monson, 112 miles of wilderness without a town.

The guide book mentioned hunting and fishing camps in the region. The telephone operator found a listing for one at West Branch Ponds and put me through. An answer came after many rings, faint, distant, interrupted by scratching static.

"... call back tomorrow ... maybe the line will be better...."

Next day I reached the owner, C. J. Kealiher. I shouted questions and strained over noisy traffic for his replies.

"... arrive before September 15 ... send box to Greenville ... cabin and three meals ... sixteen dollars a person...."

"We'll be there," I yelled. Kealiher's West Branch Ponds Camps lay just off the trail near the middle of the 112 miles.

The trail crossed the Androscoggin River north of Gorham and led steeply up through still, sunlit birch. We reached the ridgecrest after a four-mile climb and walked in silent forest past Dream Lake and on to Moss Pond. The day turned hot, yet quiet trail through suddenly remote surroundings put us again at ease. We were happy to be there, despite the terror of the tales.

The trail through the Mahoosuc Mountains was the last AT section of legendary difficulty. It had five major climbs: Dream Lake, Mount Success, Goose Eye Mountain, Mahoosuc Arm, and Old Speck. Distances between them meant we could do only one per day. Climbing amounted to nine thousand feet up and back down, and the footway tended to be rough, rocky, steep, and ungraded a good part of the way. No one we'd talked to seemed bothered by these things, however. All the attention, all the grim tales focused on but one of the twenty-four miles.

Mahoosuc Notch: a mile of horror, everyone said. We'd be there in three more days.

We descended backwards over granite ledges at Gentian Pond to reach the lean-to at the pond's eastern side. The aging structure had a pitched roof, dug-out dirt floor, and initial-scarred wood walls. And it was full.

Several of the young men inside mentioned they'd been thinking of tenting, however. I stood near the entrance, wife and daughter at my side, all of us looking ragged at the end of the day, and asked when they might decide. They moved out. We moved in. An open shelter in reasonable condition still had the edge on a two-man tent.

We crossed into Maine the next day. The climb of Mount Success took till mid-afternoon, and down the mountain's north slope we found a wooden marker in a clearing astride the state line. It was September 1; we'd been walking 165 days.

I'd expected the crossing to be a moment of excitement, some kind of meaningful passage like exiting Georgia or cross-ing the Susquehanna. We hardly took note. Kyra and I stood near the sign for pictures. Someone, Jerri, I suspect, observed that the Gotta-Get-to-Maine hiker had finally made it. Then we moved on. With many difficult peaks still to be climbed, cele-bration seemed premature.

"Do you know where the shelter is?" a woman called to us from a side trail.

"Down that trail," I said.

"I looked down there. I couldn't find it."

"It's three-tenths of a mile. Maybe you turned around too soon." The four of us found Carlo Col Shelter together.

Pam Ramsey had walked south from Katahdin. She'd been with another woman most of the way but tough going proved more than the friend could bear.

"Mahoosuc Notch did her in, I think," Pam said. "She just couldn't go on after that. I've been walking alone since then."

Pam was slender and about twenty. She had a smiling, animated face and talked with great excitement of things she'd seen. It took her only moments to learn that Jerri's birthday was a few days from her own.

"Oh!" she burst out. "A Pisces doing the whole trail! This is historic. This is *unbelievable*. Pisces *swim*, they don't walk! They dawdle, they don't stick *to* things, and they have *very* tender feet. They certainly don't walk from Georgia to Maine!"

"I bandaged my feet for five hundred miles," Jerri replied.

Mark and Ernie soon arrived. We'd met the two hiker-caver crazies at Gentian Pond and their antics left us weak with laughter. In concert with Pam, stories of the trail north and south quickly plunged Carlo Col into pandemonium. I eventually retired to the woods to catch up four days of my log. I urged Kyra to join me. Hers was even further behind. Maybe a little later, she said. Pretty likely.

Kyra's school project was suffering. Her teacher had asked for a letter once a month with a record of each day's events. Kyra's initial enthusiasm had fallen off and her log dropped a week or two behind on the trail. In town, faced with a letter to write, she would catch it up with the briefest details.

Incredible scenes we'd seen vanished in "We went over Mount So-and-So." Furious storms were reduced to "It rained." I was sure that these, along with entries like "August 29: We spent the whole day in the cabin eating McDonald's hamburgers," were less than what her teacher had in mind.

A new project was developing, however. She'd been making up stories of how various places we passed were named. Occasionally she'd give a recitation.

"One night a person dreamed he was on a flying moose," she'd told us that afternoon, "and they flew over New York City and Boston. They flew to a lake and landed right in the middle. After a swim and lunch at a handy McDonald's, the moose returned the person to his doorstep by nightfall.

"Hiking in the Mahoosucs weeks later, the person came to a lake just like in his dreams, and it even had a moose in it. So he named it Dream Lake."

In similar stories, we learned that Moss Pond was discovered by scuba-diving leprechauns searching for a lake to swim in, one with plenty of soft moss to jump on. They still lived there. Gentian Pond took its name from gentians that grew around its perimeter. They'd been planted years before by a backpacking beaver named Bonnie Gentianseed.

Kyra wrote these stories out at Jerri's urging but wasn't sure she should send them back to school. Neither was I. They were infectious, though. Soon we all began making them up.

Our day on Goose Eye Mountain brought us sights like few others we'd seen. We walked in misted alpine gardens along the mountain's rounded summits, following a path through matted foot-high spruce. We found blueberry, leaves turning red. We passed scatterings of puffy white lichen, cranberry, and Labrador tea.

Weathered slabs of rock protruded along main ridges. Haze hung on the peaks, turning even those nearby to humps of blue and soft outlines of gray. I remembered mountains forested and bald, peaks rocky and brush-grown in our climbs in fourteen states, but none had the moody character of Goose Eye.

We stayed all day, walking side trail to the mountain's 3,860-foot high point on West Peak, then crossing East Peak and a mile-long sag through patchy forest again to another summit to the north. Rain caught us as we descended. We dashed down rocky trail to shelter before damage grew severe.

The register there contained discouraging words. Weekenders had left their usual notes — "Nice place," "Great views!" — but certain through-hikers had gone on the rampage. The Appalachian Mountain Club, rechristened the Appalachian Motel Chain, had apparently done them wrong.

Serious complaining among through-hikers started in

Pennsylvania. We'd all just been "on the trail" till then, grumbling at times about rain, the trail, or the shelters. Marking halfway at the Susquehanna made us all authorities. Rocks and gypsy moths thereafter soon had through-hikers complaining about everything.

The trail was poorly routed and overgrown. Why weren't trail crews cutting brush and painting blazes? Why wasn't someone mapping easier, more scenic routes? Couldn't the ATC do its job?

Shelters were gloomy, trashed, overcrowded. Why weren't they regularly maintained? Couldn't more new ones be built?

Trail in New York and New Jersey was too urban — too many houses, too much walking on roads. Why wasn't something being done?

The guidebook had errors and caused confusion. Couldn't anyone keep that Book of Lies up to date?

And people! Trails and campsites were crowded with ordinary people! Didn't they know through-hikers were the upper class?

Policies of the Appalachian Mountain Club sent career complainers over the edge.

The AMC charged money to camp — seventy-five cents.

Unforgivable.

They told you where to camp — on the platform, partner; that ground cover took a hundred years to grow.

Preposterous!

At times, they said you couldn't camp at all — pay for a night in the hut or pay a fine to the Forest Service.

Outrage!

"Through-gripers" the hut boys called us. Small wonder.

Several northbound hikers had poured out their wrath in the Full Goose Shelter register. Covering the above points in detail, they groused about rules and people who enforced them, and about "bush-leaguers" — non-through-hikers who took up space and got in the way. No one, the grumblers said, would tell them what to do; they would camp where they damn pleased. They seemed consumed by some mission, as if hiking two thousand miles earned them special favors. As if their path to Maine should be smooth, untraveled, and free.

Amid all this turmoil, I thought I was doing pretty well. We'd just had our twelfth consecutive sub-ten-mile day. We'd walked thirty miles the last week. We could still see Mount Washington where we'd been *ten days* before. I should have been on the verge of berserk despair considering fretting I'd done about forward progress. I wasn't. In two days we'd have the hard stuff done. Katahdin would come next, then we could coast. We had it made, Tom Barringer had said, we had it made.

Evening brought ample distraction, in any case. Mark and Ernie joined us and demonstrated caving techniques.

"Here's the great caving jock working up a narrow chimney," Ernie intoned, climbing the shelter's side wall. "He moves calmly, carefully, always keeping three-point contact with the walls. He's completely under control. He sees an opening above (Ernie had reached the roof). He climbs to it and thrusts his head through.

"What does he see? What meets his eyes gazing into this dim cavern where man has supposedly never been? What glory of nature does his lantern reveal? *String!* String leads *everywhere.* It tangles his helmet, his fingers, his arms. Every caver before him has read *Tom Sawyer* and left string to find his way out. It's too much (Ernie hung upside-down from the roof). He can't go on."

Five more hikers arrived with two dogs. Ten people jammed the six-man shelter and the evening got noisier.

Jerri asked why we had such bizarre wedding anniversaries (that day was our twelfth).

And Kyra wrote history, rising to the challenge of that peculiar place:

Why Full Goose Shelter Has
Such an Extraordinary Name

Once there was a goose that lived on Mount Goose
Eye and one night he saw the full moon crying.

"What's the matter?" he asked, and the moon replied,

"I was invited to a party and couldn't go because I
had to be full moon. Could you be full moon for me?"

The goose said, "Sure."

A hiker hiking by the full moon got to the unnamed
shelter and noticed that the moon wasn't a full moon at
all, it was a full goose. He wrote about it in the register.
So, the place was named Full Goose Shelter.

"Ready for the notch tomorrow?" Mark asked.

"Sure," Jerri said. "It sounds different enough to be fun."

"It's a great place," assured Ernie. "We're going to camp at
the entrance tomorrow and spend the whole next day walking
one mile."

We crossed Fulling Mill Mountain in wispy fog next morning
and met a couple who'd spent the night in Mahoosuc Notch.
Their eyes were glazed. They seemed shaken and afraid. It was
their first backpack trip, the lady said in a discouraged voice,
and the trail had been difficult beyond anything they'd imagined. They'd planned to cover twenty miles a day but so far had
been doing only four. They were unsure of the way, uneasy in
unfamiliar territory. They'd run out of water in the Notch but
were reluctant to drink from the creek they camped near. They
looked terrified, as if they'd never again come near the woods
should they find their way out.

We gave them water and explained that creeks were safe for
drinking. They shouldn't worry about low-mileage days, Jerri
told them; the miles they'd walked were among the most difficult on the entire AT. I made adjustments to their pack straps

so their burdens would ride more comfortably, and told them the rest of their journey would seem easy by comparison. They resumed their trek south with sighs of relief. We headed north to the Notch.

Mahoosuc Notch was a sheer-walled ravine cut a thousand feet deep between Mahoosuc and Fulling Mill mountains. Refrigerator- and box-car-sized boulders filled the floor of the narrow space, fallen from cliffs above into heaps from wall to wall.

We descended into it. The trail led almost at once over, between, around, and under rocks of incredible size. We climbed massive rocks, crawled up angled slabs, descended from ledge to steep ledge. We edged through narrow cracks. We inched down steep pitches and drop-offs. We crawled in muddy tunnels, taking off packs, handing them through openings between boulders too high and too wide to climb. The trail twisted, rose, plunged, time after time. It led through arches, caves, and over heaped, jagged rocks in search of passage.

We heard a creek running below. Clouds of vapor puffed from dark openings where the sun never shined. In shadows we found ice from winters before. The temperature dropped dramatically through the notch; the sun did not visit there long.

Two hours passed, then three. We took our time and stopped often to rest and have lunch. Jerri took pictures while Kyra and I looked for the trail's next turn.

Thick clumps of moss clung to rock faces and grew on walls to either side. Trees sprang from crevices, draping roots over rocks and ledges to find soil. Fallen trees blocked our path. We climbed, wriggled, and crawled, making our way steadily on.

The creek broke to the surface at the end. Southbound hikers passed us there, about to enter the mile of trail that had taken us four hours.

"Was it awful?" one woman asked. "Was it as terrible as everyone says?"

294

"It isn't a place to hurry," Jerri said. "Take it easy and enjoy it."

Adele Joyes welcomed us to Speck Pond. The grueling thousand-foot climb of Mahoosuc Arm required to find her took another three hours, but we arrived in good spirits. Adele lived in a canvas caretaker's tent, eight feet square and set on a wooden platform uphill from Speck Pond Shelter. A red bandana hung limply from the tent's overhead crosspole. A tin marker dangled in the entryway, declaring the area a North Carolina Wildlife Refuge.

Hard-Core Adele invited us in to dinner.

"We're having tacos," she said. "I thought folks from Arizona might be hungry for something like that by now." Adele wore oval, wire-rimmed glasses, a heavy green shirt, and painters' pants that once had been white. She smiled at our surprise.

"I don't get special guests very often," she said.

"This must be like a firetower job," Jerri said after a time; "quiet, remote, not too many visitors."

"It's the quietest spot in the whole AMC system. Campers are worn out by the time they get here, from either direction. Except for those who haven't seen a woman in a while, they aren't any problem. A trail crew drops by for coffee now and then — otherwise there's not much going on. That's why I wanted to work here."

"How about through-hikers?" I asked. "A bunch of them were frothing in the register back at Full Goose."

"There was a rabid troop of them through here a couple weeks ago. They livened things up, all right — they bitched about the AMC and gave me lots of flak and I gave it right back. We had a good time, really."

Dinner was ready: tacos at Speck Pond in the Mahoosuc Mountains in Maine. Wind brushed the trees. The slap of beaver tails echoed from the pond.

"This is better than dinner in town!" Kyra said.

"You've walked a long way since I last saw you," Adele said to her. "Are you still tired of uphill and rain?"

"Uh-huh, I think the trail needs more downhill and flat."

"How did you like the White Mountains?"

"They were pretty," Kyra said. "We had good weather in the Presidentials. The huts were neat, too."

"My favorite mountain is Baldpate," Adele said, "the one beyond Old Speck. It's beautiful on top, especially when it's foggy. Be sure and stop when you get there tomorrow."

"We're going to Katahdin tomorrow."

"Oh?"

"Yes," Jerri said. "We followed spring north in the beginning; now we'll follow fall south to finish."

"The Big K, huh." said Adele. "Not a bad idea. How are you going to get there?"

"Oh, hitchhike or take a bus or something," replied Kyra. "We'll make it. We always do."

Old Speck Mountain, tallest of the Mahoosuc Range, stood beyond Speck Pond. The AT dropped twenty-six hundred feet down the mountain's north side in 1.6 miles, following the path of a landslide. Trails of six percent grade in the Smokies — six feet up or down per hundred feet forward — ranked as gentle. Climbs in the ten to fifteen percent range were steep. The trail down Old Speck had a thirty percent grade. That made it suicidal as far as I was concerned.

But we wouldn't have to take it, Adele said. A new trail, two miles longer, had been under construction all summer and would be opened in a few days. We could use it early.

And we did. Walking in woods softened by fog, we descended untrampled trail past gardens of mushrooms, lichens, and moss. We crossed a brook, passed waterfalls, pools, and cascades. The forest felt wide and open at times, close and dark at others. The newly cleared pathway led seductively ahead. Scenes of small enchantment beckoned at every turn. The path slipped easily down the slope in a roundabout way, negotiating occasional steep spots on steps of inset logs.

We met the trail crew clipping a final section of brush. We were the first to travel that way, they verified, on likely the most unspoiled piece of trail we'd ever see.

We soon reached a parking lot in Grafton Notch State Park and Maine Highway 26. There our walk north ended. Somehow in the next twenty-four hours, we would travel 250 miles to Mount Katahdin and begin walking south.

CHAPTER 26

The Big K

So you went to the Louvre: What did you see?
— TERRY AND RENNY RUSSELL

W E HITCHED A RIDE TO U.S. ROUTE 2 and another took us on to
Rumford. A third car stopped within half an hour.

"Where ya headed?" the driver asked.

"Bangor."

"You're going the wrong way."

"U.S. 2 leads right there according to my map."

"Nope, that's the wrong way."

"Where are *you* headed?" I asked.

"Augusta."

"We'll take it." It would be a bit off course, I noted, but there
we'd have a better chance of catching a bus. The driver took us
over fifty miles of back roads and reached Augusta minutes
after the bus had gone. He never let on what the "right" way to
Bangor might be.

We waited four hours and caught the next bus. Seventy
miles of Maine flew by in the night and we checked in at the
Bangor House Hotel at one in the morning. Halfway.

Another bus took us to Mattawamkeag, Maine, next morning where we transferred by van to Millinocket. Part way there the driver stopped for a hitchhiker — Doug Wilson, last seen at Homestead Camp.

"I had a feeling we'd find you up here," Jerri said as Doug climbed aboard.

"I'm sure surprised to see you guys," he said. "Heading south for a while?"

Jerri explained our change in plans.

"Jeff Menzer must be nearby if you're headed for Katahdin," I observed.

"He's with his folks in Baxter Park. I thought I'd get there before this to meet him but hitchhiking's been pretty slow."

We met Jeff sooner than expected — in Millinocket, and he had the family car. He delivered us all to Katahdin Stream Campground by early afternoon. We joined the family for dinner and at dark settled into our tent near the bank of Katahdin Stream.

I listened to water flowing by, gentle, soothing sounds in the night, and reviewed events of the day. My thoughts kept returning to two striking things I'd seen: the mountain, partially hidden by forest and clouds, yet making its presence known. And on one tree, a touch of orange. The first leaves had begun to turn.

Mount Katahdin was chosen as the trail's northern end for ample reason. It was the highest point in Maine, 5,267 feet, more than a thousand feet higher than any other mountain in the state. Forested on its lower slopes, bare rock on top, Katahdin rose more than four thousand feet above the flatness around it. That was the largest elevation gain of any mountain on the Appalachian Trail.

A plaque at the mountain's base noted words of Percival Baxter who had bought and given the mountain to the state: "Buildings crumble, monuments decay, wealth vanishes. But

Katahdin in all its glory forever shall remain the mountain of the people of Maine."

We started climbing at eight in the morning. Clouds hid most of the mountain and we walked in rain. Such weather had cleared to sunny afternoons in recent days. We couldn't wait and see; the ten miles up and back would take a full day.

The AT followed Katahdin Stream for a mile and crossed on a footbridge. We ascended gradually, passing Katahdin Stream Falls, a misty cascade tumbling among granite blocks. We paused at breaks in the trees to see foggy outlines of views. The rain retreated and returned. Tree roots formed stair steps up on the rocky trail and we found the going easy. Then trees dropped away and the climb of Hunt Spur began.

Wind and rain hit us full force beyond the forest's protection. The path led steeply forward, over and around a tumult of rocks and upward into enveloping clouds. We climbed half a mile, passing over ever-larger boulders and clinging at one point to iron rods cemented into rocks as handholds and steps. Wind and rain lashed the mountain. Cold numbed our hands and faces.

"I think we should go back," Jerri said. "This rain could freeze and turn to ice. Coming down could be treacherous."

"Let's wait a while and see," I said.

We huddled in a sheltered spot for lunch, then went on.

Landmarks indicated another two miles to the summit and we appeared to be coming out of the boulders. Perhaps the steep ridge would level off just ahead.... The gentle slope of The Tableland, a broad plateau below the summit, would lead us easily to the top from there. Rain increased and the storm grew worse.

"We've got to get off this mountain," Jerri insisted.

Kyra couldn't seem to make up her mind. Perhaps she didn't want to climb that much of the mountain a second time. Perhaps she feared we might turn back and not return....

300

I climbed on alone to see what lay beyond the next rise. Maybe we were close enough to make it.

I stopped at the last of the boulders. The trail continued upward along the steep ridge and vanished in fog thirty feet away. It gave no hint of what I wanted to see. Wind-blown rain stung my face and beat a splattering tattoo on my rain gear. The cloud held fast to the ground, blowing in snaking, undulating swirls around me. It reminded me of scenes from a movie I'd seen: *Nanook of the North.* We wouldn't make it ... not together, anyway. I turned around.

"What did you see?" Kyra asked.

"Rain," I said. "And cloud streaming over the ground like blowing snow."

"Let's get out of here," said Jerri.

"We'll try again tomorrow, I guess," I said.

"No, we'll try again when the weather is nice. I'll sit in camp a week if I have to — I want good weather next time."

We climbed back down. Rain increased to a downpour that lasted all afternoon.

Doug and Jeff returned at dinnertime. They'd started earlier, climbed more quickly, and made it to the top despite the rain. They'd leave in the morning for Harpers Ferry to complete their AT hike. I boxed our boots for Jeff's family to mail for us to Caratunk, Maine. We'd switch to canvas Viet Nam boots for the half-dozen river fords ahead and Maine's hundred miles of swamps and bogs.

I signed the climbing register again next morning. We'd been last to do so the day before; the trail had been closed shortly after we'd gone. We wouldn't be so lonely on our second try. Patches of blue showed through fast-moving clouds and many hikers were already on their way. Leaving our packs on the ranger's front porch, we started up The Big K once more.

We followed the stream, passed the falls, and climbed to rock-strewn Hunt Spur. The sky cleared by the time we emerged from the trees to grapple with the boulders. We reached the point where I'd stood in clouds the day before. It was nowhere near where I'd thought. The trail pitched up another steep ridge, then another. A chilling wind forced us into down jackets as we continued up.

In time we crossed the grassy rock flats of The Tableland. The sky had rained rocks there, Thoreau said; we followed the trail past the mountaintop spring named in his memory. Another mile of climbing — easy, almost effortless by then — took us to Katahdin's summit. A thirteen-foot pile of rocks made the mountain a full mile high. A weathered signboard told us we'd reached Baxter Peak, northern terminus of the Appalachian Trail, 2,025 miles from a similar sign on Springer Mountain. From that vantage point, on so clear a day, it looked like we could almost see that far.

Five thousand square miles of Maine lay within view, land shaded in greens and blues and Rorschach blotches of clouds. Flatland Maine, rumpled by companion peaks of Katahdin and an occasional distant ridge. Scored by hundreds of lakes in finger, dagger, and crescent shapes — elongated forms with as many identities as the clouds. We stood as through-hikers would, looking into that vast, incredible expanse.

Some had burst into tears upon seeing it, realizing their hike had ended. Many had spoken with sadness at having to leave, stop hiking, and go home. For someone who had walked those two thousand miles, that final view on that final day would leave no doubt that the end had come.

Perhaps we were lucky ... our hike wasn't finished. We had days yet to go and things yet to see. We could enjoy remaining miles with no threat of winter to worry us. But what scene ahead could compare with a mile-high view of five thousand square miles of Maine? What mountain we'd yet to climb could tell it the same way? Where else would we find such an ending? Not at Bromley Cabin, that much I knew.

Maybe I'd given up too easily. Maybe I'd made a mistake. Could we have made it? I couldn't say. But how much better it would have been if our walk had ended here.

We stayed a long time, Jerri taking pictures, Kyra chatting with other hikers. We left to climb down as our shadows began to grow long.

Rain hit us as we descended. We saw the cloud coming and donned rain gear in time to be swallowed, to become faint orange patches in a sea of mist. It passed as quickly as it came, restoring the view for our final mile above the trees. We walked into camp at nightfall. Our friends had gone. Through-hikers who'd finished that day had come off the mountain and gone. We took a shelter to ourselves for a night that quickly grew dark.

In the morning we would walk south through Maine. Though Katahdin and the Appalachian Trail charged the area with feelings of completion, though confusion over what I was seeking boiled again to the surface, I knew one thing for sure — it was too early for our hike to end. There was but a touch of orange on one tree. We had another full season to go.

CHAPTER 27

A Definition

I'll tell you how the Sun rose —
A Ribbon at a time —
The Steeples swam in Amethyst —
The news, like Squirrels, ran.
                    - EMILY DICKINSON

WE WALKED SOUTH in wide-sweeping arcs. The path led west
for a time over easy terrain, then east, then west again to cross
streams and find its way around lakes and ponds. Such routing would continue for sixty-eight miles before we climbed
another mountain. The approach seemed rather roundabout
since it traversed only twenty-six straight-line miles. Indeed, all
277 miles of Maine's meandering trail covered but 150 miles as
a crow might fly.

After side trips to Little and Big Niagara Falls, neither remotely like the original, we took a campsite at Abol Bridge. We
could see Katahdin from there, still huge on the horizon though
we were fifteen miles away.

Looking out the tent flap next morning, we watched a wispy
gray cloud drift toward the mountain and rise on an updraft.

Light from the rising sun flushed it pink as it cleared the summit. The cloud turned gray again descending the far side while another rose to catch the sun's rays.

Light struck the mountain band by band, turning eastern flanks a shadowy orange. The band lowered. Trees glowed red as if fall had come in an instant. Light shifted and balanced as it touched more of the scene. The mountain turned brown, then blue, and trees passed from orange to varied shades of green. Sun lit the stream, our camp, and began to warm us after a night that had been windy and cold.

At Rainbow Ledges, a series of rocky outcroppings among scrub timber, we sensed we'd crossed a boundary. No roads or dwellings appeared in the limitless forest around us — only trees, lakes, rolling ridges, and cotton-puff clouds. The setting suddenly felt like wilderness, like the remote back country we'd hoped to find.

We walked in showers along rough trail as we skirted Rainbow Lake. Wind stirred the water to whitecaps and brought us the haunting cry of a loon. The trail led past a group of cabins, deserted, but with roof-poles already in place on porches for the coming winter's snow. We noticed Katahdin at several points along the way, a distinct silhouette among the clouds, twenty-seven trail miles behind when we last stopped to look.

The first wading event came at Pollywog Stream. We took off our socks, put boots back on, and I held Kyra's hand to negotiate the fifty-foot crossing. The water felt suddenly cold and swift but barely came over our boot-tops. Once across, we poured water from the canvas boots and shook them out, put socks back on and continued as if nothing had happened.

Sunset at Nahmakanta Lake Shelter looked like deMille burning Rome. The sinking sun torched scattered clouds, turning them pink and rose, incendiary orange and red, and spread an intensifying glow along the black mountain ridge on the lake's far shore. The lake mirrored each shade in turn.

Clouds deepened to purple overhead. Fire on the horizon raged in a diminishing band until the sky slowly blackened to night. It was September 10; we'd walked south three days.

Hikers we met those first days had one thing on their minds — the end of the trail. We talked with Bob Hewitt and Bill Sprague on their next-to-last day out. They'd looked forward to the finish for many months but its imminence brought mixed emotions. If Alan "Two-Stick Man" Sneeringer felt such pangs, he never let on. "Tonight we rest, tomorrow we eat, and then we conquer," he wrote in a shelter register.

A couple in a jeep stopped as we walked a tote-road from Nahmakanta Lake. We exchanged generalities about the trail (people in Maine didn't say "You've walked *how* far?" — through-hikers were the usual thing), and they mentioned their hopes of going fishing.

"Too bad about the rain," I said. A light drizzle had started at daybreak.

"Rain before seven clears by eleven," the lady countered with a smile.

The rain ended promptly at noon.

"It's late," I said to Jerri.

"Daylight Savings Time," she replied.

We saw deer in the vicinity, the first since Pennsylvania, and Kyra spotted moose tracks in the mud. Asters and goldenrod grew along the road. Jerri identified pearly everlasting and she and Kyra picked a few remaining dewberries. We detoured around a beaver lodge built right in the road. As the sky cleared to a lovely blue, we stopped at Pemadumcook Lake. I listened to the quiet: no motorboats, no float planes, no people. On the horizon stood Katahdin, smaller by then, linked to us by forty-six miles of trail.

We napped on the beach at Joe Mary Lake, then went around to Antlers Camps on its opposite shore. The cabins had been abandoned years before and most were damaged or destroyed. One remained in good condition, we'd heard; passing hikers kept it so. We found it and called it home for the night.

The cabin's one room had a table, pot-bellied stove, and two double bunk beds with mattresses. A pump on the sink drew water from the lake. The screened front porch offered table and chairs and an old ice box with a clutter of utensils on top. An enameled metal pitcher full of fresh-picked sunflowers stood on the table, compliments of a recent guest. Jerri served dinner on the porch as the sun went down and squirrels chattered noisily in the yard.

Sunrise: an elongated yellow green ball rose slowly from Joe Mary Lake. It blurred to a misshapen blob, split in two, then divided again into a merging and separating column of multiple blinding lights. A bright burst of rays shot forth. An irregular chartreuse glow smeared parts of the sky and streaked a blotchy path across the lake's dark surface. The far shore shifted shape as if alternately lifting up into mountains, erupting, and sloughing off in great slides to vanish in the lake.

Someone had left a green wine bottle on the porch table. I was watching sunrise through it.

We lingered after breakfast to absorb morning quiet, heating extra cups of cocoa as we looked over the lake. When we could put it off no longer, we packed and went our way, following shoreline for a time, then rough road which deteriorated to mud and bogs.

"Swampy behind us," I told Mike DiNunzio, Fred Elliott, and Ernest "Baldman" Johns when we met later on. Baldman, a stocky, shifty-eyed character with bristling crew cut, was so named when he'd shaved his head for the summer. Nearing Joe Mary Lake, they'd come within four days of their goal.

"The worst is ahead for you," Mike said. "Streams are flooding, bogs are waist deep, and parts of the trail are impassable. You may have trouble getting through."

We met more through-hikers an hour later: John Silva, John

Laming, Gabby Dan Welch, and Damascus-to-Dalton Bob. Bob, whose adventures supplied many campfire stories, like the rainy night he'd slept in a reeking outhouse, appeared to have cleaned up his act. Perhaps he'd relinquished his quest to reach Katahdin on only four baths.

Dan filled us in on the whereabouts of other through-hikers and described the trail to the south. His cautions about flooding, deep water, and bogs echoed what we'd just heard.

"It's all easy going for you," I said.

"Nothing to it now," Dan said. "Only one mountain left."

"Have you seen it?" Jerri asked.

"Yes, from the tower on White Cap. Pretty far off then, but it's getting bigger."

Dan's words hit me like a brick. One mountain left ... getting bigger. Puzzle pieces tumbled into place....

I'd thought about Katahdin very early. I'd pictured trail's end even before our first state dropped away. Over the months and miles that followed, through Virginia, halfway, the White Mountains, and then Maine, its image grew ever stronger. Had I continued walking north, I'd have seen it as hikers we were meeting did — an image slowly becoming real on the distant horizon.

The Big K was first visible from a firetower on Moxie Bald ... small, remote, 135 trail-miles away. Seventy-five miles out on White Cap Mountain one could see it again. Sightings came more often after that — from Little Boardman Mountain at sixty-four miles, from Cooper Pond at fifty-two. At each the mountain grew larger. It gained stature day by day as one approached ... Pemadumcook Lake, forty-six miles; Rainbow Lake, twenty-seven; Rainbow Ledges, twenty-one. Soon Katahdin filled the horizon and dominated one's thoughts and attention. Standing in its presence, one could see and think little else. Climbing it brought the journey to conclusion ... the conclusion I'd felt and seen ... the end befitting a walk of two thousand miles....

But not for me. I'd first seen Katahdin from its base out the window of a car. The "mountain of the people of Maine" had been a good climb, but not the last. What might have fulfilled my summer of effort — attaining a goal in a satisfying way — I'd given up. For me, The Big K was getting smaller.

I recalled times near the Susquehanna, the Delaware, the Hudson, and at Bromley Cabin. I didn't want to break up the hike, yet couldn't say why. It should have been obvious. I should have known from what I'd seen and read.

Why didn't I make the connection? Why did I let it slip away? Missing the piece in Vermont might have been okay ... we could have walked that in either direction. *But we should have come north through Maine.* I felt as though my long walk had come to nothing. I'd let it go, let it fade away with Katahdin day by day, and I knew of no way to get it back.

"... good luck in the swamps," Dan was saying. I didn't reply. I couldn't. I turned to follow Jerri and Kyra down the trail.

We pushed on to Cooper Brook Lean-to for lunch beside Cooper Falls. Jerri wanted to stay. I didn't — we had time to reach the next shelter. We kept walking, six and a half more miles. Jerri became more upset by the hour. When we reached the shelter at dusk, she complained that we'd gone too far. I had trouble giving a damn what anybody thought.

The lean-to had the first pole bunk we'd seen — a sleeping platform made of three-inch diameter logs laid side by side. "Death boards," Fred Elliott called them. Lumpy, knobby, unforgiving ... a match for the mood I was in.

One hundred seventy-six days ... 1650 miles. That was how long and far we'd walked on the Appalachian Trail. Robert Burke and William Wills crossed Australia in 1860, walking from Melbourne to the Gulf of Carpenteria. They'd covered the 1650 miles in 176 days. Turning to walk south and retrace their steps, they'd found disappointment, tragedy, and death.

My concerns seemed small next to that, but the thought gave no comfort.

Kealiher's Camp stood in a clearing on the shore of West Branch Pond. A dozen log cabins were clustered around a central dining hall where one could look out upon the pond and White Cap Mountain beyond it. A cow stood tethered to a fence. A horse browsed in the weedy front yard. An American flag hung still on the flagpole. We found Mr. Kealiher in the office.

"We're the Lowthers," I said. "I talked to you about a cabin."

"Right on schedule, I see," he said in a jolly voice as he retrieved the food box we'd mailed from Gorham. On it I'd written we would arrive that day, September 13.

"Thanks for picking it up in Greenville," Jerri said.

"No problem at all. Most hikers don't even bother to ask."

"Is your phone always that bad?" I asked.

"Usually we can't hear at all. Here, I'll show you something." He led us outside.

"See that wire? It's strung on trees ten miles to the village of Kokadjo, then it goes another twenty on old uncovered wires to Greenville. I don't know why we even bother with the thing."

"It saved me from carrying five days' food," I said.

"It's worth something then, I guess. And you, little lady, have you walked all this way, too?"

"Yes, sir!" Kyra replied.

"A fine experience, that's for sure. Your cabin is number nine — I hope it's to your liking. Good thing you got here today. We'll fill up with fishermen tomorrow and be solid till the end of the season."

The cabin was to our liking. It had beds to sleep ten, tables and chairs, a shower, and a stove with a fresh stack of wood. The camp generator supplied power for lights. Jerri noted forget-me-nots blooming in the dooryard. We settled down to read, Jerri a month-old newspaper, Kyra and I from 1940s National Geographics.

We continued our reading after dinner. A fire kept the cabin warm and kerosene lamps gave light after the generator shut down. I paged through magazines for hours. I stared absently at pictures, thinking of what had become of my walk in the woods. Advertisements of thirty years past urged me to buy items long considered passe, to invest in motorcars whose names were but memories, to wear a precision wristwatch to be assured of catching my train. I flipped page after page as night crept by, in a cabin in the Maine north woods, in the soft glow of a kerosene lamp, while a wood fire crackled in the stove.

Kyra left early for breakfast. The Kealihers used the dining hall steeple bell to summon guests to meals and had invited Kyra to ring it. We found her chatting with the hostess as we arrived, and pulling the bell-rope that hung through the ceiling.

"What would you like this morning?" the hostess asked, seating us at a table on the porch.

"What do you have?" Breakfast was cooked to order rather than being served family-style as dinner had been.

"Bacon, eggs and toast, hot cereal, hotcakes and sausage."

"That would be fine," I said. And that's what she brought.

Mr. Kealiher stopped to chat as I paid the bill.

"The blue trail around the lake will take you right to the AT," he said. "And come back and see us again."

We would, we said. How could one pass them by?

We stopped at White Cap Mountain Lean-to to read the register (Charley had departed there a few hours before, headed north), then we climbed the mountain itself. The way was steep and bypassed the 3,644-foot summit. We took a side trail the extra distance.

On top, from the tower, we looked at mountains under overcast sky — mountains named Baker, Saddlerock, Elephant, Indian, and Little Spruce. And in the distance stood one named Katahdin, summit in the clouds, still imposing in scale. I took a last look and climbed down.

CHAPTER 28

———————

It All Makes Sense
When You Go South

*To a person uninstructed in natural history, his
country or seaside stroll is a walk through a
gallery filled with wonderful works of art, nine-
tenths of which have their faces turned to the
wall.*

                                                    - THOMAS HUXLEY

THERE WAS A MOUSE ON MY HEAD. It had run up my leg as I lay
on my stomach to write the day's log and had climbed to the top
of my head. I kept writing. A mouse could see the world that
way if it wanted to. I didn't mind.

My visitor departed the way it came, then returned. I wrote
on amid its furtive pacings, wondering if it might soon bring
friends. (Easy climb! Grandstand views from brushy summit!)
It didn't. Not while I was awake, anyway.

Beaver activity also came to our attention the next few days.
Their dams backed up streams, sending water seeping ever
deeper into marshy, low-lying terrain. Wet ground turned to

swamp. Swamps grew into ponds. Water flowed in the trail, submerging all but larger rocks, logs, and mounds at bases of trees. We hopped from one high spot to another, following each other like dancers. We took wide detours, holding to firmer ground when the trail led into open water. Lacking dry footing, however small, slippery, or oddly-spaced, we plunged directly through water and mud and more than once sank to our knees.

Dry stretches of road and trail brought occasional relief, but bogs became more frequent and extensive as we went on. The AT had been rerouted time after time to get around them, yet hardly a mile of trail passed without some part sinking into the ooze. But if our passage seemed slow and difficult, it was clear that flooding had been worse not long before. We'd already passed places where others reportedly turned back.

Fords were no problem. We waded the Pleasant River as effortlessly as we had Pollywog Stream, then crossed another once-raging creek by balancing on rocks and logs. Another time, we avoided wading a fast-moving creek by taking a side trail to a bridge we noted on the map.

Sloppy conditions were not without advantage. We met fewer people in that region and walked through much of the boundless forest in solitude. Occasional encounters with another through-hiker ranked as heavy traffic.

A blue-blazed trail led to the right at the approach to the Chairback Range.

"Shortcut," I said.

"Where does it go?" Jerri asked.

"It meets the AT in two miles and cuts out four miles and three mountains."

"Does it miss the shelter, too?" Kyra asked.

"Um ... yeah, I guess it does."

"And the stand of virgin timber I was reading of?" said Jerri.

"That, too."

"Some shortcut."

We took the white-blazed trail. We had no reason to save time anymore and the climbs would lift us out of the bogs.

The ascent took us through a collection of interesting scenes. Fog drifted through towering virgin spruce on the peaks of Chairback and Columbus mountains and viewpoints showed hazy contours of surrounding mountains and lakes. The Chairbacks marched in front of us, multiple peaks leading to 2,670-foot Barren Mountain at the end of the range. Forest stretched everywhere. Even when fog thinned we could see no houses or towns in all those rolling miles.

A plump toad in the trail on Third Mountain struggled to get out of our way. A summer of plentiful insects had left it puffed out like a balloon. It hopped forward and landed on its nose. Righting itself, it jumped to a sprawling heap again. We waited as it floundered to safety.

A pile of aluminum tubing later caught my eye. I thought it to be tent pegs at first but inspection revealed something else. A pack frame had been violently ripped apart, meticulously broken at every weld and snapped to small pieces. I pictured it breaking at an inopportune moment, the owner reacting in rage, then departing with the pack bag slung over his shoulder.

The AT met the shortcut again in the gap between Third and Fourth mountains. Judging from the note I found, written in various hands, northbound hikers we knew had paused there:

Tired of mountains so I have decided to take the Bush-Leaguer route to Chairback Camps.

Met two BLs that said it saves four miles and returns to the AT.

Good luck on the rocks if you go White like true through-hikers.

- John

I'm not a BL. I'm going White. - *Dan*

Good for you, Dan.   - Charley

The "every-inchers" were still with us it appeared.

So were the bogs. Water ran a foot deep in the trail in places and we slogged in rocky mud that extended through gaps and well up into the mountains. On Fourth Mountain, though, we noted a pleasant change. Logs laid in the footway provided easy passage through the muck, past moss growing in soft mounds, among delicate green and brown ferns nodding in the breeze. We found carnivorous pitcher plants in abundance and looked into their pitcher-like leaves for collections of trapped insects. We followed moose tracks in the mud, but saw no moose.

Jerri walked in front as always. She paused to point out plants and take in views as she'd done since the day we began. She'd stop at times to listen to the woods we had lived in so long. She became completely absorbed in each day's section of trail and was never in a rush for the next one. Kyra followed, watched, and stopped to listen, too.

I kept my disappointment to myself. The damage was done; further arguments on the subject seemed pointless. We still had many days left on the trail. There was time to keep working the problem.

We slept most nights in shelters, on the poles. They weren't that hard to survive if one avoided lying on one's back, turned over frequently, and placed shoulder and hip in grooves between the logs. Flat, dry ground would have been more comfortable, of course, had we found any, but we easily lost sight of such things under threat of rain.

The poles at Chairback Gap Lean-to defied all sleeping techniques. Its infinitely wise builder had used eight-inch-diameter logs for the bunk instead of three-inch so he wouldn't need so many. After thrashing through the night on what amounted to telephone poles, we would gladly have slept on cement.

Cloud Pond Lean-to had a sawdust floor. Though its roof leaked somewhat and the place resembled a stall from a churchyard nativity display, we had only to glance at the pond to be grateful for shelter at all. Wind beat the water to waves and a sky thick with clouds promised rain. Such overcast weather had been constant since our stay at West Branch Ponds.

We headed for Monson our 182nd day. We crossed creeks and swamps, plowed through mud and dripping brush, and rain that started in the night never slackened. Mud covered our boots and jeans and streaked and splashed our rain gear. It seemed ages since we'd last been clean. We found shelter in Nine Points Cabin for lunch. A dingy, gloomy place — I reappraised it at slightly over six.

At The Bog, where beaver works backed up a pond big enough to put on the map, the trail led right through the middle. Remembering directions in recent notes from other hikers, we swung wide to the left and found our way around without problem. At day's end, rain pounding harder than ever, we walked into town after a dismal eleven miles.

I asked about places to stay at the Post Office. See Dennis Casey, I was told, just up the street.

"Cabin?" he said upon answering the door. "Sure, I have two on Monson Pond, back up the road about three miles."

"Super," I said, "we just walked past them."

"Hop in my truck. I'll take you there."

"We have some shopping to do first, if you don't mind."

"No trouble, let me know when you're ready."

"What's the price?"

"Ten dollars — and I'll pick you up in the morning."

Mr. Casey built a fire in the cabin's wood stove when we arrived and showed us around. The place had a large kitchen, beds to sleep five, and a pleasant but rainy view of the pond.

"There are no bed linens or blankets," he said apologetically.

"Our sleeping bags will do fine," Jerri said. "We're quite used to them."

"And, um ... the john is outside, but it isn't far."

316

I paid the ten dollars. He had something else to say but was struggling with it.

"Er ... do you have any change?"

"Sure, why?"

"Well ... there's fifty cents tax."

Amazing, I thought, digging out a couple of quarters. The man delivers us to a cozy refuge from the storm, offers to pick us up next day, charges less than the usual rates, begs indulgence for "inconveniences" a step up from our normal routine, and is mortified at collecting a half-dollar tax. A life of hiking and living in the woods sure put things in perspective.

We met John Gantz on our way out of town next day. John, of Mark and John, our companions for an evening of bear entertainment in Shenandoah, said he'd recently met Ned Barr. Ned had injured his foot somewhere in New York in July and had taken a month off to recover. Resuming his walk headed south, Ned seemed excited about the prospect.

"It all makes sense going south," he told John. "Now I know why I'm doing this!"

"Why?" John asked, his own goal nearly in sight.

Ned went on at length on the subject in his usual enthusiastic way.

"Turn around and come south ... you'll see!" he'd said, sauntering on down the trail. John confessed to being more than a little puzzled.

The news explained a few things. Why we'd lost track of Ned, for instance, and what he'd meant in the card he had left us in Monson: "Hi, some northbound dudes told me you may have gone directly to The Big K to walk south. Smart move, eh what? I'm only doing about 7 m. a day!"

Turning around did make a certain sense, I had to admit. We were meeting northbound hikers once more and could share news and stories. Fall would last longer if we walked south just as spring had going north. And with the big mountains behind and but a few four-thousand-footers to go, we could see the sights as slowly as we liked.

There was a matter of convenience as well. Erosion was more noticeable on south slopes of mountains than on the north, due, in part, to the sun shining longer upon them. The approach from Georgia thus often presented gradual climbs and steep descents. Months of experience had conditioned us to prefer the reverse — steep climbs and more gentle descents.

None of these reasons outweighed my personal feelings but I had to grant the advantages. Heading south for the winter was traditional, after all.

We found moose tracks outside our door when we awoke on Breakneck Ridge. We'd been following such prints for days, hoping to catch a glimpse of the creature that left them. It apparently had stopped to look in on us in the night from a few feet away. Bear tracks had been evident recently as well, but none so persistent and regular as those of our moose.

"I wish we could have seen it," Jerri said.

"It's hiking the trail, I'll bet," Kyra said to me. "We might catch up with it later on."

"Check the register. Maybe it signed in."

"Look for a big hoofprint," Jerri said, "marked 'Through-Moose, ME →GA.'"

"Nope," Kyra said after a time, paging through the small spiral notebook. "Here's something, though ..."

"A treasure map ..."

"No, it's from Doug."

Inspired by the deep Maine woods, he'd written: "Changed my name today, to Douglas Fir Wilson. Parents named me Gordon. No vision."

The register told another story as well, one that lately was continued from shelter to shelter. Jerri thought the whole thing rather dumb. Kyra and I could hardly wait to see what would happen next.

Driven to the edge by days of walking in mud and wading through bogs and streams, three hikers signing themselves The Midnight Marauders wrote of their search for The Man Who Made The Trail. They'd hunted for days through swamp and pond in one episode but had found no trace. In another, The Man had appeared to them in their sleep and vanished with a mocking laugh. At Breakneck Ridge, they'd caught him ...

"Aha!" I chuckled vengefully (one wrote), "now we have you, O Evil Man Who Made The Trail," and we tied him securely for the fatal blow.

"Wait," the dreaded one replied. "I am beaten. You have won. Your success must first be honored."

And a table set for three appeared before us, a silver-covered platter in its center. I lifted the cover, suspecting some sinister trick.

"Oh, *no!*" we cried with one voice, weeping and sinking to our knees. "*Eggplant Parmesan!* How did you know?" And we sat down to a glorious feast we could not believe.

"So long, suckers," we heard The Man say with a cunning laugh. He had loosed his bonds and was bounding down the trail. We pursued in vain. When we returned, the table and the feast had disappeared.

"We'll get you," we solemnly vowed. And so we go on through muck and marsh, one day again to capture The Man Who Made The Trail.

We found pleasant woods and relief from continuing bogs on Moxie Bald. The trail followed open, granite ledges much of the way, affording looks at the countryside even through fog and rain. A town could be seen in the distance every thirty miles or so, yet the woods of Maine felt so large and wild that our sense of remoteness remained.

Such feelings vanished at once in lumbered areas, particularly the time a bulldozer came crunching down the trail. But in undisturbed forests and mountains, and even mucking through the swamps, we felt enjoyably alone.

Swinging around the end of Moxie Pond, we came to Baker Brook. A bridge was provided — two fifty-yard cables strung taut from bank to bank fifteen feet above the water. The hiker stood on the bottom one, apparently, held on to the top one and edged his way across. Clipping one's pack to the upper cable and pulling it behind, one could make the crossing in style. Jerri and Kyra wanted no part of high-wire acts, however. The water level had dropped enough to let rocks protrude; we stuck to the overland route.

I stepped or jumped from rock to rock, picking each one as I went. Jerri and Kyra followed. We reached dead ends, backtracked, started anew. The quarter-point passed easily, halfway less so, but stepping-stones always led somewhere. Kyra slipped at one point. After dunking one foot, she recovered.

I saw a clear course to shore at the three-quarter mark. Clear, except for the ten-foot span of rushing water in front of me. One small rock broke the surface in the center of the span. I jumped, stabbing my stick into the water as I landed. The rock did not roll; I remained standing.

Leaping the remaining distance, I hauled my pack to shore, then jumped again to the rock in the center of the current.

"Your turn, Kyra," I said.

"I can't jump that far."

"Sure you can."

"You're standing on my rock."

"I'll catch you so you don't miss."

She jumped. Her feet scored a direct hit on mine and I pitched backward. I grabbed her hand and leaned hard on my stick. We steadied each other, holding hands and walking sticks and each leaning back.

"Room for one more?" Jerri asked.

"Thank you for your interest," I said, "but all positions have been filled."

"Martha Graham should see this...."

"Now what?" Kyra wanted to know. "If you let go, I'll fall."

"Yes, I'd noticed that flaw."

"Why don't we just wade? It's not much over my knees."

"The water is cold, you know. And it's more of a challenge to beat the fords if you can."

"It's more fun to get wet all over, I suppose."

"Oh, *sure*," Jerri said. "We went to a lot of trouble to get boots you could wade in. The challenge is not to use them!"

"Put your stick behind you," I said. "Lean on it and push up when I jump. Let go of my hand when I let go."

"Okay."

I jumped, pulling her upright and letting go. She did not fall. I caught her again on the final leap and Jerri made it across with but one wet foot. We walked dirt road then, following the pond until the trail led us bushwhacking through bogs and blowdowns and up Pleasant Pond Mountain.

"I'm working on another house," Kyra said as we climbed.

"Did you sell the first one?" I asked.

"No ... it's for winter. This is a summer house in a forest in New Hampshire or Vermont."

"It rains there, I've heard...."

"Oh, but it's so nice and quiet. I have lots of land so I can wander through the woods. And there are maple trees for syrup and plenty of animals to see."

"How about moose?"

"I don't think so," she said. "It's close to the city, you know."

"What's the house like inside?"

"I don't know. I'm working on the outside. I've got a long, winding drive and wildflowers everywhere."

"Showy lady slippers ..."

"Uh-huh, if they'll grow."

"Why are you doing all this, if I may ask?"

"Doing what?"

"Spending time building houses."

"It's fun to think about what sorts of things I'll do after the trail — building houses, making things, you know."

"You seem so stuck on it," I said. "You haven't once mentioned fancy cars, handsome princes, glass slippers, or whatever girls think about. It's just different, I guess."

"Those things aren't important."

"Woods and flowers are important ..."

"Sure ... but that's not it, either," she said, thinking a moment. "I want someplace that's mine, that I've made by myself. Mom made the tent — why can't I build my own house when I grow up?"

"Has all this walking made you feel homeless?"

"Maybe ... but it was never much better before. We moved across town or across the country all the time — I've never been to the same school more than two years!"

"You haven't?"

"No."

"I'd forgotten...."

We continued our climb and I noticed we were nearing the top. Jerri had gone ahead.

"Most of all," Kyra continued, "I want a place to come home to after a trip like this. Right now our stuff is in storage. Who wants to run away to that? I want something that will stay the same while I go off to have adventures. Then I won't have to make new friends all the time. I get tired of always being the 'new kid.'"

"Do we count as friends?"

"Well ... you're different...."

"Just checking."

Another view: White Cap Mountain behind, Bigelow out

front, a hundred unidentified ridges and knobs all around like faces in a crowd. Special effects: sunlit cloud layers, a granite cliff or two, a sculptured carpet of trees, blue-white lakes mirroring light. The Kennebec River flowed out there somewhere, a thousand feet wide and five feet deep where hikers crossed.

Something else demanded attention as well — fall. A crisp wind blew steadily. Growing patches of yellow and red streaked the woods. Nights had turned cold; we wore down jackets in our sleeping bags again. And we found no one in Pleasant Pond Mountain Lean-to, on a Friday night, at a shelter on a road near a town. The trail's own notions of ending were unmistakably clear.

It was September 21. We'd been on the trail six months.

CHAPTER 29

Note Left in Passing

September 21, Day 185
Pleasant Pond Shelter

Six MONTHS AGO THIS DAY a merry band of through-hikers went forth from Atlanta to seek a mountain named Springer and a trail leading north two thousand miles. They were three in number — mama through-hiker, papa through-hiker, and baby through-hiker (age ten) — and all that day they traveled in wind and cold and country bleak and bare.

The mountain they sought bore ice in its trees and snow on its summit that first spring day, yet their spirits flagged not. Entering names in the registry as the sun descended, gazing northward to mountains row on row, they declared they would walk GA →ME.

Day followed day and mile followed mile as our merry band walked on. O'er mountains of Georgia and North Carolina they struggled (verily, even the fabled Stekoahs) in rain and fog and weather most dreary. They paused for sparse flowers and scenery by day, and to bandage mama through-hiker's blisters, and to wait for baby through-hiker who lagged behind. By night they slept with mice ... and phantoms.

Into Tennessee they marched where Great Smoky Mountains dealt snow and cold and nights of terrible shivering. Undaunted, they pressed on. Days grew warm, even hot, then snow fell once more. Still they hiked on, and though they found new friends among those who passed by, at times our merry band seemed not so merry. Indeed, they quarreled.

Flowers burst forth in sunny Virginia. They lingered to smell and admire each blossom, to name names and record each in story and image; still miles passed quickly during long days on flat ridges. Toilsome District Pedlar slowed them again, but they regained their stride in Shenandoah where small creatures (and some not so small) watched from the forest.

On through Maryland they flew, to Pennsylvania and a thousand-mile feast in the rain. There our merry band fell upon their darkest hours. Insect hordes and days of suffocating heat pursued them over insidious ridges of rocks, through ravages a plague of moths had visited upon the land. They did not falter. New Jersey fell behind, then New York as they trucked onward past all understanding, day upon day. Through Connecticut they labored, then Massachusetts, and when at last this merry band sensed delivery at hand and passed into forests of Vermont, the heavens opened and poured forth rain.

'Twas in otherwise undistinguished Bromley Cabin that the month's eighth deluge came upon them. Sadly, papa through-hiker prepared to push on as in storms before, though he found the prospect most tiresome. Mama through-hiker awoke and saw what had come to pass.

"Nuts to this!" she said. And they did not walk that day.

Bounding forward instead by bus and thumb, aided as in times past by kindhearted strangers, they reached the hamlet of Glencliff. They scaled the mighty Moosilauke, of the White Mountain Brotherhood, and stood to regard massive country stretching before them. Boldly they moved on over peak and ridge, beyond timberline on the three clearest days of summer.

Mama, papa, and baby through-hiker alike thrilled to glories on every hand as they marched to the fearsome Mahoosucs. Nothing could stop our merry band then. They scrambled unafraid through The Notch and up The Arm and walked in delight down enchanted trail to Grafton.

There more schemes lay in store. They leaped northward in mighty strides to stand before The Great Katahdin Itself. In rain they ascended, and the mountain commanded them to go back. In sunshine they strove upward again. The Big K let them pass. And lo, they saw the whole world from its summit.

Turning south, they slogged into swamps and bogs of Maine as Katahdin diminished behind. No lofty barriers barred their way and our merry band should have sung with gladness and joy. They did not. Papa through-hiker waxed glum and retreated in thought as the import of The Mountain loomed large.

Days pile upon days until now, six months on the trail, our merry band rests in Pleasant Pond Shelter — 1,783 miles behind, 248 to go. They journey again to Grafton, to skip to Glencliff and stroll final miles to a cabin at Bromley, and we wonder ...

Will they reach their goal before winter ends their days on the Appalachian Trail?

Will they amaze friends with preposterous tales of mice and bears, rain and snow, ledges and bogs?

Will mama through-hiker leave her world of green?

Will baby through-hiker get her ten-speed bicycle?

Will papa through-hiker regain his good cheer?

Stay tuned as our merry band, "The Family" to some, treks southward to The Big B. Wandering through fall, advancing before winter — tomorrow the Kennebec, then Bigelow, and beyond....

Mic, Jerrianne, & Kyra Lowther
GA →←— ME

CHAPTER 30

View from Saddleback Mountain

*The earth does not belong to man; man belongs
to the earth. This we know.*
                                    - CHIEF SEATTLE

THE LINE WAS BUSY.

"Try again in a bit," the storekeeper said, "but don't wait too long, they're leavin' town for the weekend."

We were in Caratunk, Maine, on Saturday morning, calling Harold Smith who took hikers across the Kennebec River by boat. One could wade the river, of course — water ran waist-deep until nine o'clock. A dam opened upstream then to float pulpwood logs along. We'd arrived at ten o'clock. Water would be rising and the current would be more swift. Passing logs would add hazards to what was already adventure enough. Waist- or chest-deep to me meant water to Kyra's nose. We would go by boat.

I called Mr. Smith again. He answered but sounded reluctant to delay his weekend plans. Learning there were three of us, he said to meet him on the riverbank in half an hour.

Dick Heller arrived just then, a Katahdin-bound hiker from

Indiana. The boundary of wet and dry on his clothes told he'd waded the river.

"You could have waited and taken the boat back across," Jerri said. Northbound hikers were at a disadvantage with no way to make arrangements on their side of the river.

"It wasn't so bad," he replied. "Cold, though, and slick on the bottom."

"I hope you won't mind the rain," Jerri went on.

"Rain? I thought the sun was shining."

"It is, but once we go to town, you can count on rain."

"Thanks a lot," Dick replied without cheer.

We walked to the shore and found our ferryman poling his skiff downriver from where he kept it moored. Harold Smith was seventy years old, I'd heard, but the hardy look of his face suggested no particular age. He wore an old, gray-brimmed hat, gray trousers to match, and a red-and-black checked wool shirt. A cloth patch on his sleeve proclaimed him a registered Maine guide.

"Got to be," he said when I commented on it. "You need a license to ferry people across the Kennybec."

I shoved the boat off after loading our packs aboard. Mr. Smith stood in the stern and pushed us along with a stout pole. We saw no logs afloat in the choppy water, but they would have moved quickly considering how fast we drifted parallel to the shore.

"Are you busy with hikers this year?" I asked.

"Some," he said, "but a lot of them cross on their own. They camp on the bank and ford in early morning, or build rafts for their packs from driftwood and swim alongside. It's a tricky river for that sort of thing. The bottom is slippery and the current is strong. Having a load of logs come at you is no picnic, either."

Our guide told stories as he poled across the wide expanse. He described drownings, rescues, and endless troubles people

328

had gotten into trying to get across. The Kennebec could be a treacherous place, he said. We were much better off with him. He wished us a friendly "Good hiking" as we unloaded, then made his way back to town.

Then it rained. We walked two miles, three, and stopped at Pierce Pond. Fog hung over a setting of mountains, lake, forested islands. We'd planned it as camp but had time to go on.

We reentered the forest — gloomy, scrubby, second-growth trees. Wind shook them. Rain increased to a downpour. Five miles, six. We shivered from the cold, thinking winter would overtake us in moments. Rain and wind came harder as we sped along puddled trail. Eight miles, then nine. Clouds thickened, blackened. The sky grew dark. A mile to go.

"Faster," Jerri said.

"Faster?" Kyra asked, rain stinging her face.

"The glaciers are coming."

Jerri had more news when we reached shelter at white-capped East Carry Pond.

"The bad news, troops, is that there is nothing to drink tonight but pond water. Now the good news: there's plenty of pond water."

Loons woke us early. We'd heard only one before; that morning unearthly calls echoed from many points around the pond. Jerri woke hours before dawn to hear them calling in darkness. I listened as the sky slowly brightened. Rain had gone. Though clouds remained, I felt no wind. It would be a good day. We would reach the end of a hundred miles of bogs.

But the muck did not give up easily; the worst bog of all awaited us just beyond Middle Carry Pond. I found no way to avoid it. I couldn't even see where it might end. We'd waltzed around The Bog near Monson but would have no such luck at its big brother, The Bog of Bogs — the trail led straight across.

We plunged in, crossing slippery logs part of the way and hopping between what rocks and dry spots we could find.

Grassy mounds that looked safe often collapsed. We'd leap away but water always won, gurgling into boots with an icy rush, soaking jeans to the knees. It became a dismal game in time. Jerri took pictures of Kyra doing Flying-Wallenda log-crossing routines, and of me looking morose, sunk in some great quagmire of water, mud, and weeds. White blazes led conscientiously through it all. We followed them. Soaked and slopped with mud and slime, we found our way to land in half an hour.

"How'd you get so wet?" I asked Kyra.

"I fell into the trail," she replied.

Alice and Jerry Derbyshire from Fort Worth, Texas, met us at Jerome Brook Lean-to.

"I don't believe it," Jerry said. "You really exist."

"You thought we didn't?" I said.

"We've been following you for months. You had three weeks' lead when we started but we kept whittling it down. In Vermont, we lagged only a few days and figured to catch you around Manchester Center."

"I think I know what's coming," Jerri said.

"We got to Bromley Cabin an hour after you'd gone," said Alice. "Disappeared! Skipped ahead, someone told us."

"We jumped around a bit from there," Jerri said. "Now we're coming south from Katahdin to fill in the gaps."

"People kept asking *us* where our ten-year-old daughter was," said Alice, "as if we hiked without her but signed her name. We'd begun to think Kyra didn't exist."

"You're taking lots of pictures, I gather," Jerri said, noting the couple's collection of cameras, lenses, meters, and attachments hanging here and there.

"Tons," replied Jerry. "Of everything."

"What do you plan to do with them?"

"Stuff a mattress, I think. I don't know what else they're good for."

We described the Kennebec crossing and asked about mountains ahead.

"Some tough, some not so bad," Jerry said, "but it's good to be out of them."

"We'll happily trade you," I said.

"For what?"

"The bogs."

We hiked in the Bigelows the next two days. The range rose sharply from surrounding terrain. The trail led up a rockslide to reach Little Bigelow, then plunged to a deep sag before climbing the main ridge itself. We ascended slowly over successive steep knobs, taking in views of hazy Flagstaff Lake to the north, stream-cut forests to the south, occasional gardens of rock and lichen at our feet.

We topped 4,088-foot Avery Peak late the first day. The night cooled quickly, but not so cool as it had apparently been the week before. Douglas Fir Wilson had signed in at Avery Lean-to as "Douglas Brr-r-r."

Morning brought 4,150-foot West Peak and a descent to summits called North and South Horn. I sat a long time looking down on Horn Pond, staring into valleys white with cottonball clouds. The sun shone on my back. The air felt soothing and warm. I heard no sound save a slight breeze.

Something suggested itself to me, some feeling, some distant idea I didn't quite grasp. It took shape as a question ... Why did people climb mountains? A common question, with even more common answers. I ignored it — until I realized I had no answer of my own.

Perhaps it lay in front of me ... perhaps the chance to see or listen was the reason. Perhaps standing on top let one gain a sense of the place, a sense of perspective with surroundings. I'd done those things. I'd watched, I'd listened, I'd been struck by grandeur and massiveness in the world we walked through. I'd come to regard it as worth the effort. Was there more?

I reached for something definite, something to point to and understand. But what I sought seemed to change with observation, and I found nothing different, nothing personal, nothing beyond common things I'd read. I followed the thought no further....

Getting *to* the town of Stratton was easy. We descended Bigelow Mountain to Maine Highway 27, thumbed the first passing vehicle (a flat-bed truck), and arrived downtown in minutes. After a night in the Arnold Trail Hotel, we retrieved supplies from the Post Office, at last trading Viet Nam boots for the regular ones mailed ahead.

Getting *out* of Stratton was quite another story. We stood beyond the town's last side street but within the slow speed zone. We would catch traffic headed out of town thereby, but not be bothered with cars turning off. That proved effective. Nearly every car turned before it passed. We waited. Car after car approached and turned. Of the few that actually drove by, none stopped.

Ten o'clock stretched to eleven. Turning cars all seemed headed down one particular road.

"Maybe we should be standing there," I said. "Maybe that's the usual route out of town."

"It doesn't seem likely," Jerri observed.

"What's down that road?" I asked a passer-by.

"The dump," he replied. Well, that wasn't it.

Twelve o'clock, and we waited.

"We need a sign," I said.

I made a sign that said *Bigelow Village.* The trail crossed the road there seven miles on and I thought some motorist might stop. No luck. No cars passed at all, in fact.

A Volkswagen approached, a *For Sale* sign in its window.

"Let's buy it," Kyra instantly said.

I'd thought the same thing, as had Jerri.

One o'clock.

"We could have walked there in this time," I groaned.

Two women, age nineteen or twenty, walked toward us.

"Hiking the trail, huh," one said. "North or south?"

"South at the moment," I replied, "if we can ever get back to it. We've been here three hours."

"It might be less frustrating if you walk farther out of town," said the other. "More local traffic will filter out."

"I'd thought we'd accounted for that."

"I live in Bigelow right near the trail," said the first. "If you don't have any luck, walk on down. Pitch your tent in our yard for the night and we'll have a party. You know, drink a little home brew, smoke a little home grown. Could be fun!"

"Um ... thanks," I said, fielding this wonderful line. "We'll look you up if we get stuck." The women waved and walked down the road.

We took their advice. Donning packs once again, we walked toward Bigelow soon after and got a ride in three minutes. Within the hour we'd put two trail miles behind and reached Sugarloaf Lean-to.

We filled six canteens from the spring near the shelter and started up Mount Sugarloaf, Maine's second highest mountain at 4,237 feet. I chuckled as we climbed at the invitation we'd received, quite unaware that six quarts of polluted water riding in the packs would leave us much worse off than a little home brew, and a little home grown.

Climbing easily at first, then more steeply, we struggled upward on trail that wound back and forth across the mountain's slopes. We stopped often to search for blazes on confusing, crisscrossing trails. I noticed color overtaking the forests, coming down from mountaintops just as new leaves had made their way up. We gained the summit in three hours. It gave views to the Bigelows next door and to dozens of other peaks and ridges turning blue, purple, and black as the sun sank into distant clouds.

Doors to the ski facility on top were locked. I tried one, then another. Prowling among gondola cars that hung waiting for winter, I found another door leading inside. Open. We went in.

A concrete foyer lay beyond, bright from light of several windows and warm from lamps mounted on the walls. Doors to rest rooms were open ("Heated!" Jerri called from the Women's), but all other areas were secured.

"Neat shelter," Kyra said. "No poles."

"Yeah, we won't have to hang up the packs," I said.

Outside air was unusually warm and still next morning. Odd, for late September at four thousand feet.

"It's an inversion," Jerri said. "There's a layer of warm air here on top. Valleys are probably cold." And we walked down Mount Sugarloaf in the sunshine, in shorts and rolled-up sleeves.

We awoke our 192nd day in the shelter on Poplar Ridge. Rain had beaten the roof all night but the storm had blown on, leaving clear sky. I welcomed nice weather for our traverse of the Saddleback Range.

Saddleback Junior lay in front of us, a rounded, 3,640-foot peak with patches of gold gaining prominence on its sides. The top rose briefly above tree-line. We paused to look forward and back as we had so often before, but cold wind shortened our stay. We crossed the rocky summit to a deep saddle and dropped again into trees.

The Horn stood four hundred feet higher two miles on. We stopped there to put on down jackets. The trail passed over rock ledges from that point, remaining above tree-line two miles.

Atop Saddleback Mountain itself, another hundred feet higher, we stopped again. I looked around, intently, out over the mountains of Maine. I ignored wind and cold and let the scene seep in. There was something different there.

The forest had turned. Fields of gold and orange glowed on sunlit slopes. Yellow-leafed trees dotted valleys like dandelions in a lawn. Wind had driven out the haze. I saw a patchwork of mountains, lakes, and colorful forests on to the horizon, mottled by free-form shadows of clouds blowing fast across the sky. Pretty ... but I sought something more.

Something ... I looked closer at hand.

I stood in a rocky place where scrub spruce grew short and low along the ground. Heath plants clutched fast among stone slabs, forming a dense red-brown mat that covered the summit.

Tiny flowers and tufts of yellow grass grew at my feet. The gusting wind blew them, bent them, this way and that.

I felt it bend me, too ...

Sunlight shone on each blade and leaf, then vanished in a passing cloud.

I felt the shadow come and go ...

The sequence repeated ... I watched and listened ... feeling I could almost touch the answer ... and then I knew. Standing rooted to the spot like those tufts of grass, wind-blown and sun-struck in those same eternal patterns, I knew what I'd come to find in the woods, what my walk of two thousand miles had come to mean.

We were one. The grass, the flowers, the trees, the natural world and I were one. I was a creature there just like those growing at my feet. We were each a part of the same whole. The sun shone on me, the wind blew on me, the rain fell on me even as on the world about me. I was part of it. I belonged there. I was home.

I'd felt like a guest there all that time. A stranger, a visitor, someone in the woods who did not belong. I'd come from tenderfoot to woodsman in the months that had passed ... but I'd been walking, living, surviving *in* the woods, not as part *of* them. I felt suddenly different. Not "master of all I surveyed." Not "insignificant in the cosmos." I felt one with the world, and welcomed as a friend. And I knew that was why we had come ... to see, to enjoy, to be one with the land, and to feel welcome.

This understanding had eluded me since those very first days in Georgia. I'd looked for it, tried to see it from mountain summits, tried to shape and hammer it into familiar forms: Achieving, Reaching the Goal, Witnessing Mountain Majesty. Each time I'd come up short. Each time I'd seen the parts but not the whole. Yet here the answer was, in flowers and tufts of grass warmed by the sun, soaked by the rain, beat by the wind just as I had been all this time. Here the answer was, free for the finding.

And then it didn't matter whether we walked north or south, climbed Katahdin first or last, or at all. What mattered was *being* wherever we were, *seeing* whatever we saw, feeling part of the world we all shared. I felt flooded with thought and emotion. I wanted to walk back to Georgia and see all that country through new eyes. Not as miles, schedules, or obstacles to cross ... but as the forests and mountains of my home.

I walked down off Saddleback Mountain and caught up with the others who'd gone on. Should I tell them? I wondered. Should I describe what had happened? No need, really. They'd understood it from the beginning....

I went to Rangeley next morning. It was our last supply stop in Maine and I'd hoped to hitchhike the five miles in and back quickly. Such was not to be. I could easily have walked to town in the three hours I spent getting a ride.

The Post Office had closed by the time I arrived at half-past noon. It was Saturday. I knocked on the door: no answer. I looked in the window: no one around. How would I get in this time?

The front counter, weekend tidy, had small signs at each station — *Stamps, General Delivery,* and the like — and nameplates of people who worked there. I copied down names and retired to the phone booth.

"Looking for a place to stay?"

"Huh?" I said, turning to the lady who'd nudged my arm.

"I'm Viola and I run the guest house here. I've been putting up hikers this summer. Need a room?"

"Not today, thanks. I'm just here for supplies."

"Look me up if you decide to stay. I make blueberry pancakes for breakfast, all you can eat." She smiled and walked off.

How many blueberries could a summer's worth of hikers eat? ... where was I? Oh, the postmaster.

His wife answered the phone. He'd gone moose hunting, she said, but she'd give me another number to try. A lady answered my second call and I told my story again. Her husband was still at the Post Office; she'd call him and ask him to open up. Thus I sprung our supplies and hitched back to the trail. Elapsed time: six hours.

"We thought you'd been daddy-napped," Kyra said.

"I could have had a nap between rides," I said. "But I met this lady named Viola...." And the subject turned to blueberry pancakes as we walked down the trail in the rain.

We crossed many peaks of Bemis and other mountains the next few days, moving slowly, none of us feeling very well. We'd all gotten sick the evening of our day on Saddleback, each of us getting the same queasy feeling about the same time. We blamed water we'd carried up Sugarloaf; the ski development there had polluted the spring. I'd misread warnings and loaded up anyway, thinking the bad water farther up the mountain.

We tired quickly, nursed uneasy stomachs, and made many urgent trips to the woods. Those in the middle of the night were the most disconcerting. I'd put off venturing into the cold as long as possible. At the last moment, I'd hastily try to don boots filled with pocket things, grope for the roll of paper in a hung-up pack, light a candle (our third set of flashlights had died), and dash, bootlaces dragging, to the bushes. Making such an error after being so long on the trail became more and more annoying.

But slow going made the trail last longer. Trees had gone wild by then, dazzling us wherever we walked with bursts of red, yellow, and orange. Leaves lay all along the trail. A new year's leaves, each a small portrait of fall. Shelter settings were especially picturesque. Morning and evening sunlight slanted into those secluded hollows, lighting each leaf and setting trees ablaze. We often sat merely watching the changing scene.

And so we passed into October. Feeling better at last, we started climbing along Frye Brook the morning of October 3. Ahead was Baldpate, our final mountain in Maine.

Following stone slabs that formed the creek's course, passing waterfalls, flumes, and clear, deep pools, we made our way up the mountain. We walked in no hurry. Rain in the night had left colors muted in soft morning fog. The forest had a look of magnificence, once again different from anything we'd seen.

We stood in fog on the summit. Lichen-crusted rock paved the dome beneath us, broken by patches of black moss and waving tufts of grass. Clusters of small, wind-twisted spruce led off into the mist. Red-leafed blueberry lined the path, along with other plants bearing leaves of rust to dark green. Water drops splattered leaves and hung and dripped from branches.

I experienced again what I'd felt on Saddleback. I found that mountaintop garden more lovely, more comfortable, more welcoming than any city home could be. We might have seen Old Speck, the Mahoosucs, or White Mountain Presidentials from there on a sunny day. I preferred fog. Views near at hand were also rewarding.

"Going to the woods is going home," John Muir had said. I understood it now. I felt it. I treasured it as a discovery all my own. In her way, Jerri had been showing and telling me the same thing all along. But I couldn't have just taken her word for it and felt the same way.

We descended barren ledges and walked carefully through quicksand bog to Baldpate's third summit. The trail dropped two thousand feet to the highway from there, to Maine 26, where we'd been thirty days before. We reached it at dusk. Finding no rides in the rain, we returned to the lean-to we'd passed a quarter-mile back.

"Another night on the poles," I said to Kyra.

"Hmmph," she replied. The night before was to have been the last.

"We'll get a ride in the morning. It's fifty miles to Gorham, y'know. We wouldn't have made it in the dark anyway."

"It's okay," she said. "But I want a real bed in town."

CHAPTER 31

The Man in Red Gaiters

Climb the mountains and get their good tidings.
Nature's peace will flow into you as sunshine
flows into trees. The winds will blow their fresh-
ness into you, and the storms their energy, while
cares will drop off like autumn leaves.

- JOHN MUIR

"PARSNIP," Jerri said, pointing to letters in a reverse diagonal.
Kyra circled it, along with "radish," a reverse horizontal.
"Celery," she said, making another discovery.
We were playing "hidden word." Kyra had bought a new
puzzle book to keep us occupied while waiting for rides.
We'd revised our strategy to hitchhike south from Gorham.
Kyra sat crosslegged at my feet — beaming smile, long blonde
hair in pigtails — and thumbed passing cars with upraised arm
as if answering questions in class. Jerri sat beside her. Such
resources should be used, I figured, not left on the sidelines
while I did the thumbing. The puzzle book overdid it, perhaps,
but it gave us something to do.
"Rutabaga," I said, pointing out another word. A car

stopped. A second ride later we stood thirty-six miles south of Gorham at the eastern end of the Kancamagus Highway. Perfect timing. Fall foliage was at its peak that weekend and there were so many cars a policeman directed traffic. Our third lift gave us the complete leaf-watching tour that spectacular day, all the way to North Woodstock, New Hampshire. We were left at a campground west of town. A sign on the office door said *Full*, but I paid no attention.

"Hi, I'd like a campsite," I said to the lady at the desk.

"I'm sor-"

"There are three of us and we're on foot," I went on, assuming there would be no problem.

"Um, on foot ... well, I'll check with the boss."

She went to the back room. The sky neared dark outside and every motel and guest house we'd passed had shown a *No Vacancy* sign. The manager came to the counter.

"We're full up," he said, "but I can give you a spot behind that pickup camper across the street."

"Fine. How much?"

"Four dollars." I paid it.

We got a ride nearly to Glencliff next morning and soon walked south once again. The trail led along dirt roads and wooded trail, through pastures and fields, and up whatever rugged mountains it could find. Every step passed through glorious New Hampshire fall. The sun shone. Days were warm. We had no schedule, no place we had to be. Hillsides blazed wherever we looked. Fallen leaves crunched wherever we stepped.

In camp we heard leaves fall, touching lightly one on another, and we listened as the breeze shuffled them along the ground. Such sounds awoke us one night. Footsteps, I thought, but not a large foot — certainly not a bear. Jerri raised her head to look.

"Something out there?" I asked.

"Skunk," she said. Moonlight showed a black and white tail extending from behind the fireplace.

"Oh." We went back to sleep.

We met hikers each day who stopped to talk of what they'd seen. One was Jon Mackey, an older gentleman from Burnsville, North Carolina. He had the distinguished look of a board chairman with his clipped white mustache, yet he sauntered along in red Smokey Bear hat, light jacket, and blue-jean cut-offs like one of the crowd. He was a bit reserved at our first meeting, but as we met again and again he told us more.

He'd begun walking the AT on Old Speck. He'd gotten lost almost at once, he said, was soaked in a furious storm, and somehow managed to wander on both the mountain's new and old trails. Disoriented and miserable, Jon eventually found Speck Pond Shelter. Caretaker Adele restored his well-being with a fire, dry clothes, and hot food. He'd been walking the AT south ever since. He wanted to do the whole trail, he told us, and soon.

"How near the trail do you live?" I asked Jon one evening as I baked a chocolate cake.

"Down the road from Erwin, Tennessee — about twenty miles from where the AT drops through Spivey Gap."

"Oh, yes ... Devil Fork Gap to Spivey Gap ... I'll never quite forget that section."

"Mount Mitchell is almost in my backyard. That's North Carolina's highest, you know. You should come to visit. There are ten mountains over six thousand feet within five miles of my place."

"The visiting part sounds okay," I said, "but I'll pass on six-thousand footers just now."

My Dutch oven fires went out as we talked.

"Good recovery," he said as I revived them.

"Good cake!" he said as I passed it around.

Shelters in western New Hampshire came in many styles.

342

Trapper John Shelter reminded us of those in the Jefferson National Forest. The structure was so new that not an initial or scrawled message marred its walls.

The lean-to on Mount Cube looked like a stable on the route of the Pony Express. I was sure I'd seen it in any number of movies — starring Gene Autry, perhaps, or Gabby Hayes. Its outhouse afforded an exceptional view.

Named "The Second Al Merrill Memorial Privy," after the Dartmouth ski coach (Dartmouth Outing Club maintained this section of trail), it had neither roof nor walls. It was a box painted orange on a platform over a pit. Functional. A box seat in the woods from which to view the world.

We went to Hanover October 10. Things started going wrong fairly early in the day; trail markings vanished for long stretches and kept us guessing at the way. We occasionally backtracked when we sensed we'd wandered from the path. The route to Velvet Rocks — the name sounded so inviting — dragged us steeply over ridge after ridge for no compelling reason, only to leave us on the same flat road from which we'd begun. Another pointless relocation, we sputtered as we straggled into town.

No problem now ... we'd retrieve the box from the Post Office, buy a few things at the store, and be on our way. So it might have been, but the box wasn't there.

We'd passed through Hanover before. Our destination had been Gorham then and we'd left a mail-forwarding card. Traveling now in the reverse direction, we'd forgotten about the card. The box we'd mailed from Gorham four days before had thus been sent back.

"There's no way to get it today," the postmaster told us. "You'll have to wait a day or two or have it sent to you somewhere else."

"Isn't this great," I said. "Our first problem with the mail in nineteen hundred miles and we can't even blame the Post Office." We forwarded the box to Rochester.

To the store: Jerri improvised four days' menus on the spot and put us back in action in an hour or so. That still left five and a half miles to do at four in the afternoon. We hit the trail.

Two miles of road passed in under an hour. We slowed on undulating forest path yet continued to make good time. Darkness neared. Kyra complained of a headache. We had no water but stopped for aspirin when we found a spring.

Darkness came. We entered a dense stand of pine. The crunch of leaves that had marked our progress gave way to muffled tread over layers of duff. Quiet. Dark. We could barely see. The forest seemed alive as though a host of Disney characters lurked in the trees. We couldn't see the Dartmouth Outing Club's orange and black blazes, yet we sped along winding path as though we knew the way well.

Jerri spied a light — the DOC's Happy Hill Cabin. I could well imagine seven dwarves living in a place like that.

Instead we found Jon, tending a roaring fire, and Jim Morrisey, a hiker from Illinois.

"I thought you might be here soon," Jon said with a sly smile.

"Why," I asked, "because it's late?"

"Yes," he said. "We've shared three camps and each time you've stumbled in after dark. Another night you didn't show at all."

"Real tourists, huh."

"Nice place you have here," Jerri said. "And it's warm!"

"I got this little fire going to take off the chill."

"*Little* fire," said Jim. "You should have seen it when I got here. I thought he was going to roast a hog."

We walked in pastoral country the next few days, through gentle hills and fields of Vermont. Groves of birches, maples, and other hardwoods colored the forests. Though the peak had passed, scenes of red, orange, gold, green, and brown remained a stunning sight.

344

We watched a herd of grazing cows and heard the dinging and donging of real cowbells tied about their necks. We passed a tall white teepee pitched with a ridgetop view. We walked on Podunk Road, crossed Podunk Brook. We stopped at a roadside cemetery — two short rows of bleached headstones under a fiery oak. Miles beyond, we saw a sign that read *Slow — Children Playing, also Ducks, Horses, and Dogs.*

Jon and Jim walked at their own pace during the days, but evenings found us together, usually only eight or nine miles on. Jim would take it easy and often meet us on the trail. Jon would hit camp around noon. Rather than forging on as he could have easily done, he would build a fire and while away the afternoon.

"There's something very wrong," Jerri said one evening.

"Hmmm?" I replied.

"We've just been to town."

"Yes."

"And tonight is full moon."

"I guess so."

"It hasn't rained."

Nor did it. We'd had rain with every full moon till then and in thirty-seven of forty-one towns. Perhaps the two events together canceled the effects....

We camped another time in a meadow white with erupting milkweed pods. Kyra waded knee-deep among them, picking handfuls of feathery fluff to toss on the breeze. She watched them drift, then ran to pick more to toss in the air, and more. Light from the setting sun glowed orange in her hair and cast long, shadowy patterns about her. She seemed so completely happy — shining face, playful smiles and giggles — so completely involved in what she was doing.

She'd been on quite a journey ... from tearful child lagging behind on uphill, to through-hiker obviously at ease living in the woods and sleeping on the ground. She'd contemptuously said "I thought this was supposed to be *fun!*" yet walking the Appalachian Trail was now something she enjoyed. She'd remember it ... at eleven years old she'd probably learned as much about feeling at home in the woods as I might ever know. I ran after her then, to throw handfuls of down and laugh, too.

As we neared the top of a hill the following day, she started picking and tossing fluff again.

"It must be Kyra," Jim Morrisey's voice boomed from beyond the crest.

"How'd you guess?" she kiddingly asked.

"When I saw that fluff flying, I knew it could only be you."

"I'm really into fluffs!" she replied.

"How did you ever get this far walking so slow," he said. "I've seen faster turtles."

"We weren't even trying at first, it was so far," I told him. "Then we tried too hard. I think we've got it about right now."

"It's a good pace if you're not going anywhere, like me, but for two thousand miles I think I'd get a little nervous."

"We've had discussions along those lines," I said. "Whether we should go fast or slow, walk in the rain or not, and like that. We ended up doing some of each — sixteen-mile days some times, so slow other days I thought I'd fall asleep. It all worked out, I guess. Here we are in Vermont with seventy miles to go."

"Maybe you do have it right...."

"We don't *waste* time," Jerri said. "We just use all there is."

That day was no exception. We stopped for everything that looked even marginally interesting and rested at the slightest provocation. I read aloud the better lines from the guidebook. We were crossing "unnamed Topman Hill," I announced at one spot, and I noted scenes termed "attractive," "charming," and "extremely fine panoramic." I also found mention in the guide-book of a record eight-pound trout — caught nearby, in 1943.

"No wonder these books are so heavy," I said....

Next morning I found a note on the Cloudland Shelter wall:

Dear Tooth Fairy,

   Yesterday I pulled a tooth and slept with it under
my pillow all night long and it was still there this
morning. I hope you didn't have trouble following the
trail. I will be at Gulf Shelter tonight. Please forward
my dime.

Good luck with the blazes,
Baby Through-Hiker

Hikers camped with us read the note and laughed.

"Try again tonight," Jerri told her. "I'm *sure* you'll have
better luck."

Resting on a steep climb later, Kyra began to write notes on
fallen leaves. "Hi!" said one in large block letters. "Hill, use low
gear," others combined to read. She'd cleared a space in the
trail to arrange them.

"What are you doing?" I asked.

"I'm *leafing* messages."

"Are you leaving them for other hikers?" asked Jerri.

"I believe so."

"Good idea," I said. "Your notes will alleviate concern about
this climb."

"Uh-huh, and give people behind us relief."

Kyra found a dollar under her pillow next morning. She
acted properly delighted, but was also prepared. Later she
showed us another message, written in a familiar hand:

Dear Baby Through-Hiker,

   Sorry I missed you but I had an awful time finding you in the dark. This certificate is good for 25
cents. Redeem it at your nearest daddy.

Good hiking,
The Tooth Fairy

Leaves. Weather. Both had been uncommonly beautiful for weeks. We hikers exulted in it. People we met in farmyards and on country lanes never failed to mention it. "Splendid," they would say, and "Gorgeous!" Ah, but we were still in Vermont.

"We'll pay for't this wintah," one farmer cautioned.

But the glory was fading. Trees were stripped on mountaintops and again we could see into valleys through the branches. Each day the barren gray line moved farther down the slopes. Geese flew overhead. Their formations looked ragged, out of practice, but they flew — going south. When a storm finally came, burying hillsides in a blizzard of leaves, we knew the driving wind and piercing chill belonged to no spring rain.

October 14 dawned clear and cold — the 208th day Kyra hadn't had to clean her room. She kicked already deep leaves into a huge pile and jumped in. So did I.

"I'm going to town at Sherburne Pass," Jon Mackey said. "Maybe I'll see you later."

Dressed smartly as usual, wearing the skin wine flask he'd found and a new pair of red gaiters, he posed for a departing picture.

"You know," he told Jerri with a wink, "nothing makes an old man feel quite so sexy on a cold and frosty morning as a new pair of red gaiters."

We never saw Jon on the trail again but we heard from him regularly over the next year.

Hampton, Tennessee, to Springer Mountain in winter.

Hampton to Roanoke, Virginia, in spring.

Roanoke to the Susquehanna in summer.

Katahdin to Grafton Notch, Sherburne Pass to Duncannon and the last of the Appalachian Trail in fall.

"It must be those red gaiters," he said. "They're working! They're working!..."

The sky alternately threatened and cleared as we walked due west through Vermont. Rain fell for a time, and we noticed the bleak look of our early days in Georgia stealing upon the land. There would be warm days left, but not many.

Our destination that day was the Long Trail Lodge. We'd been reading about it lately. The proprietors didn't care for hikers, registers warned: "no packs, no boots — a real snob place." No home, it seemed, for the unwashed. We turned south through Sherburne Pass in late afternoon. The AT joined the Long Trail there and the lodge stood a short distance on.

Hikers leave packs outside, read its sign. We left our packs outside.

No boots. We left them on.

We walked through the door and stood side by side at the front desk. The man behind it eyed us with obvious distaste.

We had cash. We got a room.

CHAPTER 32

Crossroad

I left the woods for as good a reason as I went there. Perhaps it seemed to me that I had several more lives to live, and could not spare any more time for that one.

- THOREAU

WE PUT ON OUR BOOTS OUTSIDE. The man at the desk had retrieved our supply box with the lodge mail, the waitress at breakfast brought us a second round without charge, so we sat on the steps of the Long Trail Lodge and put on our boots outside. Forty-seven miles of Appalachian Trail remained. Forty-seven miles of trail we had walked since well before spring. Sun shone on our faces, sparkled on the lawn, lit patches of marigolds and windrows of bright leaves blown around the building. It warmed us for almost the last time. Clouds, stiff winds, and frequent rain soon moved in to stay the next four days.

We walked in hardwood forest through a gradually fading scene. We climbed mountains in the two- to four-thousand-foot range, crossed over Mount Pico and windy Mount Killington. We passed shelters, lodges, cabins, once four in a day. We met hikers on occasion, hikers in no hurry, a few friendly faces on an almost deserted trail.

Jim Morrisey joined us the first night in Governor Percival W. Clement Shelter. A distinctive name, we thought, until we discovered its outhouse — the Lieutenant Governor Jarvis Snodgrass Memorial Gazebo.

The trail led us October 16 to the edge of Clarendon Gorge. The flooding Mill River had ripped out the trail's suspension bridge there in July, leaving it tossed aside like so much driftwood. Warning signs directed us temporarily west some unspecified distance to cross on Vermont 103. The river looked placid. I carried rocks to complete a stepping-stone trail and we crossed without incident.

"Scenery is slacking off," I said to Jerri next afternoon. We walked through leaves that lay deep in the trail. Around us, forest stood ready for winter.

"We're seeing the full cycle," she said in her philosophical way. "There's still color in the valleys, but soon we'll be back to bare trees like when we started."

"Sure, but we need something to liven things up."

"Why? We've seen the seasons from beginning to end. We started with juncoes, blue jays, and woodpeckers, watched things come and go, now we're back to juncoes, blue jays, and woodpeckers."

"Uh-huh."

"What did you have in mind?"

"Maybe a billboard."

"Right."

"That might be a *bit* crude. How about Burma Shave signs? There's a real part of the land."

"Two hundred-some days he lives in the woods, in a natural world of wonder, and he wants Burma Shave signs!"

"Maybe I'll write them on markers we pass from time to time — 'Rip a fender off your car ...'"

"Hopeless!" But she was laughing, and so was Kyra.

"'Mail it in for a five-pound jar'...."

We crossed White Rocks Mountain then and camped on an island in Little Rock Pond. Hikers who joined us there left un-washed pots and pans on the picnic table overnight.

Enter raccoon.

Bulges in tin sheathing that protected the table from porcu-pines yielded to the raccoon's weight — BONK — then popped out again — CLUNK. Pans rattled as well. Our stealthy midnight visitor became a one-raccoon band.

BONK, rattle, CLUNK, rattle-rattle, *BONK*.

No one slept long through that.

"Hey, get outta here," one fellow yelled.

"Get some rocks," said another. They threw rocks and sticks.

CLUNK, rattle-rattle, THUMP, klonk, THUD ... the raccoon scampered away.

An hour later: BONK, rattle, CLUNK ...

"It's back!"

The lesson seemed obvious, yet confrontations continued through the night.

Next day it rained. We followed trail that was easy and flat around Griffith Lake, wearing rain gear that felt like we'd worn it since the day we began. I saw a stream ahead at one point, and across it, a sign. Unusual shape — several rectangular boards on a post. No, surely not....

"I don't believe this," I said, reading,

> Walking on this
> bridge of rocks
> Keeps the water
> from my socks
> *Burma Shave*

Rain became sleet by afternoon and we took refuge in Peru Peak Shelter. Nine miles of Appalachian Trail remained — one last sub-ten mile day. I expected hikers behind us to appear, but as darkness descended and the patter on the roof went on, none did. Few besides us would walk in a full day of rain. We set about evening routines in silence. No one had much to say.

"Where were we a month ago?" I said.

"Maine, I guess," Kyra said.

"That really narrows it down, y'know. We were in Maine a month."

"Monson?"

"Right, in rain just like here. How about August 18, two months ago?"

"Probably the White Mountains," Jerri said.

"Eliza Brook Shelter — the day after Moosilauke. Three months?"

No one remembered. The game was harder of late, and one day from the end, no one felt like playing.

"Just tell us the rest," Jerri said.

"We camped at Dutch Hollow Road in New York on July 18, a few days before Homestead Camp. On June 18 we visited Harpers Ferry."

"We stayed with Annie there," Kyra said.

"We were in Symms Gap in Virginia on May 18, straining water by the thimbleful through a bandana. And April 18, six months ago, we were with Adele, Jonathan, and Al[2] in — "

"Hot Springs," Kyra answered.

"We'd been on the trail nearly a month then. March 18 we were driving to Atlanta. Long trip, huh."

No one replied. Peru Peak Shelter fell silent again save for the sound of steady rain.

Odd, being so near the end. Two thousand miles had once seemed impossibly far. Two hundred days had once seemed uncommonly long. All but one day had passed. What now?

What would we take away? Did it have to end? I sorted through thoughts and feelings as if cleaning out a drawer.

It was time to leave. We would finish the trail, reach the goal, winter would come, our savings would be gone. We had no reason or way to go on. Facts and Logic: set those aside for now.

We would go to the city, drive cars, get jobs. I'd sit at a desk, answer telephones, wear a tie. What if I didn't want to? I rather liked the AT. I'd just come to know the place; why should I have to leave? Dewy Sentiment: common on such journeys — disregard.

I belonged here. I felt at peace with the land; I felt a closeness with the natural world. I felt at home and welcome. Life was *real* here and I still had much to learn. Revelations on a Mountaintop: keep those.

Questions had answers here. Could we reach the next shelter? Should we wear rain gear? Would the Post Office be open? Few decisions were much harder. Though life on the AT wasn't easy, neither was it complex. Yearning for the Good Old Days: not much use, still ...

I'd worn one shirt for seven months, one pair of jeans. I'd carried what I needed in a pack, slept in a bag on the ground, in shelters with roof and three walls. Those things were enough. One needed little to be happy, really. To be warm, dry, safe, and not hungry was richness indeed. Simplicity: that was it ... getting somewhere ...

We'd suffered rain, snow, wind, cold, heat, bugs. We'd crossed rivers and bogs, rocks and mud. We'd climbed mountains, gained seventy-five *miles* of elevation and given it back. We'd lived with mice, bears, snakes, skunks, porcupines, raccoons. We'd supplied our own food, had not gotten lost, had not given up. Together, we had made our own way.

This was what we'd found on the Appalachian Trail. The simple way of life, peace with the land and each other, confi-

354

dence that we could handle whatever came along. This was what I wanted to hold.

I fell asleep in the darkness. Very soon rain turned to snow.

Dawn. Honking geese. Sunshine in clear blue sky. Snow had melted on contact around us but peaks wore white. We would walk through a day of winter to the finish.

"This is perfect," Jerri exulted. "We started in snow and we'll end in snow. It's everything I wanted!"

Peru Peak rose in front of us, 3,429 feet. We climbed to a faint dusting of snow, then pushed on as it deepened to several inches. Snow hung in trees, tumbled down our necks as packs struck the branches. We hardly cared. We walked as though weightless, not feeling our packs or the cold.

We were almost there.

Nothing could stop us anymore.

We gained the summit, passing through incredible sunlit scenes, recalling wintry days on Roan Mountain and Cheoah Bald. Had we met such a storm on Katahdin, we would never have been able to finish.

We crossed Styles Peak and to the south saw Bromley Mountain. We climbed it, too — one last "Ascend steeply" for one last peak — and stood atop its observation tower.

The view from The Big B looked bleak, barren, and brown. Snow frosted trees on upper slopes. A forest of bare branches swept on to mountains we'd left behind. Every leaf had fallen. Even trees in the valleys were bare.

Jim Morrisey met us for the final two miles downhill. We passed the signpost at Bromley Cabin in mid-afternoon, completing the Appalachian Trail. Jerri and Kyra cheered and turned down the path to the cabin.

"Tell me, sir," Jim said, thrusting an imaginary microphone into my face, "how do you feel about finishing your long walk?"

I could not think of one thing to say.

"Hey, this cabin is a dump," he went on.

"Give it a couple hours," I said. "With a little rain, you'll think it's great."

Connie Cross, a friend from Phoenix, was to join us our last night on the trail. She lived fifty miles away in Putney, Vermont, and I'd given her directions by phone from the Long Trail Lodge. By dark she hadn't arrived.

Jerri and Kyra sat at the cabin table, speculating on where she might be. I traded comments with Jim and another fellow named Stan as we each arranged gear in bunks. A wood stove warmed the twelve-foot-square cabin and our candle lantern hanging at the window shed the only light.

"We shouldn't be hard to find," I said to no one in particular. "She only has to follow the blazes two-thirds of a mile from Vermont 11." But we'd followed blazes for many days. We hadn't done so well at first, either.

Hearing a knock, I knew she'd arrived. No trail hiker knocked on cabin doors. She'd found the trail without problem, she said, but darkness came before she'd walked a hundred yards. Only by chance had she noticed the light in the window as she passed.

October 20, our 214th day — the Appalachian Trail was business as usual. Two hikers tenting outside wondered when they could move into the cabin. Rain through the night caught them with no tent fly.

Stan milled about in an agitated state, stuffing things into his pack, taking them out. He paced back and forth, moving items from bunk to table, from table to bunk, moving them back. He thought he might hike on, then he decided to stay. Maybe, he fretted, he would just quit.

"I've just *got* to get it together!" he finally said.

A bag of granola had burst in his pack the night before. He began to sift through it by handfuls.

"Lose something?" Jim asked.

"No, just a bunch of loose cereal here I don't need floating around my pack." He scooped it into a new plastic bag and began packing to walk the thirty miles to Bennington.

"Are you awake, Connie?" Jerri, still in her bag, said to the bunk above.

"You mean you *slept* on these boards?" came the answer.

"I suppose we have gotten used to them."

"I've been awake for hours."

"I had the strangest dream," Jerri said. "We woke up here in Bromley Cabin thinking we'd finished the Appalachian Trail, only we had two hundred more miles to do, somewhere in Europe!"

"Are you sure you're awake now?" Connie asked.

"I think so. Are we finished?"

"Hey, hey," said Jim, "you sure are! And tomorrow's my birthday. You know what that means."

I did. I unclipped my carabiner pack hangers — he'd been eying them since Hanover — and gave him one as promised.

"Happy trails," I said. "Now you can hike first class."

Toward noon we donned packs a final time and walked to the highway. Connie would drive us to Manchester Center. From there we'd hop a bus, roll off a day's miles every ten or fifteen minutes, and be in Rochester, New York, by evening. We'd have a month to make our way back to Phoenix. I loaded packs into the car. While Jerri, Kyra, and Connie got in, I stood at the door and took a last look at the trail we'd come to call home.

A carload of hikers tied boots, hoisted on packs, adjusted waistbelts for a weekend walk north. Jim would soon be along to hitchhike to town. Stan, together at last, had headed south. Life on the AT went on.

The trail led north to Katahdin, south to Springer. All along its length that day, the next, and for years to come people would walk, climb, camp, see, and perhaps know the simple life we'd known. The Appalachian Trail was a world to itself. One could escape there for a time for any reason he or she might choose: to walk, to achieve, to regain something lost, or to find something one never knew was there.

We'd stood at the entrance to that world exactly seven months before. It was a crossroad of sorts, where pavement from a familiar world met a dirt path through a place that felt foreign.

In that last minute on Vermont Highway 11, I knew we'd reached a crossroad again — but the path through the wood was now the familiar way, and the world along the pavement was foreign.

"C'mon, Dad," Kyra said. "Let's go to town."

Town. That's right, we were going to town. It was starting to rain.

Epilogue

*It is years now
but I
still lie awake and listen
in the mornings.*
- LOREN EISELEY

THAT WAS SIXTEEN YEARS AGO. We returned to Phoenix as planned but left there a year later for Alaska. Jerri and I have traveled the whole state since then, as part of and vacation from our respective trades of photo-journalism and computer systems analysis. We've added the Arctic, the parks and forests, the outlying islands and villages, and every mile of every road to our record of places seen, along with such exotic finds as snowy owls, lynx, arctic fox, and pink-spotted lady slippers. While some of that might make good reading, the real story is Kyra's.

Kyra finished grade school and high school in Alaska, then attended the University of Virginia in Charlottesville. She obtained her undergraduate degree from the Architecture school there, then received a two-year research assistantship to M.I.T. She earned a Master's degree in Visual Studies (computer graphics) there in 1985 and is now employed as a computer wizard in California where she lives with her cat, Wichita.

Kyra grew more confident and comfortable in the woods on her AT hike, she says, and more self-reliant, but she tells of her most lasting lesson this way:

"I remember watching you and mom make decisions, working with available data, considering options, deciding what to do on the fly. Children don't often see their parents making family decisions; I did and even got to take part. The most valuable lesson for me was learning the willingness to go on when you don't have all the information — learning to look at a situation, take your best guess, and go for it.

"The outcome of our hike was committed to those decisions. You made them and stuck with them. You were ready for opportunity when it came along and took it, saying 'Let's see what happens.'"

Wisdom from the so-much-talked-about ten-year-old.

I've been asked many times if I would hike the trail again. My feelings on that have changed over the years. At first I said my next adventure would be a cruise of some sort where I could sit down most of the time and have people bring me things. I did that, on the Alaska ferry between Juneau and Sitka, which was long enough. Just recently I've taken to hiking again and think often about walking the AT or some other long trail. Some things would be different next time, however.

We were, I think, the best-equipped hikers on the trail that year. I've since replaced nearly all my gear with new products so would be even better equipped if I walked the AT again.

If I kept a journal I would write about different things — what I saw, who we met, what I was thinking and feeling, not what we ate for breakfast and our statistical rate of travel.

I would do about the same amount of planning next time: not so little I was caught unprepared, not so much the walk lacked adventure.

I doubt I would "take more time," as most hikers vow when asked; we took most all the time there was, 214 days, starting in snow and ending in snow. But I would try to use the time more profitably, thinking more about the moment, about what was happening now, rather than being so intent on how far we needed to get that day, how we would get through the White Mountains, or whether it was snowing yet on Mount Katahdin.

My reason for returning would be to recapture that view from Saddleback Mountain, that feeling of being at home, of being part of the natural world. I can't help but think that insight was just an introduction and that some wider vision lies beyond it.

Anchorage, Alaska   Mic Lowther
December 1989

Second edition note:

I published thirty-four hardcover copies of this book in 1990. I gave most of them away to family and friends but saved five to lend to anyone who might wish to enjoy this adventure. Those five copies have since traveled all over the US to a steady list of readers.

Appalachian Trail Internet sites have lately generated even more interest along with many requests to make the book generally available. Thus encouraged, I at last located a publisher interested in producing this edition. It contains the entire original text of *Walking North*, unchanged except for this note.

August 2000

Sources

Abbey, Edward. *Appalachian Wilderness: The Great Smoky Mountains.* Photographs by Eliot Porter. New York: E.P. Dutton, 1970.

Baker, Raymond. *Campfires Along the Appalachian Trail.* New York: Carlton Press, 1971.

Bartlett, John. *Familiar Quotations.* Boston and Toronto: Little, Brown and Co., 1968.

Borland, Hal. *Twelve Moons of the Year.* New York: Alfred A. Knopf, 1979.

Brower, David, ed. *The Place No One Knew.* Photographs by Eliot Porter. San Francisco: Sierra Club, 1966.

Carroll, Lewis. *Alice's Adventures in Wonderland & Through the Looking Glass.* New York: New American Library, 1960.

Dillard, Annie. *Pilgrim at Tinker Creek.* New York: Harper's Magazine Press, 1974.

Eiseley, Loren. *Notes of an Alchemist.* New York: Charles Scribner's Sons, 1972.

Fisher, Ronald M. *The Appalachian Trail.* Photographs by Dick Durrance II. Washington D.C.: National Geographic Society, 1972.

Garvey, Edward B. *Appalachian Hiker: Adventure of a Lifetime.* Oakton, Virginia: Appalachian Books, 1971

Godfrey, Michael A. *A Closer Look.* San Francisco: Sierra Club Books, 1975.

Guide to the Appalachian Trail in the Great Smokies, the Nantahalas, and Georgia. Washington D.C.: The Appalachian Trail Conference, 1971.

Guide to the Appalachian Trail in Tennessee and North Carolina, Cherokee, Pisgah, and Great Smokies. Washington D.C.: The Appalachian Trail Conference, 1971.

Guide to the Appalachian Trail in Central and Southwestern Virginia. Strasburg, Virginia: Shenandoah Publishing House, 1972.

Guide to the Appalachian Trail and Side Trails in the Shenandoah National Park. Washington D.C.: The Potomac Appalachian Trail Club, 1970.

Guide to the Appalachian Trail from the Susquehanna River to the Shenandoah National Park. Washington D.C.: The Potomac Appalachian Trail Club, 1972.

Guide to the Appalachian Trail in Pennsylvania. Concordville, Pennsylvania: Keystone Trails Association, 1970.

Guide to the Appalachian Trail in New York and New Jersey. New York: Walker and Co., 1972.

Guide to the Appalachian Trail in Massachusetts and Connecticut. Harpers Ferry, West Virginia: The Appalachian Trail Conference, 1972.

Guide to the Appalachian Trail in New Hampshire and Vermont. Strasburg, Virginia: Shenandoah Publishing House, 1968.

Guide to the Appalachian Trail in Maine. Kents Hill, Maine: The Maine Appalachian Trail Club, 1969.

Hare, James R., ed. *Hiking the Appalachian Trail.* Emmaus, Pennsylvania: Rodale Press, 1975.

Herbst, Robert L. "We Must Protect the Appalachian Trail," The Living Wilderness. Washington, D.C.: The Wilderness Society, June, 1980.

Hesse, Hermann. *Siddhartha.* New York: New Directions, 1951.

Leopold, Aldo. *A Sand County Almanac.* New York: Sierra Club, Ballantine Books, 1970.

Melham, Tom. *John Muir's Wild America.* Photographs by Farrell Grehan. Washington, D.C.: National Geographic Society, 1976.

Milne, A.A. *Winnie-The-Pooh* New York: E.P. Dutton, 1954.

Patterson, Freeman. *Portraits of Earth.* San Francisco: Sierra Club, 1987.

Russell, Terry and Russell, Renny. *On the Loose.* New York: Sierra Club, Ballantine Books, 1967.

Sherman, Steve and Older, Julia. *Appalachian Odyssey: Walking the Trail from Georgia to Maine.* Brattleboro, Vermont: The Stephen Greene Press, 1977.

Snyder, Gary. *Turtle Island.* New York: New Directions Publishing Corp., 1974.

Sutton, Ann and Myron. *The Appalachian Trail: Wilderness on the Doorstep.* Philadelphia and New York: J.B. Lippincott Co., 1967.

Thoreau, Henry David. *Walden.* New York: Milestone Editions.

Whitman, Walt. *Leaves of Grass.* New York: New American Library, 1958.